WOMEN
and
ELECTIVE OFFICE
Past, Present, and Future

edited by
Sue Thomas and Clyde Wilcox

New York   Oxford
OXFORD UNIVERSITY PRESS
1998

Oxford University Press

Oxford   New York

Athens   Auckland   Bangkok   Bogotá   Bombay
Buenos Aires   Calcutta   Cape Town   Dar es Salaam
Delhi   Florence   Hong Kong   Istanbul   Karachi
Kuala Lumpur   Madras   Madrid   Melbourne
Mexico City   Nairobi   Paris   Singapore
Taipei   Tokyo   Toronto   Warsaw

and associated companies in
Berlin   Ibadan

Copyright © 1998 by Oxford University Press, Inc.

Published by Oxford University Press, Inc.,
198 Madison Avenue, New York, New York, 10016

Oxford is a registered trademark of Oxford University Press

Library of Congress Cataloging-in-Publication Data
Women and elective office : past, present, and future /
edited by Sue Thomas and Clyde Wilcox.
p.   cm.
Includes bibliographical references.
ISBN 0-19-511230-X (cloth). — ISBN 0-19-511231-8 (paper)
1. Women in public life—United States.   2. Women in politics—United States.
3. Women political candidates—United States.
I. Thomas, Sue, 1957–   . II. Wilcox, Clyde, 1953–   .
HQ1391.U5W63   1998
320'.082—dc21   97-27331
CIP

1 3 5 7 9 8 6 4 2

Printed in the United States of America
on acid-free paper

Contents

Illustrations

Tables

Acknowledgments

No book is ever completed without the help of a great many people apart from those whose names appear as editors or authors. We would like to offer heartfelt thanks to Emma Craswell for all her painstaking work making 15 separate pieces one seamless document. Thanks also go to the anonymous reviewer of the book as well as the editorial staff at Oxford University Press.

Contributors

The Editors

SUE THOMAS is Associate Professor of Government and Director of Women's Studies at Georgetown University. Her research interests center on women and politics, with a particular emphasis on women officeholders. Her most recent works include *How Women Legislate* (Oxford University Press, 1994) and coeditorship of *The Year of the Woman: Myths and Realities* (Westview, 1994). Dr. Thomas is currently working on a book about the intersection of the personal and the political in legislative careers.

CLYDE WILCOX is Professor of Government at Georgetown University. He is coeditor of *The Year of the Woman: Myths and Realities* (Westview, 1994) and coauthor of *Between Two Absolutes: Public Opinion and the Politics of Abortion* (Westview, 1992). He serves on the editorial board of *Women & Politics*. His other research interests are religion and politics, campaign finance, and public opinion.

The Authors

BARBARA BURRELL is a researcher and head of survey design at the Wisconsin Survey Research Laboratory. Her scholarly interests focus on women as candidates for elective office, and her most recent work is *A Woman's Place in the House: Campaigning for Congress in the Feminist Era* (University of Michigan Press, 1994). Dr. Burrell's forthcoming book is titled *Public Opinion and Hillary Clinton*, which is being published by Garland Press.

JOHN M. CAREY is Assistant Professor of Political Science at Washington University in Saint Louis. He is the author of *Term Limits and Legislative Representation* (Cambridge University Press, 1996) and coauthor of *Presidents and Assemblies: Constitutional Design and Electoral Dynamics* (Cambridge, 1992), as well as a number of articles on electoral systems and legislative behavior.

JANET CLARK is Professor of Political Science at West Georgia College. She has published extensively on women officeholders, and among her most recent works is her coauthored work *Women, Elections, and Representation*

(University of Nebraska Press, 1994). She is also the editor of *Women &
Politics.*

ELIZABETH ADELL COOK is coeditor of *The Year of the Woman: Myths and
Realities* (Westview, 1994) and coauthor of *Between Two Absolutes: Public
Opinion and the Politics of Abortion* (Westview, 1992).

MARSHA DARLING is Assistant Professor of Women's Studies and History at
Georgetown University. Her research interests include the role of minorities
as officeholders and the impact of emerging biomedical technologies on
reproduction in African-American females in the United States and abroad.
Recent publications include "African American Female Reproductive Sexuality: Normative, Ethical and Public Policy Issues and Challenges" in *Black
Women Scholars/Work and Struggle: Selected Papers from the 1994 Black Women
in the Academy Conference.* Among her many awards, honors, and services to
the community, Dr. Darling served as a consultant on the *Eyes on the Prize*
documentary series.

DEBRA DODSON is Senior Research Associate and Assistant Professor at the
Center for the American Woman and Politics at the Eagleton Institute,
Rutgers University. Her numerous publications focus on the influence of
abortion in gubernatorial elections and the impact of women in elective office.
She is coauthor of *Reshaping the Agenda: Women in the State Legislatures* with
Susan J. Carroll, and editor of *Gender and Policy Making: Studies of Women
in Office.*

KATHLEEN DOLAN is Assistant Professor of Political Science at the University
of Wisconsin, Oshkosh. Her primary research interests include gender politics,
public opinion, and political behavior. Her work in these areas has appeared
in *American Politics Quarterly, Political Behavior,* and *Women & Politics.* She
is currently working on a project on public attitudes toward congressional
candidates in the 1990s.

GEORGIA DUERST-LAHTI is an Associate Professor of Political Science at
Beloit College, where she teaches American government and women's studies
courses. Her research focuses on gender and bureaucracies and women at
state-level government. Among her recent publications are *Gender Power,
Leadership and Governance,* edited with Rita Mae Kelly (University of Michigan Press, 1995) and *Women and Men of the States,* edited with Mary Guy
(M. E. Sharpe, 1992). She is also on the editorial board of *Women & Politics.*

LYNNE E. FORD is Assistant Professor of Political Science at the College of
Charleston. Her research interests and publications focus on women and politics, political socialization, and service learning as it relates to civic education

and participation. Her articles have appeared in *American Politics Quarterly* and *Women and Politics: Outsiders or Insiders?* (Prentice Hall, 1993).

MALCOLM JEWELL is Professor Emeritus of Political Science at the University of Kentucky. His research interests include legislative politics, political parties, interest groups, and elections. Among his numerous publications is the coauthorship of *Legislative Leadership in the American States* (University of Michigan Press, 1994). Dr. Jewell is also past president of the Midwest Political Science Association.

LYN KATHLENE is Associate Professor of Political Science at Purdue University. She has published articles on women officeholders and the public policy process in the *American Political Science Review*, the *Western Political Ouarterly, Journal of Policy Analysis and Management, Policy Sciences*, and *Knowledge in Society*, as well as contributed chapters to several edited volumes. Her current research interests include violence against women, women as political elites, feminist methodology, and citizen participation.

NICOLA MAZUMDAR is a doctoral candidate at the Claremont Graduate School's Center for Politics and Economics. She is currently working on a philosophical analysis of the effects of rhetorical strategies and linguistic style during the Clarence Thomas confirmation hearings. Her primary interests are in political philosophy, political sociology, and women's issues. She is currently adjunct faculty in political science at several California colleges.

RICHARD G. NIEMI is Professor of Political Science at the University of Rochester. He is coauthor or coeditor of *Comparing Democracies: Elections and Voting in Global Perspective* (Sage, 1996); *Vital Statistics in American Politics*, 5th ed. (CQ Press, 1995); *Controversies in Voting Behavior*, 3rd ed. (CQ Press, 1993); *Classics in Voting Behavior*, (CQ Press, 1993); and *Minority Representation and the Quest for Voting Equality* (Cambridge University Press, 1992). He has written extensively on voting behavior, political socialization, and legislative redistricting.

BARBARA NORRANDER is Associate Professor of Political Science at the University of Arizona. She writes frequently for academic journals on the topics of presidential nominations, public opinion, and voting behavior. She is the author of *Super Tuesday: Regional Politics and Presidential Primaries*.

LYNDA W. POWELL is Associate Professor of Political Science at the University of Rochester. She is coauthor of *Serious Money: Fundraising and Contributing in Presidential Nomination Campaigns* (Cambridge, 1995). She has published articles on women in politics, campaign contributors and campaign finance, congressional and presidential elections, and congressional representation.

JEAN SCHROEDEL is Associate Professor of Political Science at the Center for Politics and Economics at the Claremont Graduate School. She is a contributor to *The Year of the Woman: Myths and Realities* and the author of *Alone in a Crowd: Women in the Trades Tell Their Story* (Temple University Press, 1985) and *Congress, the President and Policy-Making Over Time* (M. E. Sharpe, 1993).

CINDY SIMON ROSENTHAL is an Assistant Professor of Political Science at the University of Oklahoma. She is completing a manuscript on women's leadership roles in state legislatures.

MARCIA WHICKER is Professor of Public Administration at Rutgers University, Newark, and she is coauthor of *Legislative Leadership in the American States* (University of Michigan Press, 1994).

LEONARD WILLIAMS is Associate Professor of Political Science at Manchester College. He is a contributor to *The Year of the Woman: Myths and Realities* and editor of *Political Theory: Classic Writings and Contemporary Views* (St. Martins, 1992).

Introduction

Women and Elective Office: Past, Present, and Future

SUE THOMAS

Where do women candidates and officeholders stand in 1997, after the "year of the woman" and the "year of the angry white male"? What progress has been made toward storming the statehouses and the national legislature? What impact have women had in these positions? What advantages and disadvantages do they face? What are their goals, successes, and challenges? What are their dreams for the future?

These questions are at the heart of *Women and Elective Office: Past, Present, and Future*. Each assumes that having women in elective office is an important goal. Why is women's representation important? Why are we concerned about women being represented among those who make policy decisions for our government at the local, state, and national levels? As long as elected representatives are aware of and care about the interests of all their constituents, does it matter that legislatures, governors, and presidents are predominantly male?

It matters very much, for several reasons. First, a government that is democratically organized cannot be truly legitimate if all its citizens from all races and classes and both sexes do not have a potential interest in and an opportunity for serving their community and nation. Second, if all citizens are seen to have an equal opportunity to participate in the decision making that affects their lives, there is a greater likelihood that the polity will be stable and that citizens will have a reasonable degree of trust in and support for it. Third, women constitute a large pool of talented leaders, and their abilities, points of view, and ideas can only be utilized by a society that selects its leaders from among both men and women.

It is important for women to be included among our public officials for symbolic reasons as well. If children grow up seeing women and men in the political sphere, each sex will be likely to choose from the full array of options when preparing for their adult lives. Finally, it is important for women to have full access to the public sphere because they have different life experiences from men. Because our society still operates with divisions of labor between the public and private spheres, women and men tend to have some different life experiences and points of reference. This can translate into a distinctive way of viewing existing legislative proposals and can lead to different agendas. It is important, then, that women inhabit our legislatures and executive offices so that their concerns contribute to policy agendas.

For all these reasons, then, it matters very much that women have access to and assume elected positions. The extent to which this has been true over the course of U.S. history is explored in the following section.

History

Although women were not granted national suffrage until 1920, famous suffragist Elizabeth Cady Stanton made an unsuccessful run for Congress in 1866. Fifty years later, Jeanette Rankin of Montana became the first woman to win a congressional seat. She served twice, from 1917 to 1919 and again from 1941 to 1942. Rebecca Latimer Felton of Georgia was the first woman senator. She was appointed in 1922 and served for only one day. Ten years later, in 1932, Hattie W. Caraway of Arkansas earned the distinction of becoming the first woman elected to the Senate—or rather, reelected to a seat to which she was originally appointed. It wasn't until 1978, however, that Nancy Landon Kassebaum of Kansas became the first woman to enter the Senate by election rather than by appointment to fill an unexpired term. Nine years later, in 1987, Barbara Mikulski of Maryland became the first Democrat to do so (CAWP, 1995b; Foerstel and Foerstel, 1996).

The first women in state politics broke into political office earlier than their counterparts on the federal level. In 1895, Clara Cressingham, Carrie Clyde Holly, and Frances S. Klock all earned seats in the Colorado statehouse. Their election was due, in part, to a record number of women who went to the polls; 78 percent of eligible women voters turned out in that election compared to 56 percent of the eligible men. And, foreshadowing a pattern prevalent today, once in office, these three representatives made a priority of enacting legislation related to women, children, and families. Together, they ushered legislation through the statehouse that gave mothers equal rights to their children, raised the age of consent from 16 to 18, and created a home for delinquent girls (Cox, 1994; CAWP, 1996c).

Nellie T. Ross of Wyoming was the first female governor. She served from 1925 to 1927. To date, only thirteen women have ever served as governor: nine elected in their own right and four appointed to fill unexpired terms. The largest number to serve simultaneously was four: Joan Finney of Kansas, Ann Richards of Texas, Barbara Roberts of Oregon, and Christine Todd Whitman of New Jersey (CAWP, 1996c) all served in 1994.

Several firsts occurred only recently. In 1968, Shirley Chisholm of New York became the first African-American woman elected to the U.S. House of

Representatives. In 1974, Ella Grasso of Connecticut became the first woman to win the governorship without succeeding a husband in that office (CAWP, 1996a). And a famous first was Geraldine Ferraro, who, in 1984, was the first woman to run for the vice presidency on a major party ticket.

Important firsts also occurred in this decade. In 1991, Ileana Ros-Lehtinen of Florida became the first Hispanic woman elected to the U.S. House of Representatives. In 1992, Carol Moseley-Braun of Illinois became the first African-American woman elected to the U.S. Senate. Only in 1995 did Nancy Landon Kassebaum of Kansas became the first woman to chair a major Senate committee (CAWP, 1996a; NWPC, 1995b).

All these pathbreaking victories led to an electoral situation in 1996 in which 10 percent of the U.S. Congress was female and 21 percent of state legislators were female. The most recent figures available (from March 1995) show that 18.2 percent of mayors of cities with populations over 30,000 are women (CAWP, 1995b).

At the time of this writing in November 1996, 172 women (110 Democrats and 62 Republicans) have served in the U.S. Congress. Twenty-three have been in the Senate and 149 in the House of Representatives. Of these, nineteen women of color have served in Congress. Fourteen were African-Americans, two were Asian American/Pacific Islanders, and three were Latinas (CAWP, 1995b, 1996a, 1996b).

Women have a long history of breaking barriers to participation in the policy-making process, and in making contributions to policy. The next section explores the difficulties of that path.

Women As Candidates for Electoral Office: Obstacles and Challenges

Despite the gains made by women over the course of history, women continue to be vastly underrepresented in elective office for their proportion of the population. Why is this the case? Scholars have explained this fact by focusing on barriers to women's participation. Some of these barriers have been largely overcome, but others continue to make it more difficult for women to win elected office.

In the not-too-distant past, it was not uncommon for women candidates to face discrimination by party elites. Party leaders did not recruit women to run for office, they directed those women who wanted to run toward seats in which they were sacrificial lambs, and they failed to support women's candidacies. As a consequence, women had difficulty in fund-raising and in being perceived as credible candidates by the media and by voters (Gertzog, 1995).

The most recent studies (including Darcy, Welch, and Clark, 1994; Burrell, 1994; Carroll, 1994; Duke, 1996) suggest that such discrimination has diminished considerably. As Georgia Duerst-Lahti discusses in Chapter 1, whereas women may once have lost their elections more often than their male counterparts, that is not the case today. When factors such as party and incumbency status are taken into account, the evidence is clear that women win races as often as men. Hence, when women decide to present themselves to the public as candidates for local, state, and national offices, their chances of winning are as good (and sometimes better) than those of men.

Part of the reason women candidates are competitive with their male counterparts has to do with the rise of the individual entrepreneurial candidate (Mayhew, 1974; Fenno, 1978; Jacobson, 1992) and of alternative fund-raising sources such as EMILY'S List and WISH List—two political action committees (PACs) that provide funding for women candidates (Cook, Thomas, and Wilcox, 1994). As Barbara Burrell shows in Chapter 2, in recent election cycles women have been as successful or even more successful in fund-raising than men at every stage of the process from early money through the general election.

Voter hostility toward female candidates has also been documented. In the past, substantial percentages of citizens felt that women's place was not in elective political positions. More recent research (Darcy, Welch, and Clark, 1994; Burrell, 1994; Carroll, 1994; Duke, 1996) finds that women politicians have largely overcome these barriers. Some citizens are still somewhat less supportive of women candidates, but the proportion of the population feeling this way has shrunk dramatically (see Chapter 4 for more detail), and even when such feelings persist they are often overcome by party loyalty or incumbency status. Hence, women's share of the vote, controlling for party, incumbency, and other variables, is equal to men's.

Beyond vote parity is the possibility that women candidates for office might even be advantaged compared to men, as evidenced by, for example, the recent fund-raising success of women. Is it possible that the much publicized gender gap, which advantages the Democratic Party and its candidates, also inclines female voters to be more supportive than male voters of women who run for office? In Chapter 4 Elizabeth Cook reports that in some cases this is true, but the effects of party, ideology, and incumbency on vote choice are generally greater than the effects of the candidate's sex. Thus, while women candidates, in the aggregate, are not advantaged compared to men, the fact that even some are attests to the abolition of previous obstacles.

Studies focusing on voter choice, fund-raising records, and elite treatment of female candidates have concluded that when women run, they win political office as often as men do. But the elimination of some barriers does not mean that women and men operate on equal or even similar playing fields. Obstacles to women's representational equality still exist and help to account for why comparatively low numbers of women run for office. These obstacles include electoral structure, the social eligibility pool, socialization effects, media coverage of candidates, and the strength of the incumbency factor.

The social eligibility pool concerns expectations citizens have about the backgrounds of those who are quality candidates. Often this includes certain occupational backgrounds, military service, educational accomplishments, type and number of previous electoral experiences, and the like. Although there has been much progress, women today are still less likely than men to come to office from legal careers, for example, and are more likely to have entered politics from community volunteerism or women's groups. Hence, women may be viewed as less viable candidates. Although the effects of the social eligibility pool have lessened over time and women candidates are competitive with men, the differences in these factors mean that women still have greater or different hurdles to overcome to reach the same goals (Darcy, Welch, and Clark, 1994). Georgia Duerst-Lahti in Chapter 2 refers to the pipeline of potential candidates for national office—composed primarily of women in state and local office. Although women have made gains in these offices, it remains true that a majority of those in the pipeline are men.

One ramification of the differing backgrounds and credentials is that women are less inclined to see themselves as viable candidates for public office. The type of socialization that impels fewer women to seek careers in corporate businesses or law firms also results in their lower levels of confidence about becoming candidates for political office. A recent example helps make this point. The National Women's Political Caucus conducted research that targeted voters in occupations that have traditionally been pipelines to politics. The results suggest that women are much less likely than men to consider running for political office. Those surveyed said that women have a harder time than men winning office, that women are more concerned than men about their own qualification levels, and that women, more than men, tend to lack confidence about their ability to win. All this indicates that not only do women need role models, they need the sort of candidate recruitment and training conducive to developing perceptions of their own viability (NWPC, 1994). As Barbara Burrell concludes in Chapter 2, the challenge for the future is to convince more women to run for office.

One reason why potential women candidates exhibit reluctance to run may be related to media treatment of those who do. Studies of media treatment of women and men on the campaign trail show that women, especially those running for high-level offices such as the U.S. Senate, receive less coverage than men, and when they are covered it is in a negative fashion. Emphasis is placed on low probabilities of success rather than on issues or candidate appeal. Further, the press is more likely to cover the policy priorities of men than of women (the priorities of both sexes are detailed later in this chapter) and more likely to highlight the personality traits emphasized by men (Kahn and Goldenberg, 1991; Kahn, 1992, 1994a, 1994b).

Given these findings, it is not surprising that women who are considering running for office think twice about how they and their campaigns will be portrayed and how best to effectively convey their message. In Chapter 3, Leonard Wiliams evaluates gender differences in TV advertising strategies of candidates. Blending existing literature and original analysis, Williams details the areas in which gender differences are detectable as well as where the literature is mixed. Consistent with the findings on media treatment of candidates, much appears to depend on the political climate during the election cycle, the type of race involved, and the level of office sought. As Williams emphasizes, more research needs to be done to sort out the ways in which women and men running for office respond to electoral conditions, social perceptions of women's strengths and weaknesses, and expectations of women's proper societal roles.

Electoral structure may also contribute to low proportions of women in office. Results of recent research (Welch and Studlar, 1990; Darcy, Welch, and Clark, 1994; Matland and Brown, 1992; Rule and Zimmerman, 1992) indicate that women have more success in multi-member districts (several officeholders chosen in a single district) than in single-member districts (one winner per district). Theories about why this is true suggest that when voters can make several ballot choices rather than one, they are likely to want to balance and diversify those choices. Since the trend in U.S. politics has long been toward creating single-members districts out of formerly multi-members ones, women candidates are rarely in a position to take advantage of the more favorable structure.[1]

Analysis of the effect of electoral structure is also relevant with respect to female candidates of color. As Marsha Darling concludes in Chapter 10, African-American women face a number of barriers that are different from the experiences of white women legislators. Structural impediments such as at-large elections, lower levels of registration and voting among black populations than white populations, difficulties in financing campaigns, and gerrymandering have been and remain obstacles to greater access.

One recent phenomenon indicates that the future may bring greater opportunity for women seeking political office. In Chapter 14, Schroedel and Mazumdar highlight the widespread success of the term limits movement. Because the United States historically has high incumbency return rates, any newcomer group has a hard time breaking into political office. However, as of December 1994, 22 states have imposed term limits for state legislative office (Foerstel, 1994). The term limits effort at the national level has been struck down by the U.S. Supreme Court, but several legislators are pursuing a term limits amendment to the U.S. Constitution. Further, the fact that term limits do exist for some state and local offices means that newcomer groups will have more access at those levels than they would have previously. Whether women will ultimately benefit from the term limits movement will depend, of course, not only on an increased proportion of open-seats, but on the type of women candidates who present themselves to the electorate (Carey, Niemi, and Powell, this volume).

1992—The Year of the Woman

As Table I.1 shows, underrepresentation of women has not been a phe-nomenon only of the distant past. Before the 1992 elections, women made up just 6 percent of the U.S. Congress and 18 percent of the membership of state legislatures. After November 1992, although women were still a

TABLE I.1
Percentages of Women in Elective Offices[*]

Level of Office	1975	1981	1987	1991	1993	1995
Congress	4	4	5	6	10	10
Statewide	10	11	14	18	22	25.9
State Legislature	8	12	16	18	20.6	20.7

[*]Information provided by the Center for the American Woman and Politics, Eagleton Institute, Rutgers University.

minority in the electoral arena (10 percent of Congress and 20 percent of state legislatures), a watershed was reached. In congressional races, a record number of women candidates competed for seats and a record number won. One hundred six women won major party nominations for the House and 47 women won their general election races. In the Senate, 11 women ran and 6 won, increasing women's representation to ten percent of the U.S. Congress. Never had there been such a large one-time increase in candidates or in winners (Cook, Thomas, and Wilcox, 1994). Journalists and other observers quickly dubbed 1992 the year of the woman.

After the 1992 election, women also began to crack the leadership glass ceiling. Barbara Kennelly (D-Conn.) was appointed one of four chief deputy whips in the House of Representatives and Barbara Mikulski (D-Md.) was appointed assistant floor leader in the Senate (Hook, 1993:2708; for discussion of the ramifications of having few women in leadership in legislatures, see Norton, 1995).

Why was 1992 different for women? For a variety of reasons, the 1992 elections presented extraordinary opportunities for newcomers, and women, who had made their way up the political ladder by running for local and state offices, were primed to make the jump to the national level. Most important was the unusually large number of open-seats resulting from retirements and redistricting following the 1990 census. open-seats are the best opportunities for newcomers to break into office (Jacobson, 1992). Moreover, 1992 was a good year to challenge incumbents because the House bank and post office scandals made them especially vulnerable. Combined with the anti-incumbency mood of the nation, challengers were more viable than usual.

Another way in which the general political climate had changed was that interest in domestic issues was high and it is on domestic issues that women are seen as particularly skilled. Coupled with the domestic agenda focus of presidential contender Bill Clinton, such issues received heavy media emphasis.

A highly charged and highly visible event focused the nation's attention on the low percentages of women in Congress and the consequences of under-representation: The face-off between Anita Hill and Clarence Thomas over his nomination to the U.S. Supreme Court. This event may have indirectly spurred interest, attention, participation, and the flow of money to help elect more women to Congress. (Cook, Thomas, and Wilcox, 1994).

As several chapter authors note, an example of this burst of enthusiasm for women candidates is that EMILY'S List (a fund-raising organization for Democratic women) membership rose from 3,500 in 1990 to 24,000 in 1992 and a record 6.2 million was raised to distribute to candidates. WISH List, the Republican counterpart to EMILY'S List, attracted 1,500 members in 1992, its first year of operation, and raised $250,000 (Broder, 1993; Mathis, 1993).

The drama of the coverage of the Year of the Woman, which concentrated on federal races, obscured the fact that women also continued to make progress on the state and local levels. For example, more women ran for state legislative seats and won than ever before: 2,373 ran and 1,516 won, bringing the proportion of women in state legislatures to 20.4 percent (the 1990 level was 18.4 percent). Though the increase on the state level was less dramatic than on the federal level (mostly due to a higher proportion of women in statehouses at the outset), progress was being achieved and women were continuing to make their way up the political ladder (Thomas, 1994a).

In the 1992 elections, rather than having their sex be perceived as a disadvantage to be overcome, women candidates, possibly for the first time, were advantaged. Voters wanted change and women, as collective outsiders, represented an aspect of that change.

The Elections of 1994

The momentum of the historic elections of 1992 was not sustained. After women's historic gains, fewer voters perceived the need to elect more women to Congress. Reported pollster Celinda Lake, "Some of the hype is gone. Last year, 63 percent of the voters agreed with the statement that it would be better to have half the government offices filled by women. Now, it is 53 percent" (Broder, 1993). In addition, many of the new women representatives had to compete as freshman incumbents, which is an extremely vulnerable position. Twenty-two of the 24 newly elected women in the House of Representatives won in open-seat races and many were targets in 1994 (Broder, 1993). Moreover, the fact that the 103rd Congress, in conjunction with the president, was perceived as achieving very little change resulted in voter willingness to once again shake up the political landscape. Voter anger was said to be rampant and the results at the polls brought dramatic change. Both the House and Senate changed hands and the Republicans led Congress for the first time in 40 years. Many of the Democratic women who swept into Congress in 1992 lost. But women candidates on the whole were successful: in the House 11 Democratic incumbents lost but 11 Republican newcomers won, making 1994 a break-even year for women in Congress (CAWP, 1995b; NWPC, 1995a).

After the 1994 elections, women made up 10.3 percent of Congress, holding 55 seats. Eight women served in the Senate: two Democrats from California, Dianne Feinstein and Barbara Boxer, Carol Moseley-Braun (D-Ill.),

Kay Bailey Hutchison (R-Tex.), Nancy Kassebaum (R-Kans.), Barbara Mikulski (D-Md.), Olympia Snowe (R-Maine), and Patty Murray (D-Wash.). Forty-seven women held House seats. And one woman (Democrat Eleanor Holmes Norton) served as the nonvoting delegate from the District of Columbia. Thirty of the women serving in the House were Democrats and 17 were Republicans. This compares to 36 Democrats and 12 Republicans in 1992. Further, 14 women of color sat in the House of Representatives: 10 African-Americans, 3 Hispanics, and 1 Asian American (CAWP, 1995b; NWPC, 1995a).

Women in the 104th Congress also made gains in leadership positions. Senator Nancy Kassebaum from Kansas headed the Senate Labor and Human Resources Committee, Senator Barbara Mikulski of Maryland was appointed Democratic Conference Secretary, U.S. Representative Jan Meyers of Kansas chaired the House Small Business Committee, Representative Barbara Kennelly of Connecticut was appointed vice-chair of the Democratic Caucus, and Representative Susan Molinari of New York was appointed vice-chair of the Republican Conference (NWPC, 1995a).

In 1995, women held 25.9 percent of statewide offices (84), up from 22 percent after the 1992 election cycle. However, only one women served as governor, Christine Todd Whitman, Republican of New Jersey. Women were most represented among lieutenant governors: 19 women held these positions as a result of the 1994 election cycle. Six percent (five women of color) served in statewide elective office during this time and Vikki Buckley (secretary of state in Colorado) was the first Republican African-American woman to be elected statewide (CAWP, 1996c).

The national legislative trend was mirrored at the state level. Women ran in numbers just slightly greater than their records in 1992 and, although Republican women won in greater numbers than Democratic women, the overall totals for women's representation held constant. As a result of the elections of 1994, 20.7 percent of state legislators were women. That is, 1,534 of the 7,424 state legislative positions were held by women (18 more seats than after the 1992 election cycle).[2] Women held 17.2 percent of state senate seats and 21.9 percent of lower chamber slots. There were 220 women of color (14.3 percent of all women serving) in state legislatures after the 1994 election cycle. All but 10 were Democrats. African-American women made up the largest proportion of women of color in statehouses and held 167 of those seats (CAWP, 1995b).

There was a fair amount of variation in the proportions of women serving is state legislatures. The five states with the highest percentage of women in the statehouse were Washington (39.5 percent), Nevada (34.9 percent), Colorado (31.0 percent), Arizona (30.0 percent), and Vermont (30 percent). The five states with the lowest percentage of women in the statehouse were Alabama (3.6 percent), Kentucky (8.0 percent), Louisiana (9.7 percent), Oklahoma (10.7 percent), and Virginia (11.4 percent) (CAWP, 1996c). In Chapter 6, Barbara Norrander and Clyde Wilcox examine the factors associated with the proportion of women in state legislatures. They find that the best predictors of women's presence are the ideology of the electorate, the political culture of the state, and the predominant religion.

The 1996 Cycle

At this writing, the outlines of the 1996 election are just beginning to come into focus. It is clear that the Republican Party continues to dominate both chambers of Congress. Women in the 105th Congress will comprise at least 11.3 percent of the House (49 members out of 435) and 9 percent of the Senate (9 members out of 100). This is a very small gain over the 104th Congress, but it indicates that women continue to hold their own as strong, viable, and successful candidates. Moreover, two women now serve as governors. In addition to sitting governor Christine Todd Whitman of New Jersey, New Hampshire is now served by Jeanne Shaheen.

In sum, the excitement and gains of 1992 were not replicated in 1994 or 1996. However, the good news was that women held their own and proved to be successful regardless of which party claimed power. That fact that women achieved success in the very different political climates of 1992 and the subsequent two elections bodes well for their future.

Do Women Make a Difference?

The trend toward increasing the number of women candidates and office-holders on the national, state, and local levels leads directly to the question of whether women in office operate any differently than their male counterparts. Certainly, the theoretical arguments about why women ought to hold office, offered at the beginning of this chapter, suggest that such potential exists. As Kathleen Dolan and Lynne Ford recount in Chapter 5, empirical research gathered over the past twenty-five years confirms that women's increased representation has resulted in a significant impact on politics, which manifests itself in a variety of ways.

Policy

Results from several attitudinal indicators provide the foundations of women's distinctive impact. First, women officeholders are more likely than men to consider representing the interests of women to be very important and to take pride in accomplishments that further the status of women (Thomas, 1994a). Women politicians of both parties also tend, more often than their male peers, to be supportive of issues relevant to women, including funding for domestic violence shelters, funding for medical research on women's health issues, and child support enforcement (Thomas, 1990, 1994a; CAWP; Saint-Germain, 1989; Dodson and Carroll, 1991; Welch, 1985). Finally, as Carey, Niemi, and Powell illustrate in Chapter 6, women, regardless of party, tend to be more liberal than their male counterparts.

Most tellingly, attitudes translate into direct legislative support. Women legislators tend, more often than men, to make priorities of issues of women, children, and family and to introduce and successfully usher those priorities through the legislative process. It is important to note that women in politics do not limit themselves to only certain kinds of issues; they are involved and successful in the full range of items in the political arena. What is clear, however, is that women are more active and involved than men in issues that flow from their different life experience (Thomas, 1994a; Dodson and Carroll, 1991; Tamerius, 1995).

An example of the impact of women's issue support comes from the state level. Women's presence in Virginia's statehouse was a historical high in 1996; 14 women were in the House of Delegates and 7 women were in the Senate. The *Washington Post* reported:

> Their presence has helped to drive some of the significant debates of this year's General Assembly session, from barring mandatory hospital maternity stays of only 24 hours to requiring police to make an arrest in domestic disputes involving an assault. All 21 supported a bill to give women in managed-care health programs direct access to gynecologists and eliminate the need for referrals. (Nakashima, 1996)

An example from the congressional level of the sort of interest women representatives take in legislation dealing with issues of women, children, and the family comes from the 103rd Congress. The increase in women holding congressional seats as a result of the 1992 campaign, combined with the presence of a newly elected Democratic president, resulted in a burst of women-related legislation. A news release from the Congressional Caucus for Women's Issues (1994b) noted that the 103rd Congress broke all records for passing women-oriented legislation—66 measures of importance to women and families became law. Caucus cochair Pat Schroeder of Colorado was quoted as saying:

> In 1992, the voters said they wanted change and as a result, the number of women in Congress nearly doubled, going from 31 to 55. The list of accomplishments we are releasing today represents a healthy return on the voters' investment, one that should finally put to rest the question, "What difference does having more women in Congress make?"

Included in the list of successful measures were family leave; expansion of a tax credit for the working poor (the Earned Income Tax Credit); the right to safe access to reproductive health clinics; expansion of domestic violence and sexual assault services; funds for research on breast cancer, osteoporosis, and menopause; improved federal contracting opportunities for women-owned businesses; legislation to improve gender equity in education; increased Head Start funding; and increased child support enforcement.

In Chapter 9, Debra Dodson provides the background on women's impact in the 103rd Congress. She offers readers the in-depth story of the congresswomen's contribution on women's health issues, abortion rights, and health care reform. Whether it was bill introduction, committee mark-up, floor scheduling, or floor action, women members of Congress were instrumental at all stages of the process, and their energy, effort, and effectiveness on behalf of these legislative issues is evident.

The story does not end there, however. As Janet Clark shows in Chapter 8, the replacement of Democratic women in the House of Representatives with Republican women has not resulted in the neutralization of women's impact. Clark's roll call voting studies show that women and men in Congress still vote differently from each other, with women being more supportive of issues relating to women, children, and the family. It is true that the degree of difference has diminished in the 104th Congress, but the fact that it has not been eliminated indicates that women's presence, regardless of party or ideology, is important for policy reasons.

If differences among female legislators in party and general political ideology do not erase their tendency to support issues of importance to women, what about their self-identification as feminists or nonfeminists? In Chapter 5, Kathleen Dolan and Lynne E. Ford show that more than a majority of women in state legislatures (58 percent) either sometimes or frequently call themselves feminists, and that feminist women are more likely than nonfeminists to include women's issues among their priorities. These scholars also find that feminist women legislators are more likely than nonfeminists to engage in mentoring behaviors to encourage other women to enter and succeed in political careers. Taken together, these results indicate that the progress women legislators have made in bringing private-sphere issues to the public agenda is dependent, at least in part, dependent on the election of feminist women to office.

Process

Recent studies of women in elective political office indicate that women's impact on politics may go beyond the policy dimension to include the process by which policy is made. Specifically, female politicians have been found to be more likely than their male counterparts to conceptualize public policy problems broadly and, as a result, to seek different types of solutions. One example concerns crime. As Lyn Kathlene explains in Chapter 13, whereas male officeholders tend to view the problem as one of individual flouting of legal mandates, females representatives are more likely to search for societal antecedents of criminal activity. Hence, women's legislation is more likely than men's to address the roots of the problem rather than its most recent symptoms.

Another aspect of altering political processes concerns efforts to further diversify legislative bodies. Current research suggests that women in politics are much more likely than men to support increasing the proportion of women in office and to participate in recruitment and training efforts (Thomas, 1994a). Perhaps this quote from Missouri representative Bonnie Sue Cooper, ranking Republican on the House Budget Committee and president of the National Order of Women Legislators, says it best: "Those of us in leadership have a responsibility to pave the way for more young women to be elected. We need women who are competent and capable of assuming the leadership available to them as we begin the second hundred years" (Cox, 1994:18). Representative Cooper's vision for the future may well become reality; Carey, Niemi, and Powell show in Chapter 6 that women's levels of political ambition are quite high and their high levels of professionalization indicate an ability to achieve success.

A final way in which process changes may occur as a result of women's presence in politics concerns how their actions are affected by varying levels of representation. Theories of critical mass suggest that when a large enough group of newcomers or a unified group is present in an organization, their attitudes and behaviors will permeate the mainstream. My research on passage of legislation dealing with women, children, and the family in state legislatures suggests that the presence of either a formal women's legislative caucus or a relatively high percentage of women in the legislature is associated with higher rates of bill passage in those areas (Thomas, 1991b, 1994a; see also Berkman and O'Connor, 1993).

Women As Leaders

Do women lead differently than men? Two of our chapters focus explicitly on this question. First, in Chapter 11, Whicker and Jewell find that women at all levels of state legislative leadership, more than men, exhibit a consensus style rather than a command and control style. In Chapter 12, Rosenthal's study of leadership styles of state legislative committee chairs suggests that women chairs place more emphasis than men do on getting the job done and doing it in a team-oriented way rather than relying on positional authority or raw power. Together, these chapters indicate that women in leadership positions make a difference in the way legislative business is done.

The debate about women's ability to change the legislative arena in this way yields some disagreement, however. Contributors Lyn Kathlene (Chapter 14), Cindy Simon Rosenthal (Chapter 12), Marcia Whicker and Malcolm Jewell (Chapter 11), and John Carey, Richard Niemi, and Lynda Powell (Chapter 6) all indicate that women officeholders have a greater propensity than men toward cooperation, communication, coalition building, and facilitating. One way to interpret this evidence, argue Whicker and Jewell and Rosenthal, is that as more women storm statehouses and the national legislature as rank-and-file members and as part of the leadership, the process will more closely conform to their styles. Kathlene argues, however, that the fact that political institutions are themselves gendered means that women's full inclusion into the process or a change in the process itself may still be impeded by backlash and inertia. She notes that the complex interactions of gender, structure, norms, and rules suggest that should women attempt to change the process, it will take more than winning increasing numbers in office and in leadership. When the analysis of the intersectionality of race, gender, and class, offered in Chapter 10 by Marsha Darling, is added to the discussion of the gendered nature of institutions, the complexity of institutional change is further illuminated.

Conclusion

In spite of ongoing obstacles and problems encountered in changing the norms and rules of legislative life, the answer to the question "Do women make a difference?" is still an emphatic "Yes." That women have done so in an environment that was created without their input or perspectives in mind, an environment that is gendered and racially biased, is all the more remarkable. Do women officeholders have more to accomplish in the future and more challenges to face? The debate highlighted in the previous paragraph suggests that this is certainly true.

In Chapter 14, Jean Schroedel and Nicola Mazumdar highlight the challenges women officeholders of the future will face. They note that term limitations, changes in campaign finance laws, shifts in voter mobilization, changes in electoral structures (such as the rise of single-members districts), the diversity of women elected to office, and the devolution of political responsibility from the federal government to the states and localities will all have an impact on the proportions of women in office, the role they play, and their impact. The hard work women at all levels of political office have devoted to carving out a place for themselves means, however, that whatever changes on the political horizon are in store, women's voices will be heard.

Notes

1. Research also shows that multi-member districts are more conducive than single-member districts to the election of minority candidates. Hence, choices about electoral structure affect diversity on several fronts.

2. Party breakdowns after the 1994 election reflect trends toward Republican gains mirrored on the national level. Democrats held 55.1 percent of statehouse seats and Republicans held 43.9 percent. Independents held .3 percent and non-partisans .8 percent. The nonpartisan figure reflects the fact that the Nebraska legislature is a nonpartisan unicameral (CAWP 1996c).

1

The Bottleneck
Women Becoming Candidates

GEORGIA DUERST-LAHTI

Most people believe that women have a tougher time winning elections than men do. At this writing in October 1996, only 8 percent of governors are female, the U.S. Congress has only 10 percent women members, and even state legislatures, which are relatively easy to access, count just 21 percent women in their ranks (CAWP, 1996b). These numbers exist in spite of the fact that 53 percent of voters are women. At face value, the numbers indicate that women have a tougher time winning office.

Most people also believe that women who run for office face bias or discrimination. Politics has long been seen as a man's game and those women who try to play it face trouble. Few politically active people cannot tell at least one story about an instance of discrimination against women. Accounts by female candidates of blatant sexism or gender-based questioning add to the belief that women face different treatment because they are women. Given society's treatment of women, the association between politics and masculine activities, and the low numbers of women in office, women do appear to face more obstacles in running for public office, especially at higher levels.

Anecdotes and face value are often deceiving, however. Political scientists know that the incumbency advantage is a primary explanation for the paucity of women in office (Jacobson, 1992). Women have a tougher time winning elections not because they are women, but because they are not incumbents (Darcy, Welch, and Clark, 1994; Carroll, 1994).

The pipeline is another explanation for the shortfall of elected women. It refers to the fact that experience in one elected office is seen as providing credentials for other offices. Serving in elected or appointed office at a local level creates credentials for county or state office. For this reason, the number of women who serve in local office is a critical indicator of the number of women who will be seen as credible candidates for higher office. Since 1972 women have come to occupy a far greater proportion of local offices, but although the proportion varies widely, it still falls far short of 50 percent in most locales. Hence, the trend is in the right direction, but the pipeline is still not close to full capacity (Darcy, Welch, and Clark, 1994; Carroll, 1994).

How quickly the proportions of women in local, state, and federal office will increase is unclear. On one hand, a 1994 study conducted by pollster Celinda Lake for the National Women's Political Caucus (NWPC) found that two-thirds of voters believe that women have a tougher time winning elections than men do (Newman, 1994:3). This belief was based on assumptions that "good old boys" keep women out, women will not vote for women, voters cannot see women as top executives, and female candidates cannot raise enough money (NWPC, 1994). This suggests that potential female candidates might be reluctant to run for office and proportions of women will not increase dramatically or quickly.

On the other hand, since 1972 the number of women in state legislatures and Congress has charted a steady upward course (CAWP, 1996b). The pipeline may not yet be full, but such gains create a steady stream of women with a key qualification for higher political office.

Societal attitudes about women continue to change also. Women have entered law, executive positions, and other professions that traditionally create the pool for candidates (Darcy, Welch, and Clark, 1994). Proponents of the pipeline explanation see a bright future as more women establish themselves. Perhaps more fundamental, election results show that the acceptable routes to office have broadened to include more occupations common to women such as teaching and nursing. Reflecting these changes, the 1992 "year of the woman" in politics captured media attention and furthered the sense of women's forward momentum. But female candidates for Congress in 1992 did not appear overnight. They came from the pipeline of qualified women, which had grown far fuller than most had acknowledged. Realities had changed as well as attitudes.

In sum, there is a discrepancy between conventional wisdom about why so few women relative to men hold political office and whether they do poorly or well as candidates and the systematic evidence of their progress. The remainder of this chapter is devoted to exploration of additional evidence of women's status as candidates and how their performance compares to that of men.

Success Rates: How Women Fare As Candidates

Most studies of candidate success rates have compared male and female candidates in the aggregate. Of all men and women who ran in a given election, such an investigation asks, how many and what proportion of men won and how many women won? Women candidates generally do not fare well by these measures, winning at much lower numbers and rates than men.

But does this mean that women have a tougher time winning office? A closer look at the data reveals that men are advantaged because most incumbents are men. Studies should contrast women and men in comparable circumstances—incumbents with incumbents, challengers with challengers, open-seats with open-seats. Only a few studies have adopted this approach, and those that have looked only at small samples. To have an accurate understanding of how women fare, we needed a comprehensive study of candidates over time. Ideally, the study should cover a variety of offices, encompass the universe of all candidates, and analyze comparable races.

NWPC Takes a Careful Look

In order to fulfill their goal of getting more women into elective and appointive office, NWPC set out to determine the success rates of female candidates through a careful study of comparable races. In the largest data-gathering effort to date, Jody Newman, then executive director of NWPC, compared the actual experience of women and men who were candidates.

The database included every major party candidate who ran in a general election, with information on the office, year, party, sex, and whether he or she was an incumbent, challenger, or candidate for an open-seat.[1] For the posts of U.S. House, U.S. Senate, and governors, the data included all candidates from 1972 through 1992. For state house and state senate, the database included all candidates in general elections during 1986, 1988, 1990, and 1992. Information on a total of 50,563 candidates was used.

The findings proved startling. "When women run, women win as often as men" (Newman, 1994). NWPC found success rates to be almost identical in all comparisons. In state houses, incumbent women won 95 percent of their races compared to 94 percent for incumbent men. Women and men running for open-seats won, respectively, 52 percent and 53 percent of the races. As challengers, female candidates won 10 percent their races compared to male challengers who won 9 percent. At the state senate level, women did as well as men or better. Female and male incumbents won 91 percent and 92 percent, respectively. In open-seat races, women won 58 percent compared to 55 percent for men. Female challengers won 16 percent of their races compared to men's 11 percent.

For U.S. House, female incumbents won 96 percent of their races compared to 95 percent for men. open-seats have success rates of 48 percent for women and 51 percent for men. As challengers, women succeeded in 4 percent of races in contrast to 6 percent for men. None of these differences proved statistically significant.

The numbers of women who have run for U.S. Senate and governor are too small—53 and 33, respectively—to provide meaningful comparison. Nevertheless, no evidence suggests that women were less likely to win these offices than men.

These findings surprised even savvy political operatives, and decidedly contradicted widely held beliefs that women have a tougher time winning office. The study's conclusion stands out starkly: "The reason there aren't more women in public office is not that women don't win, but that not enough women have been candidates in general elections" (Newman, 1994:2).

A few other findings were less surprising but are still worthy of note. First, even during the 1992 year of the woman in politics, success rates between women and men running in the general election were very similar. More women won in 1992 because more women ran. Second, at every level of office through 1992, more women ran as Democrats than Republicans. Third, during the entire period under study, incumbents were far more likely to win than challengers. For example, U.S. House members won their reelection bids 95 percent of the time, 16 times as often as challengers. The least successful incumbents, governors, won reelection 77 percent of the time, three times as often as challengers.

Two additional findings are sobering. First, women constitute a small minority of candidates for all levels of office. During the past four election cycles, women have made up just 20 percent of state legislative candidates. Since 1972, a mere 7 percent of candidates for U.S. House and Senate and 6 percent of gubernatorial candidates have been women. There is a striking similarity between the percentage of female officeholders and the percentage of women who were candidates.

Second, regardless of a candidate's sex, the study found that candidates for open seats—seats where no incumbent is running—were two to nine times more likely to win than challengers. For example, 45 percent of those elected governor in the study won in an open-seat race. Although open seats offer the best opportunity to win, NWPC found that women constituted "only 7 percent of open seat gubernatorial candidates, 8 percent for U.S. Senate, 10 percent for U.S. House, 19 percent for state senate and 24 percent for state house" (Newman, 1994:1–2). Open seats are the single most important key to winning higher office, and NWPC's findings show us just how few women have run for open seats.

The Best Chance

Because open seats are so much more easily won, the chance to run in such a race can be considered a relatively rare opportunity. The difficulty women have winning party nomination for open seats constitutes an important bottleneck that slows the flow of women into higher office. Women who seek election for the first time must either challenge an incumbent or run in an open seat contest. Challengers win less than 10 percent of the time, while open-seat candidates win slightly more than half the time, so clearly it is far preferable to run as an open-seat candidate. Yet fewer than one in four candidates in state house, state senate, U.S. House, and U.S. Senate races in recent years have run in open-seat contests.

Table 1.1 shows the total number of candidates in general elections for each office for the specified time period. State houses, for example, have had a total of 32,257 candidates in general elections since 1972. Each of these

TABLE 1.1
Percentage of All Candidates Who Ran for Open Seats, by Sex and Office

	Total Candidacies			
	All Candidacies	Open Seats	Percentage of Open-Seat Candidacies	Percentage of Open-Seat Female Candidates by Level
State house (1986–1992)	32,257	7,468	23	24
State senate (1986–1992)	8,246	2,081	25	19
U.S. House (1972–1992)	8,782	1,038	12	10
U.S. Senate (1972–1992)	714	145	20	8
Governor (1972–1992)	564	255	45	7

candidacies represents an opportunity to win office. Of these state house candidates, 7468, or 23 percent, of all candidates have captured the best possible opportunity to run for office. The smallest bottleneck is for the U.S. House, at 12 percent open-seat opportunities. The largest is for governor with 255 candidates or 45 percent of all chances to win being in open-seat opportunities. (Two candidates for one seat is the most common pattern, but some also ran unopposed.)

The right-hand side of Table 1.1 shows the percentage of open-seat candidates for each office who are women. Women comprise only 24 percent of open-seat candidates for state house races, and 19 percent of open-seat candidates for state senate contests. The numbers are even lower for the U.S. House and Senate and for gubernatorial contests. The conclusion is clear. Too few women run, especially in open-seat races. In either case, the single most intractable obstacle for women's political parity is the unwillingness of women to become candidates. If women don't run, they can't win elections.

Recruiting Women to Become Candidates

Efforts to recruit women to become candidates have been made at least since the revival of the women's movement in the 1960s. Party organizations try to convince women to run: in 1984, the Republican Senate Campaign Committee offered $17,500 in start-up funds to any women willing to step forward as a candidate (Newman, 1995). In recent years both parties have made major efforts to encourage women's candidacies.

In 1990, the National Organization for Women and the Fund for a Feminist Majority attempted to field a women to run in every race. This effort sent the clear message that women can and should run for office, gave more women experience with the campaign process and, not inconsequentially, increased the pool of women in the pipeline with candidacies to their credit. Although many women who were recruited through this effort were not viable, overall there were clear benefits from this strategy.

National efforts generally were not prominent during 1991 and 1992, although prior efforts percolated in at least some states.[2] However, the Hill/Thomas Senate hearings created a momentum as many women responded to the all-male Senate Judiciary Committee (Duerst-Lahti and Verstegen, 1995; Cook, Thomas, and Wilcox, 1994) and the media paid special attention to the increased number of women candidates. Overall, feminist organizations played the momentum much more than creating it.[3]

During 1993 and 1994, the National Women's Political Caucus made a concerted effort to recruit candidates from its national office by working closely with state and local caucuses. It hired a field director, Michelle Parish, who created training material and coached state and local leadership (NWPC, 1995a), and political director Mary Beth Lambert consulted with state leadership about important races and potential candidates. Yet ultimately the "year of the angry white male" yielded no real gains for women in Congress.

In late 1994 the NWPC switched its focus to the states. Beginning at its fall National Steering Committee (NSC) meeting, NWPC began a series of training events for state leadership focused on learning from current campaigns and identifying candidates and campaign managers for future campaigns (Duerst-Lahti, 1994). The clarion call of its biennial convention in August 1995 was the urgency of candidate recruitment. Prior to the convention, outgoing president Harriett Woods made a swing through 23 cities, giving a "wake up call and guidance" on candidate recruitment (Newman, 1995). A refrain was sounded in the recruitment campaign: "Women can't win if they don't run." Further, Woods declared that women "weren't seizing the best opportunities—open seats" (press conference, August 3, 1995, Nashville). The Caucus identified several models of candidate recruitment and showcased them throughout these efforts, buttressing state and local descriptions with insights from professional trainers from both political parties including Robin Wright, Heidi Von Szeliski, and Heidi Bunkowske. These models of candidate recruitment warrant a closer look.

Recruitment Strategies: Three Steps

All successful efforts to recruit female candidates share three components, identifying winnable seats, finding credible candidates, and having something to offer individuals in their campaign.[4] Knowledge of the district and of incumbents' records is a key to targeting seats. Incumbents may be vulnerable for a variety of reasons such as scandal, poor health, or weak job performance. To identify winnable seats, districts must be analyzed for a variety of factors, including partisan composition and voting history and turnout.

Credible candidates must have a background suited to the particular office as a result of either substantive experience or personal resources. Substantive background can include education or training or civic activity, for example, a neighborhood watch group leader taking up crime issues on the city council. Personal resources include the ability to speak well, an established base of support, positive name recognition, a capacity to raise funds, and the absence of scandal. Recruiters should look to civic organizations, other offices, past candidates, staffers for other politicians, attorneys, and academia to find such individuals.

For the 1996 cycle, Democratic pollster Celinda Lake advised recruiting women who have started their own businesses, become prominent in community-based organizations, or served in local offices, especially school boards and other appointive or elective boards such as those dealing with health care, safety issues, and environmental regulation. Because women are still seen as outsiders in politics, according to Lake, alternatives to usual sources of candidates serve women well (Lake, 1995).

As an inducement to potential candidates, those doing the recruiting need to offer desirable resources such as money, endorsements, volunteers, organization of campaign events, political expertise, campaign software, or help with the press.

Models of State and Local Initiatives

The following four models illustrate the ways in which these principles have been put into practice.

California has been using a system for identifying optimal seats called D.I.R.E. DIRE identifies seats where officeholders have died, have been indicted, are retiring, or have reached term limits. Unlike other states, California has an ample number of women willing to step forward as candidates, so the California Caucus found that the most important intervention it could make was to simply publicize a list of these attractive seats.

NWPC-Wisconsin employs a joint strategy of targeting seats and identifying potential candidates called "political mapping." The effort began by dividing the state into practical political regions—for example, Milwaukee, Dane County, Lake Shore, Central, Northeast, Northwest, Fox River Valley. In each region, a core of political insiders worked from comprehensive county directories that identified every elected office and incumbent. Between three and five activists identified seats likely to be open in the next election and contacted women with good credentials to run for these offices. The Caucus then offered training sessions, mailing lists, endorsements, and funds. Even if only a handful of those contacted chose to run, those women who did so ran in contests where they had the best chance of success.

Moreover, recruiters believed that the list of potential candidates would be useful in the future as other seats opened and as individual women came to think about themselves as capable of taking the plunge. So a one-time effort to identify credible female candidates can have long-term effects.[5]

Power 2000 in Michigan is part of a five-year Caucus building plan. The recruitment task force has so far functioned for one year, from June

1995 to May 1996. Those involved believed that a limited time period would bring more vigor to the plan's efforts. The task force grew out of the NWPC but is larger than the Caucus, drawing on individual women and representatives of other organizations. Its central purpose was to change the atmosphere for female candidates using the press as its prime vehicle. Power 2000 selectively endorsed viable female candidates, then spotlighted those candidates as they signed policy statements, served as mentors, worked on recruitment coalitions, and collected resources for other female candidates. Power 2000 systematically approached editorial boards of newspapers to educate them on the dynamics surrounding female candidates and their differential treatment. By centering on extraordinary female candidates, the task force attempted to improve opportunities for all women who might run.

Project Suffrage began in Tucson, Arizona, after the 1994 election, with the goal of majority representation on the city council. It used a strategy of research on message, fit, and consistency with the district to achieve its ends. Project Suffrage formed into a tax-exempt organization to create and support its library on voter information and attitudes, district history, incumbent background and opposition research, candidate profiles, and the like. It also conducts training on local and state politics for its candidates. Homework is the key to its success.[6]

These models illustrate different approaches to recruiting and supporting female candidates, tailored to suit various locales. But despite such well-designed efforts, too few women run for office.

Why Don't More Women Run?

If efforts to recruit women to become candidates are to succeed, understanding why so few women now run is essential. As noted in the Introduction, Celinda Lake explored that question in detail through a national survey of 1,000 voters in July 1994 and a pilot study of 212 voters drawn from the pool of likely candidates: women and men with legal or executive backgrounds and women activists. Her findings help to explain women's reluctance to run for office.

First, women are less than half as likely as men (8 percent and 18 percent, respectively) to have considered running for office. Within the recruitment pool sample, only 36 percent had ever considered public office: 58 percent of activist women, 38 percent of male lawyers and executives, 25 percent of female lawyers and executives. Again, not enough women run because not enough consider running.

Second, both women and men are concerned about the impact of running on their families. Both the amount of time necessary for a successful campaign and the public scrutiny involved are chief concerns. Both also are concerned about adequate financial backing. Among recruitment populations, female executives and lawyers are more concerned on every factor than men or women activists. Time is the most important reason for not running for these women (30 percent). For men (23 percent) and activist women (17 percent), exposure to public scrutiny is the number one reason.

The Lake study also found that women are less confident about their chances than are men. Lake's research shows that women are more likely than men to believe themselves unqualified and incapable, and to think themselves less likely to win.[7] While the NWPC study demonstrates that women win as often as men in comparable races, that message has not gotten through to potential candidates.

Training and support are key factors distinguishing women and men in the recruitment pool. Two-thirds of women compared to one-third of men cite training as a factor in deciding to run. Women were more likely than men to stress three types of support: a mentor to show them how to run, help in raising money, and the support of community organizations. Training and support, then, are "critically important to encouraging women to run for office" (NWPC, 1994).

A few other findings are worthy of note. First, younger women are much less likely than older women to worry about their qualifications, even though they still worry more than men. Thus, the future looks promising. Second, men are asked to run more often than are women, and are more likely to be asked to run by friends and colleagues whereas women are more likely to be asked by family members. Finally, women who have considered running for office worry less and about different concerns than women who have not considered running.

Some Actions to Unclog the Bottleneck

Together, these findings suggest insights and several courses of action. For example, activist women are more similar to activist men in their willingness to consider running for office than are the female executives and attorneys to their male counterparts. It may be that activist women have already experienced politics and therefore bring a better understanding to it than women who have not had such close encounters with elected office. Also, activist women have already been subject to public scrutiny in a variety of ways and they have sacrificed family time for their activism. In short, activist women are more politically involved and therefore know the costs.

The larger gender differences in willingness to run among executives and attorneys suggests that special efforts should be made to reach out to female executives and attorneys. Perhaps a long-term strategy would be to involve these professional women in some form of activism as a first step. Given such experience, they should become more likely to consider running.

Another effort involves asking. If women are asked to run only by family members, they may readily dismiss this encouragement to run because of the source. Colleagues, friends, and party officials need to undertake a systematic strategy to ask women to run, especially women executives and attorneys. "Recruitment is really the phone calling," according to Celinda Lake (Lake,

1995). Ultimately recruiting involves getting on the phone to ask women to run for office. Someone must make recruiting female candidates a priority and take the initiative. Although women in campaigns may occasionally face sex discrimination, it does not prevent them from winning as often as men win in comparable races. Women need to know this fact. open-seats are the key. Efforts should be directed toward identifying potential open-seats and matching a credible candidate to each.

Women say that they want training, and several sophisticated training programs exist. The NWPC holds training sessions across the nation. EMILY's List, a PAC that targets Democratic pro-choice women, offers sessions for congressional candidates. Women who want training can get it, but they must be told where to find it.

Finally, those who want more women in public office should take heart. Younger women are more confident than their older sisters, female candidates are increasingly common, and women candidates are accepted by voters. The pipeline of lower-level offices offers a ready pool of candidates for higher office. All of these suggest that rapid progress may be possible.

Like men who succeed in politics, women must work for their success. We know now that when women run, women win. We also know that most female candidates squander their efforts on difficult races, so we must target our efforts more strategically. And finally, we know why more women do not run. Our work to open the bottleneck must include training, mentors, and other support. In the end, according to Jody Newman, we may have reason to take heart. Young women in office now talk openly about their desire to run for higher office and they are positioning themselves to do it successfully. "Societal, historical and political forces are bigger than anything an individual or organization can do to encourage women to run for office. But those who care can create the climate for that change by our work" (Newman, 1995).

Notes

1. All data were double-checked for accuracy and the study used lists of all female candidates from the Center for the American Woman and Politics to ensure that women were accurately identified. For further methodological details, see Newman, 1994: 6–8.
2. In Wisconsin, for example, NOW remained a central organizer of a coalition to recruit and support pro-choice female candidates.
3. We should not underestimate the importance of the NWPC *New York Times* advertisement picturing Anita Hill before fourteen female senators. See Duerst-Lahti, 1993.
4. These three components were presented by Robin Wright on August 4, 1995, in Nashville.
5. The California and Wisconsin models were presented at a training session for the NWPC National Steering Committee, February 24, 1995, in San Diego.
6. The Michigan and Arizona models were presented at the NWPC convention in Nashville, August 4, 1995.

7. Fifty-five percent of women and 34 percent of men thought themselves unqualified, 37 percent of women and 26 percent men thought themselves incapable, and 71 percent of women but only 63 percent of men thought that they were less likely to win. Within the recruitment pool, 54 percent of men, 48 percent of activist women, and 36 percent of female attorneys and executives thought they could win. In terms of feeling unqualified and not sufficiently knowledgeable, men (8 percent) and activist women (10 percent) were not concerned, but 26 percent of female attorneys and executives were quite concerned.

2

Campaign Finance

Women's Experience in the Modern Era

BARBARA BURRELL

As Georgia Duerst-Lahti discusses in Chapter 1, both students of politics and women's rights activists have long tried to understand why such a small percentage of elected public officials in the United States is women. Two themes predominate in attempts to address this puzzle—the scarcity of women running for office and, when women have run, the extent to which they have faced discrimination in acquiring the resources needed to be successful. One of the key resources for elections in America is money. In this chapter, I provide an overview of women's experience in campaign finance in the modern era and then concentrate on the 1994 elections. First, I review what we have learned from empirical analyses about the financing of men's and women's campaigns for the national legislature elections prior to 1994. Second, I discuss women's presence as candidates in the 1994 election, and third, I analyze the financial basis of their campaigns compared with that of male candidates. It is important to remember that election to national office is a two-stage process involving winning a party nomination and then winning the general election. Thus, I focus on women's presence and performance both in primary elections to receive a party's nomination, and in general election campaigns as party nominees, and on the role of money at each of these stages.

The role of money in campaigns for public office in the United States has become a subject of major concern and debate. As Jean Schroedel and Nicola Mazumdar discuss in Chapter 14, campaign finance reform is a major agenda item for the U.S. Congress. The amount of money that different individuals and groups have to spend on politics influences who gets heard, what issues are debated, and how they are addressed. The ability of candidates to raise sizable amounts of money to finance a campaign helps to determine who gets elected.

Traditionally, it was thought that a major reason why so few women were elected to the U.S. Congress was that they did not enjoy the same levels and kinds of financial assistance as men—at either the primary or the general election stage. Many believed that potential donors were less likely to give to women candidates, women candidates were psychologically less predisposed to ask for donations, and women did not have the same access to big money givers.

Contrary to conventional wisdom, empirical evidence has shown that while differences in financial support existed during the contemporary era, current women candidates now raise and spend as much or more than their male counterparts. The small group of female major party nominees (32 candidates) in contested U.S. House races in 1972 began the era raising and spending nearly as much money as male nominees. As their presence in elections expanded from the 1974 to 1980 elections, female nominees raised and spent approximately three-quarters of what male contenders acquired and spent. In the 1982–86 period, women achieved near equality with men in the financing of their campaigns. In the 1988 election, a major breakthrough occurred when female nominees raised and spent greater average amounts of money than male nominees. In fact, they raised 119 percent of what male candidates raised. In 1990 female nominees raised 97 percent and spent 102 percent of what men raised and spent, and in 1992 they raised 111 percent and spent 108 percent (Burrell, 1994).

Examining the campaign process at an earlier stage of the political process —during the primaries—also reveals that women in the modern era have not been disadvantaged compared to men. Analyses of the financial structures of men's and women's campaigns in open-seat primaries for the U.S. House of Representatives in recent elections show that female candidates have held their own. A comparison of the average amounts of money male and female major party open-seat contenders raised in the first and second reporting periods of the 1988–1992 campaigns showed female contenders doing better than their male counterparts. A larger percentage of these female candidates reported having raised funds at the end of the first reporting period in each of the three years, and women had larger average campaign treasuries in the early stages of their election cycle (Burrell, 1994). These early reporting periods are critical to nonincumbent candidacies, for it is then that successful candidates introduce themselves and their issue priorities to the voters. Thus the message on campaign finance is similar to the message on electoral results: when women run, they can raise the money they need to win.

The 1994 Election

Unlike 1992, the "year of the woman," no defining event crystallized the 1994 election for women candidates and women voters. Media coverage of the election evidenced little celebration of (or criticism of) the difference women could bring to political leadership, and the coverage that appeared was mixed. On one hand, journalists argued that since many women incumbents were Democrats and freshmen, women might face difficulties in that anti-Democrat, anti-incumbent, anti-progressive ideological campaign. On the other hand, the media sometimes talked about women's potential to extend their victories of previous years. When all the votes were tallied, the outcome was similar to women's experiences in recent elections—when women run, they do as well, if not better, than male candidates.

In 1994, 200 women entered Democratic and Republican Party primaries for seats in the U.S. House of Representatives—12.9 percent of all major party candidates. The 200 women seeking nominations were slightly fewer than the 218 women who had run in 1992, but they constituted a slightly higher percentage of all candidates in 1994 than in 1992. Women's presence in 1994 was the highest percentage ever of female candidates for the U.S. House of Representatives.

The increase in women's presence was, in large part, due to the record number of women who had been elected in 1992 and were running for reelection. All of the women who were first elected in 1992 ran for reelection in 1994. Two incumbent women retired from the House in order to run for higher office and one female incumbent retired from public office completely. Thus, the pool of female candidates in 1994 consisted of 44 incumbents seeking reelection compared with 27 in 1992. Added to the female incumbents seeking reelection were 21 challengers to their party's incumbents, 81 opposition party candidates, and 54 open-seat contenders.[1]

Women's Presence and Performance in Open-Seat Primaries

Creating a presence in open-seat primaries is critical if women are to expand their numbers in Congress. In 1994, fewer than half of the open-seat primary contests within both political parties had a woman candidate. Voters had an opportunity to choose a woman in only 45 percent of the Democratic and 47 percent of the Republican contests if they desired to do so. These figures represent an expanded opportunity among Republicans but a lessened opportunity among Democrats compared with earlier elections.

How successful were the women open-seat candidates relative to their male counterparts? Twenty-eight percent of the women won their primaries compared with 25 percent of the men. Two female Democrats had no opposition in the primary. Six Democratic men and four Republican men had no primary opposition for an open-seat. In contested primary races, women won an average 26.8 percent of the vote compared with 22.6 percent for men. This finding is consistent with results of analyses of other recent elections (Burrell, 1992, 1994). Once again we find women, a small percentage of all candidates, outperforming their male counterparts.

Democratic primaries continue to be more friendly than Republican primaries toward women candidates. Nearly a third of the Democratic female candidates won their primaries, compared with roughly a quarter of male Democratic candidates and male and female Republican candidates.

Republican women were the least successful group in winning open-seat primaries, but in contested primaries they did not lag behind other groups in obtaining votes. Democratic women in contested open-seat primaries obtained an average 27 percent of the vote, Republican women obtained 26 percent, Republican men obtained 24 percent, and Democratic men obtained 21 percent.

Overall, in open-seat primaries in 1994, women continued to be a small minority of all candidates, but their presence did not decline compared with other recent elections. Republican women increased their presence while Democratic women decreased theirs. However, among those who did enter primaries, Democratic women did better than their Republican counterparts. Most important, overall, women did better than men; they won a larger percentage of their primaries and they obtained, on average, a larger share of the vote. The bottom line is that, once again, it is not poor performance but the lack of women in open-seat primaries that accounts for the low representation of women in Congress.

Open-Seat Primaries and Early Money

How did female candidates in open-seat races do in raising dollars in the beginning of the campaign season of 1994? Data from the first and second reporting periods of the election cycle (supplied by the Federal Election Commission) reveal that women open-seat primary contenders raised a mean amount of $43,075 compared with $49,211 for male open-seat primary contenders. This was the first election season in which women candidates did not outperform men candidates at this stage of the campaign process in fund-raising since we have been able to conduct such analyses. However, if we compare the median amount raised instead of the mean amount, women continued to do better than their male counterparts. Taken together, comparing the mean and median amounts suggests that women are at least as successful as men in raising money. By the second reporting period, women were outpacing men in both mean and median amounts raised.

PAC and Individual Contributions   In the first reporting period of 1994, political action committees (PACs) were not as generous with women open-seat candidates, on average, as they were with men. This is a reversal of what had occurred in 1988 and 1992. By the second reporting period, however, women had once again surged past their male counterparts. They also raised more in both reporting periods from individual donors than male candidates did in 1994 (see Table 2.1).

Party and Fund-raising   Both Democratic and Republican women lagged behind men in acquiring money (measured by mean receipts) in the first reporting period of 1994. But by the second reporting period Democratic women surged to a substantial lead while Republican women continued to lag behind (Table 2.2).

As the table shows, Democrats were much more likely to obtain PAC money than were Republicans. In the first reporting period, they acquired an

TABLE 2.1
Financing of Male and Female Open-Seat Candidates for the U.S. House of
Representatives, First and Second Reporting Periods*

	First Period				Second Period			
	Mean		Median		Mean		Median	
	Men	Women	Men	Women	Men	Women	Men	Women
1988	$42,475	$45,942	$13,256	$13,492	$97,160	$103,863	$39,905	$109,766
1990	37,607	43,910	5,232	17,862	84,215	135,259	24,854	95,430
1992	29,228	35,854	0	873	78,350	104,397	28,071	39,440
1994	49,211	43,075	11,169	26,857	107,729	113,399	48,660	104,671
	PACs		Individual		PACs		Individual	
	Men	Women	Men	Women	Men	Women	Men	Women
1988	$3,632	$9,540	$26,224	$31,271	$11,334	$21,675	$56,440	$109,766
1990	5,681	5,513	23,579	23,675	14,386	23,436	46,538	74,259
1992	3,596	3,937	19,893	28,493	9,547	17,973	44,784	64,259
1994	4,912	3,056	30,951	31,776	13,123	14,629	60,096	71,526

*Data from Federal Election Commission

TABLE 2.2
Mean Receipts, First and Second Reporting Periods, Open-Seat Primaries for
the U.S. House of Representatives by Sex and Party, 1994

	First Reporting Period	Second Reporting Period
Democratic men	$54,000	$111,033
Democratic women	43,848	123,589
Republican men	44,514	104,487
Republican women	42,244	102,425

average of $6,400 compared with $2,885 for Republicans. The gap narrowed
only slightly by the end of the second reporting period. At that point,
Democrats had obtained an average of $18,139 and Republicans had obtained
an average of $8,555. By the second reporting period, Democratic women
were the leading recipients of PAC donations (mean of $20,127), followed
by Democratic men (mean of $17,777). Republican women also acquired a
slightly higher amount than Republican men ($8,707 vs. $8,529).

Women's Performance in the General Election Votes

On election day in November 1994, how did women candidates do at the
ballot box compared with men candidates? The election of 1994 had the
distinction of having an unprecedented number of general election contests

for the U.S. House of Representatives in which the nominees of both parties were women—11 races. All these races pitted a female incumbent against a female challenger. Those 11 races are excluded from this first piece of analysis so that I can compare the votes women get when running against men.

Men as a group did slightly better obtaining votes than did women U.S. House nominees in 1994. They obtained an average 49.6 percent of the vote compared with 46.2 percent for the women nominees.[2] As Table 2.3 indicates, however, when we control for party and candidate status, women outpaced men in four of the six pairings. Only Republican female challengers and open-seat contenders slightly trailed their male counterparts. Female Democratic open-seat nominees obtained a substantially higher share of the vote than male Democratic open-seat nominees.

Table 2.3 also describes the general election success rates of Democratic and Republican male and female U.S. House candidates in 1994. Not one Democratic challenger—male or female—defeated a Republican incumbent. Republican challengers, on the other hand, although only winning a small minority of the time, did better than they have in the past two decades (see Burrell, 1994:144). In addition, open-seat Republican candidates, especially male Republicans, did exceptionally well. Male Republicans won 83 percent of their open-seat races and female Republicans won 67 percent of theirs. For both groups, that was their highest success rate in over 20 years. Female Democratic open-seat nominees did better than their male counterparts, who were particularly unsuccessful, winning only 21 percent of their races.

Female Democratic incumbents did poorly in 1994 compared both with other incumbent groups and with their success rate in previous elections. Eight of the 23 female Democratic incumbents were defeated. Democratic women

TABLE 2.3
Mean Percentage of the Vote and General Election for the U.S. House of Representatives Success Rate by Sex, Party, and Candidate Status, 1994

	Democrats		Republicans	
	Men	Women	Men	Women
Challenged incumbents				
Percent of vote	60	60	67	70
Success rate	177/148	23/15	114/114	5/5
	(.84)	(.65)	(100%)	(100%)
Challengers				
Percent of vote	31	32	39	36
Success rate	95/0	24/0	185/28	16/3
	(.00)	(.00)	(.15)	(.19)
Open-seats				
Percent of vote	44	50	53	51
Success rate	42/9	10/4	46/38	6/4
	(.21)	(.40)	(.83)	(.67)

had done particularly well in 1992 when 21 of them were newly elected to the House. It may be that this group of new "insiders" was disproportionately vulnerable in 1994 given the "backlash" atmosphere of that election. The question of disproportionate vulnerability can be partially explored by comparing the success rate of first-term Democratic women with that of the newly elected male Democrats. Forty-two male Democrats were newly elected to the 103rd Congress in 1992. Ten of the men were defeated for reelection, for a 76 percent success rate. The success rate for first-term Democratic women was 74 percent. Thus, we can say that the backlash of 1994 resulted in the defeat of first-term Democrats in general, not just female Democrats: the women were no more likely to have been defeated than their male counterparts. First-term female Democrats facing major party opponents won 54.2 percent of the vote compared with 59.5 percent for the male Democrats.[3] These women were advantaged, however, through national support in the financing of their campaigns. They raised an average of $803,922 compared with $585,188 for the men. They collected an average of $366,243 in PAC donations compared with $299,892 for the men.

The Financing of the 1994 Campaigns

Women major party nominees once again slightly outpaced their male counterparts in the financing of their campaigns. Women nominees with a major party opponent as a group raised an average of $438,256 compared with $433,303 that male nominees raised.[4] Women incumbents, women challengers, and women open-seat nominees all did better than men in those groups. Female Democratic nominees raised more than their male Democratic nominees in each status category, and female Republican challengers and open-seat nominees bested their male counterparts. Only female Republican incumbents raised a smaller average amount than male Republican incumbents. The six female Republican open-seat nominees raised $863,413 compared with only $567,324 for the male Republican open-seat nominees. But they did not suffer at the ballot box, as indicated by Figure 2.1.

Female Nominees versus Their Opponents

It has been argued elsewhere that comparing female candidates with male candidates as a group is not the most appropriate comparison to assess women's equality in obtaining campaign funds. Instead, female candidates should be compared with their male opponents (Herrick, 1995).

In 1994, the 15 female open-seat nominees raised 95 percent of the average of their male opponents. But, the average for men was especially high because one male candidate raised $2,420,786, far more than the other candidates. If we compare median amounts raised, female nominees in open-seat races in 1994 outpaced their male opponents—$614,078 to $488,579. Further, female nominees did better than their male opponents in 10 of the 15 races. In this overwhelmingly Republican year, the nine female Democratic

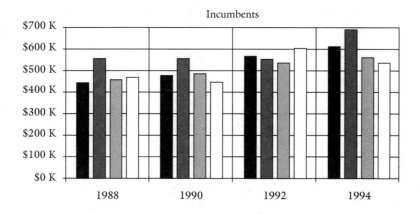

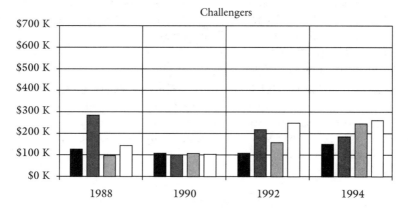

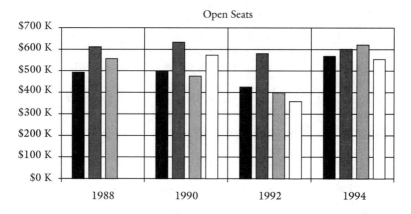

■ Democratic Men ■ Democratic Women ▨ Republican Men ☐ Republican Women

Figure 2.1. Mean receipts by party, sex, and incumbent status for major party nominees, 1988–1994.

open-seat nominees raised substantially more their Republican opponents, while male Democratic open-seat nominees raised substantially less than their male Republican opponents. In 1994, no evidence exists to suggest that female nominees suffered in comparison with their male opponents.

PAC and Individual Contributions   In the 1994 election cycle, 4,618 political action committees registered with the Federal Election Commission (FEC) contributed $189.4 million to federal election campaigns (FEC data). As Table 2.4 shows, women major party nominees, on average, raised more money in PAC contributions than their male counterparts. Women incumbents, women challengers, and women open-seat candidates all raised more than male candidates in comparable situations. Male and female nominees raised virtually the same average amounts in individual contributions ($224,718 vs. $224,051) in 1994. Women incumbents and women open-seat candidates raised a greater average amount than male incumbents and male open-seat candidates in individual contributions, but female challengers raised less. Female Democrats in all three candidate status groups raised a greater average amount in individual contributions than their Democratic male counterparts, but female Republican nominees raised less in each candidate status group.

Political Parties' Financial Support   Political parties are another source of campaign money, in addition to raising funds from political action committees and from individuals and using one's own financial resources. The Federal Election Campaign Act limits the financial support political party organizations can give to their candidates. National party organizations and state party committees also can make coordinated expenditures, on behalf of their candidates.

In each of the elections between 1980 and 1990, Republicans contributed a larger average amount to their female candidates than to their male nominees in U.S. House campaigns. In four of the six elections, they were also more generous to their female nominees in their coordinated expenditures. Democratic female nominees also did better in acquiring direct contributions and coordinated expenditures from their party in four of the six elections (Burrell, 1994:97).

Table 2.5 presents party contributions and coordinated expenditures to male and female nominees in 1992 and 1994. The table compares donations to candidates by status group, that is, incumbents, challengers, and open-seat

TABLE 2.4
Mean Political Action Committee Contributions for U.S. House of Representatives Races

	1988	1990	1992	1994
Men	$120,646	$128,829	$139,807	$150,576
Women	124,625	121,059	137,776	157,999

candidates. In 1992 both parties contributed more money to nonincumbent women nominees than to nonincumbent men nominees. Democratic open-seat male and female candidates received virtually the same amount in coordinated expenditures, and Democratic female challengers received substantially less than their male counterparts in coordinated expenditures. Republicans on the average gave more to their candidates and favored their women candidates in almost all candidate status categories.

In 1994 the Democratic committees were more generous with their female incumbents than their male incumbents, but slightly less generous to their nonincumbent female nominees in their direct contributions. They were substantially less generous to their female open-seat nominees but contributed more to their female challengers in coordinated expenditures. Republicans in 1994 gave more to their male nominees in both direct contributions and coordinated expenditures in all status categories except open-seat coordinated expenditures. In half of the 24 comparisons of party contributions and coordinated expenditures the parties, on average, advantaged their female candidates, and in the other half they gave more to their male candidates. Once again we find no evidence of systematic party bias against female candidates.

TABLE 2.5
Average Party Contributions and Coordinated Expenditures for U.S. House of Representatives Races by Party, 1992–1994

	Contributions		Coordinated Expenditures	
	Men	Women	Men	Women
Democratic incumbents				
1992	$1,778	$1,742	$7,362	$7,017
1994	3,167	4,851	17,100	17,870
Democratic challengers				
1992	$1,840	$2,623	$17,310	$13,572
1994	2,677	2,296	16,167	19,316
Democratic open seats				
1992	$2,094	$3,568	$12,847	$12,891
1994	6,698	6,058	45,344	36,882
Republican incumbents				
1992	$4,578	$3,568	$26,565	$34,286
1994	1,871	1,578	11,239	1,629
Republican challengers				
1992	$3,902	$5,342	$24,001	$27,120
1994	5,123	4,811	22,975	20,952
Republican open seats				
1992	$5,602	$6,943	$27,696	$33,256
1994	9,218	8,789	46,550	66,760

Source: Federal Election Commission. The 1992 figures were reported in Biersack and Herrnson (1994).

Women's PACs   Increasingly women have been organizing on behalf of women candidates and this phenomenon has been a major boost to women's fund-raising potential. In 1992 six national organizations including EMILY's List gave a total of over $7 million to women candidates for national office (Burrell, 1994). In 1994 *Campaigns & Elections* magazine listed 54 state and national women's PACs.

In 1994 EMILY's List distributed $8.7 million to pro-choice Democratic women candidates in national and state races, including 41 women running for federal office. EMILY'S List was the third highest PAC money raiser in the 1994 election cycle, and was second in spending. The WISH List, which was established in 1991 to support pro-choice female Republican candidates, distributed $370,000 to women candidates in 1994 (an increase from $230,000 in 1992). Thirty-three women running for Congress received help from the WISH List. Joining the primarily pro-choice women's PACs in 1994 was the Susan B. Anthony List which was established to assist pro-life women candidates. According to FEC records, the Susan B. Anthony List distributed nearly $34,000 to federal election candidates in 1994. All three of these PACs encourage their members to write checks directly to women candidates, and then they gather them together and distribute them in a bundle. This "bundling" process enables the PACs to provide far more help to candidates in close races than would be allowed if the committee only made direct contributions. The majority of funds distributed by all three PACs were bundled contributions from their members.

In addition, in 1994 the Women's Campaign Fund, a bipartisan organization and the oldest of the women's PACs, founded in 1974, gave $1,474,355 to female candidates for federal office. The National Women's Political Caucus contributed $125,762 and the National Organization for Women contributed $326,324. (See also Nelson, 1994; and Burrell, 1994, for further historical material on these women's PACs.)

Conclusion

Progressive women candidates have come to have an advantage over their male counterparts. They now have access to a pool of money for primary and general elections and a network of supporters who are becoming increasingly sophisticated in operating in electoral politics. Of course, money alone is not the goal of electoral campaigns; votes are. As evidence in this chapter indicates, women are successful compared to men in winning votes and winning seats.

Does all this mean that women's presence in the U.S. House of Representatives will soon approach parity? Unfortunately, the answer is no. The first barrier to rapid parity is the power of incumbency. As illuminated throughout this book, the incumbency advantage is a powerful one and because men are the vast majority of incumbents, women remain underrepresented. In addition, the fact that women are successful money-raisers does not mean that all in the political world are convinced of their viability and attractiveness as candidates. As Sue Thomas noted in the Introduction to this book, research suggests that potential women candidates are still hesitant to run, in part because of the difficulties of fund-raising. Party leaders and other political influentials must be sensitive to this hesitancy and help overcome that reluctance by convincing women that they can raise enough money to win. Surely, women's success in money-raising and vote-getting is an incentive for other women. As the social and political environment comes to greater acceptance of women's role in political representation, one thing will is clear: women can and do raise money and votes as successfully as their male counterparts.

Notes

1. Women seeking reelection constituted 11.4 percent of incumbents running. Women represented 11.3 percent of challengers to their party's incumbents, 12.9 percent of challengers to incumbents of the other party, and 14.8 percent of open-seat candidates.

2. The correlation between sex and votes was .07, suggesting that the sex of a candidate had little impact on the votes of the public. The closer the correlation statistic is to 1, the stronger the relationship.

3. The correlation between sex and votes obtained among first-term Democrats was .22.

4. These figures do not include nominees with no major party opponent. They include contested races only.

3

Gender, Political Advertising, and the "Air Wars"

Leonard Williams

Observers have long noted that in the masculine world of politics, military metaphors abound. Yesterday's party bosses and today's political consultants have planned and conducted campaigns, recruited and organized platoons of volunteers for action in the field. Candidates fight for their political lives and engage in battles over budgets. Since electoral victories are won by controlling this or that territory, it is not surprising that reporters adopt a "game schema" that discusses politics in strategic terms (Patterson, 1994; cf. Joslyn, 1990; and West, 1994). Nor is it surprising that enterprising consultants read books with such titles as *The Art of War* or assert that today's campaigns "have taken on all the aspects of a video war" (Luntz, 1988:18).[1]

If modern election campaigns may be described as a video war, then the weapon of choice has been the spot ad, the 30-second political commercial. With their spots, candidates spend millions of dollars to win the hearts, minds, and votes of millions of people. In the last few decades, though, a new set of candidate gladiators has entered the arena. Women, long relegated to support positions in political campaigns, now occupy both the front lines and the command centers (Boneparth, 1977). In today's campaigns, women hold many of the most visible positions—pollsters and press secretaries, media wizards and managers, consultants, and, more importantly, candidates. What has this new role for women meant for the conduct of political campaigns? Do the women running for office employ the same strategies and tactics as the men who run? Are there significant gender differences in the ways candidates present their qualifications or criticize their opponents?

Fortunately, scholars in communication studies and political science have begun exploring the content of ads for female and male candidates for public office. Most research has focused on campaigns for federal or statewide office, where television ads are more widely used than radio or newspaper advertising.

This chapter will review the academic literature concerning gender influences in televised political advertising. The discussion will focus on three areas: (1) the situational demands and expectations faced by women running for office; (2) the special case of "attack politics"; and (3) the videostyles employed in the ads of male and female candidates. In addition to reviewing previous studies, I will also share results from a qualitative study of ads for selected gubernatorial and senatorial candidates in elections from 1990 to 1994. Finally, I will conclude by highlighting some avenues for further research.

Women's Reality

Not surprisingly, faced with the problem of how to persuade large numbers of voters to support a candidate, campaigns typically use television advertising to perform a basic set of communicative functions. On the positive side of the campaign, candidates tell their "stories," explain their positions on the issues, and reinforce the favorable images held by their supporters. In a more negative vein, candidates attack opponents in order to set a rhetorical agenda, produce a defensive mood in the opposition camp, or simply undermine any positive image the opponent might have among the voters. In response to attacks, candidates either refute or counterattack (Trent and Friedenberg, 1995:128–134).

Though most candidates face similar situations, women running for office have usually confronted additional barriers to political advancement. Despite the fact that women now comprise a remarkable talent pool of political leaders, the political situation for women has not changed completely. Women running for office must continue to deal with the legacy of gender socialization and stereotypes. The way these operate in media aspects of campaigns are particularly stark. Whereas a female candidate in the 1970s was warned that she "must be shown as assertive rather than aggressive, attractive without being a sexpot, self-confident but not domineering," a similar candidate today is told to "craft a message and a public persona that persuades party, pundits, and public that she can be as clear and independent a decision maker as any man, but more caring and trustworthy" (Paizis, 1977; Witt, Paget, and Matthews, 1994). The image-oriented advice for women remains the same: strike a careful pose—one that delicately balances both stereotypically masculine and feminine qualities.

The trick, of course, is to walk this tightrope in the very public and highly charged atmosphere of the "air wars." As Kern and Edley (1994) put it, the task for women candidates "is to appear strong and competent, when the conception established by the public/private paradigm is that women may be honest and compassionate, but strong they are not." How do women running for office manage to negotiate their way through these contradictory demands? How do women candidates resolve the tensions inherent in a conflict between stereotype and ambition? To answer these questions requires a look at political advertising and videostyles of women and men.

The Paradox of Negativity

"Politics ain't beanbag," Will Rogers reminded us, but today's politics appears even more unseemly and harsh than its earlier variants. Negative campaigning, attack politics, dirty politics, mudslinging—these words are most commonly used to describe contemporary election campaigns. Why so much negativity? For one thing, attacks on one's opponent may help frame the issues of a campaign, draw contrasts between the candidates, and weaken an opponent's base of support. Second, a negative approach can be especially useful for challengers facing entrenched incumbents not only for the reasons just mentioned, but also because negative ads can be cheaper to produce. Finally, negative spots have become a favored campaign technique because they have had demonstrable effects on public opinion polls; in short, they "move the numbers" (Jacobson, 1992:87–91).

For female candidates, the issue of "going negative" in their political advertising is a difficult one. Going negative usually means slinging mud and fighting with one's opponent—just like "the boys," and may pose problems for women that are not faced by men. Indeed, for Ronna Romney and Beppie Harrison (1988:64), postelection analysis of the 1986 campaigns (especially the senatorial campaigns of Harriett Woods in Missouri and Linda Chavez in Maryland) indicated that "particularly for women, the dangers of going negative might outweigh the possible advantages." Going negative thus has all the trappings of engaging in politics as usual, and may hurt the women who engage in such tactics.

Women running for office routinely face a *paradox of negativity*. A negative media campaign is a political necessity for almost any candidate in a hotly contested race, and certainly for one in a race against an incumbent. Yet, both candidates and consultants believe that women pay a high price for going negative, because in doing so they risk being tagged as shrill, strident, vicious, unfeminine, even "bitchy" (Benze and Declercq, 1985; Procter, Schenck-Hamlin, and Haase, 1994; Trent and Friedenberg, 1995). Men, on the other hand, are seen as fighters. As a result of this paradox, scholars have often focused their attention on when and how women candidates use negative advertising.

Using Negative Advertising

Do female candidates use negative ads, despite the paradox of negativity? Research into gender-related differences in attack strategies has yielded mixed results. One study of gubernatorial and senatorial races in 1990 found that women were twice as likely as men to air negative ads (Procter, Schenck-Hamlin, and Haase, 1994). Other studies, though, have found that women use negative appeals in only about 20 percent of their ads (Johnston and White, 1994; Trent and Sabourin, 1993b). Still other studies of congressional and senatorial campaigns have noted few differences in the frequency with which men and women running for office go negative—with anywhere from one-third to two-fifths of ads classified as negative (Benze and Declercq, 1985; Bystrom, 1994; Williams, 1994).

How can we explain these mixed results? We should note, first, that any finding that women are more likely to use negative spots probably is shaped by the fact that women running for office typically are challengers, while men have usually been incumbent officeholders. Challengers often perceive the need to attack the incumbent's record in order to lower the public's positive evaluation of the incumbent and thereby increase their odds of winning. In this respect, what appears to be a gender-related difference is a difference in candidate status. Second, we have to acknowledge that scholars have not yet agreed on what constitutes a negative ad. For example, while Judith Trent and Teresa Sabourin (1993a:26) regarded as negative any ad whose "content focused on the failings of the opponent rather than on the positives of the candidate," Montague Kern (1989) saw as negative those ads whose primary affect-laden appeals worked to sever bonds of trust between the public and a candidate.

To help resolve the issue, I conducted a qualitative study of 69 ads produced for fifteen senatorial and gubernatorial campaigns from 1990 to 1994.[2] Each campaign pitted a female candidate against a male candidate; three female and eight male candidates were incumbents, and four races were for open-seats. Though not drawn from a random sample of campaigns, the ads screened generally reflect the messages presented by senatorial and gubernatorial candidates in different regions of the country. Further comparison with ads from other campaigns in other years suggests that the spots were not abnormal.

Each ad was coded for the presence of particular kinds of negativity. First (following Benze and Declercq, 1985), I examined ads for the presence of an attack upon an opponent's issue stands (positions), performance (actions), or personality (character). Second (following Kern, 1989), I noted the dominant affective appeals made by each spot, both negative and positive. Table 3.1 shows that no matter how negativity is measured, male and female candidates go negative with a similar frequency. Coding for the presence of overt attacks on an opponent, we find that all candidates did so in a little more than one-third of the spots. When we measure negativity by looking at affective appeals,

TABLE 3.1
Negative Spots by Sex of Candidate

Measure of Negativity	Sample	Males	Females
Overt attack[*]	36%	36%	37%
Affective appeal[**]	32%	29%	34%
Number of ads	69	28	41

[*]Ad attacks an opponent's issue stands, performance, or personality.
[**]Ad contains negative appeals such as fear, anger, uncertainty, or guilt.

again we find that about one-third of the spots contain either a primarily negative appeal or a negative appeal mixed with a positive one.

Character versus Substance

Although they use negative ads with about the same frequency, do male and female candidates take a different approach when they go negative? There is some evidence that women candidates attack their opponents in a more substantive vein than do men. For example, one study found that female candidates seem to prefer to attack an opponent's issue stands rather than an opponent's character (Benze and Declercq, 1985:283). In another study, women running for office were found to focus on issues, whereas male candidates were "likely to adopt more general appeals that include both trait and issue attacks" (Kahn, 1993:492). Perhaps women's campaigns live up to the perennial claims of campaign managers, who rarely admit to engaging in "negative politics" since they believe in talking about "the issues."

Not all evidence supports these findings, however. Another study of negative spots used in the campaigns of 1990 concluded that women running for governor or U.S. Senate did not use issue attacks more frequently than image attacks (Procter, Schenck-Hamlin, and Haase, 1994). A 1994 study found that women running for office could be aggressive in their ads, and that men were the ones who attacked their female opponents on the issues (Bystrom, 1994).

The study conducted for this chapter supports the idea that men and women are more alike than not in their approach to negative ads. Of the 25 spots that contained overt attacks on the opponent, nine of the fifteen ads for female candidates focused clearly on their opponent's issue positions or performance in office, and each of the ten spots aired by male candidates did so.

Softening the Attack

Since women do indeed use negative ads, do they find some way of preempting or overcoming the paradox of negativity? Perhaps women running for office "make an effort to avoid the appearance of defying normative behavior even while using a campaign tool as blatantly 'unfeminine' as negative advertising" (Trent and Sabourin, 1993a:23). After all, given the dangers for women of going negative, it seems reasonable that they might soften the attack by employing humor or by using a surrogate to disassociate themselves from the attack.

Despite the reasonableness of a cautious approach, one study indicates that women's campaigns do not generally differ from men's campaigns in their approach to negative advertising (Procter, Schenck-Hamlin, and Haase, 1994). For both men and women, report ads are preferred to softer, alternative formats; neutral reporters are used more frequently than surrogates or the candidates themselves; and typically an unseen narrator delivers the attack, using largely undocumented evidence. It seems, then, that efforts to soften the negative character of ads are generally not made.

The negative ads aired by female candidates are just as hard-hitting as any produced for a male candidate From the ads I screened for this chapter, one good example can be seen in a spot, entitled "Friends," produced for Bonnie Campbell's Iowa gubernatorial campaign in 1994 (see Appendix B). The ad carefully blends issue and character concerns about incumbent governor Terry Branstad, and it uses headlines from "newspaper clippings" (though the sources are never documented) to raise the specter of killers on the loose because of undue political influence by campaign contributors. Although there are no longitudinal data to confirm this, it is entirely likely that if a reluctance by women to go negative did exist at one time, that reluctance has been overcome.

Are There Gender Differences?

Ads such as Bonnie Campbell's suggest that the techniques of going negative are widely shared by candidates and campaigns across the spectrum. Indeed, the only conclusion seems to be that "gender differences are secondary to other concerns when constructing negative political campaign advertising" (Procter, Schenck-Hamlin, and Haase, 1994:17). Chief among those other concerns are a candidate's status (challenger, incumbent, or open-seat) and his or her place in the horse race (ahead or behind). The mood of the times may well be another factor in deciding whether or how to go negative. In some election years, going negative is somewhat fashionable; this seemed to be the case in 1986 and 1988. In other years, though, more positive appeals might be better suited to an electorate soured on the excesses of negative campaigning. Perhaps candidates (or their managers and consultants) simply follow the crowd in their use of negative ads. If so, this pack mentality probably overrides substantial gender differences in political advertising.

On the other hand, a recent study of negative ads used by men and women running for office in the 1980s offers some reason to doubt the conclusion that gender differences are secondary. Trent and Sabourin (1993a) found that whereas male candidates overwhelmingly used "assaultive ads" that directly attack an opponent's character or motivations, female candidates were as likely to use "comparative ads" as assaultive ones. When criticizing an opponent men tend to be harsh, unforgiving, and "opponent-centered," whereas women highlight not only the negatives of their opponents but also the positives of their own candidacies. In short, women are both "opponent-centered" and "candidate-centered." By using advertising in this blended mode, women running for office lessen the paradox of negativity. In other words, they "accommodate gender-based stereotypes of femininity even while using a campaign tool that is inherently aggressive, confrontational, argumentative, or, in other words, stereotypically masculine" (Trent and Sabourin,

1993a:36). A Kathleen Brown ad discussing the "Wilson recession" in 1994's California gubernatorial race provides a good example of this kind of blended attack, one that is simultaneously negative and positive (see Appendix C). The literature is still, therefore, mixed. Although women seem to be adopting the tactics necessary to win in the existing environment, some gender differences may still prevail.

Videostyles

Videostyles are the approaches candidates use to present themselves to the public at large, the means by which candidates not only give information to the voters but also establish some degree of intimacy with them. As Dorothy Nesbit (1988:20) has observed, videostyle simply "encompasses what is said (the verbal message), what is shown (the visual message), and how it is presented (production techniques)." As such, videostyle refers both to the communication strategies evident in political advertising and to the overall narrative presented by and within the spots themselves.

Production Techniques

With regard to communication strategies, one important aspect of the manifest content of ads is their use of certain production techniques. Anne Johnston and Anne Barton White (1994:327) note that senatorial candidates generally have chosen "strategies that focused on their positive attributes and used verbal, nonverbal, and production techniques which assisted in informing voters of their ideas, their qualifications, and their competence." Specifically, female Senate candidates in 1986 tended to air introspective or testimonial spots that emphasize philosophy and qualifications. They relied upon a combination of cinema verité (documentary-style footage) and direct address in order to convey information to the voters. Indoor and outdoor settings were used equally, and the candidate was most often pictured in a "feminized" business suit.

There remains some dispute among scholars as to the kinds of gender-related differences found in the production techniques respectively used by male and female candidates. For example, Trent and Sabourin (1993a:36) discovered that compared to ads used by male candidates, the negative ads used by females "showed the candidate in professional clothing less often, did not picture the opponent, and less frequently showed the candidate in a close-up at the time of the attack." However, my study of both negative and positive ads from the 1992 senatorial campaigns largely supported the views of Johnston and White.

In that study, I coded ads for the presence of various production values such as the use or print or a voice-over, the use of film footage or still photos, and the type of camera angle employed. For the 1992 campaigns, I found that ads for men and women running for office were almost equally likely to use indoor settings and picture the candidate speaking directly to the camera, but that women were somewhat more likely to appear in more formal dress and use male voice-overs (Williams, 1994:201). Further, as Table 3.2 indicates, gender-related differences in production techniques are somewhat more evident in the sample of ads studied for this chapter. Female candidates in elections in 1990 and 1994 appeared much more likely to speak on camera, wear formal or business attire, use a male voice-over or announcer, and use an indoor setting for the ad. Although male candidates appeared more likely to use cinema verité in this sample of ads, females were much more likely to employ a mix of photographic techniques—cinema verité, stills, and film.

Despite the differences of opinion, most researchers agree that women running for office are more likely than men to show other people (both men and women) in their ads. For the senatorial campaigns of 1992, a similar finding led me to speak of "connected activity" to refer to the pattern of women using the presence of others in their ads to show, rather than merely state, a message of empathy (Williams, 1994:210). However, in the spots viewed for this chapter, advertising by male and female candidates indicates no major differences in its use of other people. Though women may be slightly more likely to show other people in their ads, this means of showing connectedness seems to be more universal than it first appeared.

TABLE 3.2
Production Techniques by Sex of Candidate

Production Technique	Sample	Males	Females
Cinema verité	38%	48%	32%
	(24/63)	(12/25)	12/38)
Combination*	22%	8%	32%
	(14/63)	(2/25)	(12/38)
Neutral camera angle	94%	95%	94%
	(51/54)	(19/20)	(32/34)
Candidate speaks on camera	70%	65%	80%
	(23/33)	(7/13)	(16/20)
Candidate in formal dress (business attire)	72%	65%	78%
	(34/47)	(13/20)	(21/27)
Male voice-over	84%	75%	91%
	(36/43)	(15/20)	(21/23)
Indoor setting	55%	36%	69%
	(27/49)	(5/17)	(22/32)
Other people**	51%	47%	56%
	(18/35)	(9/19)	(9/16)

*Ad uses many photographic techniques, employing a mix of cinema verité, still photos or slides, and film footage.
**Ad pictures people other than the candidate, the candidate's family, or government officials.

Family and Identity

It is common for candidates, when presenting themselves for office, to show their social stability and personal character by making at least some reference during the course of the campaign to their families. Yet for women, the family represents one of the areas in which they encounter a sort of double-bind not faced by men. For example, since women are generally held responsible for meeting daily family needs, the very fact of running for office signifies a woman's willingness to break out of traditionally defined gender roles. Though men seeking office often highlight their families in television and print ads, political consultants have acted as if "drawing family members into women's ads has been taboo" (Kern and Edley, 1994:87). Indeed, female candidates are sometimes asked how they propose to care for their children if they win office or whether their husband approves of their political life.

Still, one cannot forget the critically important role that a supportive and cooperative family plays in furthering the careers of women in politics (Cantor, and Bernay, with Stoess, 1992; Carroll, 1994; Kirkpatrick, 1974; Mezey, 1978a). Since a woman's family plays a key role in encouraging her candidacy, does she then feature them or acknowledge their contribution in her political advertising? The conventional wisdom is that she should not do so, because that would only highlight her difference and provoke the very questions she should avoid. Few studies of political advertising have reported findings on this question, presumably because women have followed the conventional wisdom.

Nonetheless, some women have begun to use family members in their spots. In the 1994 gubernatorial campaign in California, for example, Kathleen Brown used a spot in which she specifically introduced her mother and her husband, and also mentioned her children and grandchildren, primarily in order to demonstrate her concern for the plight of middle-class families generally. Similarly, Governor Ann Richards of Texas used a video of her grandchildren on a porch swing to underscore the theme that all elections are about providing a better future for our children and grandchildren. Still, women running for office lag behind their male counterparts when it comes to portraying their family connections in their political advertising. In my study, in ads that pictured people other than the candidate, only 11 showed a candidate with members of his or her family—including 7 of 19 spots for male candidates and 4 of 16 for females.

Another concern for women running for office is whether or not they should "run as a woman." As Representative Pat Schroeder of Colorado once noted, in one sense they have little choice in the matter. But the question focuses not so much on biology as on the gender identity of the campaign. Very few campaigns explicitly take on the gender identity of a "woman's" campaign. Two obvious exceptions may be found in the senatorial races of 1992, namely, the primary campaign of Lynn Yeakel in Pennsylvania and the

"Cagney and Lacey" campaigns of Dianne Feinstein and Barbara Boxer in California (Cook, Thomas, and Wilcox, 1994).

If few campaigns adopt gender identification as their main focus, fewer still proclaim that identity in their political advertising. The most notable exception is a spot aired for Olympia Snowe's 1994 senatorial campaign in Maine, in which she adopted the slogan "A Woman's Place is in the House . . . and in the Senate" and highlighted (through film of the candidate with women of all ages in various settings) the difference she had made for women during her service in Congress. Despite the merits of this sort of appeal, women are rarely featured in spot ads either for female or for male candidates. For example, in an earlier study of 1992 senatorial campaign spots, I found that 18 of 59 ads portrayed women other than the candidates (Williams, 1994:201). However, that proportion may have been exceptional, for among the 69 ads viewed from the 1990–1994 senatorial and gubernatorial campaigns, only 10 featured women—primarily, though, in nontraditional roles. This may suggest that women candidates will run explicitly as women when electoral conditions are favorable (as in the "year of the woman"), but that in most elections they will run as individuals.

Issues and Images

Walking the tightrope between the demands of stereotype and ambition, women not only face the paradox of negativity and the double-bind related to family, but they also confront the choice between airing issue ads or image ads. At one time, the hope was that all political advertising would focus discussion on the issues. It quickly became clear, however, that "candidates typically use televised spot advertisements to communicate appeals about personality traits, performance while in office, and cultural beliefs and icons; they seldom use ads to reveal policy preferences, ideological predispositions, or partisan identities" (Joslyn, 1990:107). Indeed, we cannot overlook the fact that the "way that candidates approach issues, and even which issues they attend to at all, are indicators of the way in which they view the world" (Whillock, 1991:35).

Although political advertising clearly links issues and images, the key question is whether or not there are gender-based differences in such linkages. One early study found that men and women running for office do indeed stress different dimensions of candidate image. Moreover, they do so in ways consistent with our gender-role expectations: "Male candidates emphasize toughness in their ads three times as often as females, while the latter stress their compassion and warmth in ads more than twice as often as men" (Benze and Declercq, 1985:283).

However, other studies have demonstrated that when it comes to crafting personal images, the prevailing approach is decidedly masculine. Both men and women (more so for women than for men) emphasize stereotypically masculine traits over stereotypically feminine ones. Johnston and White (1994), for example, found that issues were emphasized in more than half of the Senate ads they screened and that toughness was given priority over compassion and warmth. In her study of ads for U.S. Senate candidates in 1984 and 1986, Kim Kahn (1993) found that both men and women running for office focus on policy rather than image, and when personality is discussed, both highlight their own strengths rather than an opponent's weaknesses.

Kahn has also discovered that men and women running for office do indeed develop different campaign messages. Women are somewhat more likely than men to discuss issues in their advertising, and when issues are discussed, women candidates stress a different set of them than men do. Her study shows that, predictably, "men are more likely to discuss economic issues such as taxes and the federal budget, in their spot ads, while women spend more time talking about social issues and social policy, such as education and health policy" (Kahn, 1993:489). Yet, when one includes gubernatorial ads with senatorial ones, a slightly different picture emerges (see Table 3.3).

In order to augment this line of research in my study, I coded each of the 1990–1994 spots for any mention of various issues common to recent election campaigns—for example, the economy, the deficit, education, welfare, crime, or government spending. These issue mentions were then grouped into the categories that Kahn used. Contrary to her results, among the spots screened for this chapter, I found little difference in the rate at which women and men speak of social programs (10 percent compared to 12 percent) or in the rate at which they talk about economic issues (25 percent versus 22 percent). Nonetheless, there is a major difference between female and male candidates in their references to "social issues" (29 percent compared to 41 percent)— a difference that is particularly evident because crime (a significant issue for gubernatorial races) is included in that category. The results obtained in this and other studies make it hard to escape the conclusion that gender-related

TABLE 3.3
Issue Mentions by Sex of Candidate

Issue Category*	Sample	Males	Females
Social issues	34%	41%	29%
Economy	24%	22%	25%
Social programs	14%	12%	15%
Authentic voice	11%	10%	12%
Government reform	9%	2%	14%
Other	8%	12%	5%
Number of codings	106	41	65

*Issue categories are drawn primarily from work by Kahn (1993:490). "Social issues" includes discussion of such issues as crime, drugs, abortion, and family values. "Economy" includes discussion of the economy in general, jobs, taxes, the deficit, and the debt. "Social programs" includes discussion of education, senior citizens, health care, and welfare. "Authentic voice" includes discussion of the incumbent's record and the need for representation of the state's interests. "Government reform" includes discussion of reform proposals, government spending, and government management.

differences in the discussion of issues in campaign ads largely depends on the prevailing context of a given election year.

The same cannot be said, however, about gender-related differences in candidate images (see Table 3.4A). Using the personality attributes identified by Richard Joslyn (1986:162–172), and assuming that ads sometimes present multiple traits of a candidate, I coded ads for any image-oriented traits they presented. As expected, male candidates stressed images related to strength and integrity. Consistent with previous results, women running for office emphasized traits such as empathy, integrity, and activity. Further, if we categorize these personality attributes as stereotypically masculine or feminine images, we find again that masculine traits are stressed by both male and female candidates (see Table 3.4B). Still, women running for office continue to be more likely than men to emphasize "feminine" traits.

Narratives

Without question, the traditional stereotypes about women in general and about women running for office persist. However, as the 1992 elections showed, women clearly have begun to campaign in a different voice that

TABLE 3.4A
Image Traits by Sex of Candidate

Image Trait[*]	Sample	Males	Females
Compassion	5%	5%	5%
Empathy	21%	11%	28%
Integrity	21%	18%	23%
Activity	20%	18%	21%
Strength	22%	27%	18%
Knowledge	14%	20%	10%
Number of codings	105	44	61

[*]Image trait categories are drawn from work by Joslyn (1986:162–72; cf. Williams, 1994:207–9, 215). percentages may not add up to 100 due to rounding.

TABLE 3.4B
Gendered Image Traits by Sex of Candidate

Gendered Image Trait[*]	Sample	Males	Females
Feminine	26%	16%	33%
Neutral	21%	18%	23%
Masculine	56%	66%	49%
Number of codings	105	44	61

[*]Image trait categories are drawn from work by Joslyn (1986:162–72; cf. Williams, 1994:207–9, 215). percentages may not add up to 100 due to rounding.

both accentuates and undermines those stereotypes. This ambiguous result highlights the fact

> that American women are undergoing an immense, and complex, transition. On the one hand, women have been engaged in an effort to rescue female traits from derision, and are vigorously protesting the tendency to undervalue women's work and women's activities. On the other hand, women are also attacking the privileged position that male traits or values have occupied in American political life. (Witt, Paget, and Matthews, 1994:269)

Witt, Paget, and Matthews (1994:223) also point out that toughness could be shown in stories of overcoming personal adversity—for example, Ann Richards's struggle with alcoholism; Dianne Feinstein's experience with the impact of political assassination; and, lest we forget, Patty Murray's acquired identity as "just a mom in tennis shoes."

The notion that women campaign "in a different voice" leads to a focus on the narratives present in political advertising. It highlights, in a very direct manner, the constraints and confines of gender roles and stereotypes. Because of those roles and stereotypes, women seeking office end up speaking in two distinct voices. On the one hand, they speak in a woman's voice that focuses on an "ethic of care," which emphasizes nurturant symbols and stresses social welfare issues. On the other hand, they must also speak in a more masculine voice that emphasizes strength and competence. However, their attempts to combine these voices do not necessarily bring success; instead, they often lead to a complicated, disjointed, and fragmented narrative that makes it difficult to communicate the sort of "complex, hermaphroditic persona" a woman running for office must present "in the fast and furious 30-second political spot" (Kern and Edley, 1994:93).

How can this problem be overcome? Kern and Edley's suggestion is that women concentrate on presenting their narratives through a series of advertisements, rather than through a single spot. Character development over time, then, is their answer. One difficulty with this strategy is that today's campaigns, with all the trappings of a video war, may not allow the luxury of time. If attacks begin early, as they increasingly do, a campaign simply will not be able to present its candidate's story as a coherent narrative. Waiting to fully present the candidate may well permit the opposition to define her first, and to do so, of course, in a rather negative light.

Of Typologies and Things

Political advertising has been studied by scholars in part because it has been assumed to have some impact on elections. Although direct effects on voting behavior have not been demonstrated, there is some evidence that political ads exert their influence primarily "by altering underlying views about the candidates, which in turn [may] affect the vote" (West, 1994:1056). When voters in the 1992 Senate races in California saw ads, they were more able to recognize a given candidate, but they were not necessarily more favorably disposed to that candidate. Indeed, in the U.S. Senate race between Barbara Boxer and Bruce Herschensohn, while people who saw Herschensohn's spots saw him as more electable, people who saw Boxer's ads regarded Herschensohn less favorably and were less likely to support him at the ballot box (West, 1994:1066–70).

Even this indirect influence, though, must be placed in context. As many have suspected, the impact of political spots is greater in nomination contests—where the cues provided by party labels are unavailable. Moreover, advertising may produce its effects in conjunction with, rather than instead of, press coverage and other sources of information about the campaign. Women candidates who, in their ads, emphasize "female" issues such as social welfare and social policy often do not realize that such issues receive less attention in the press. Even when reporters focus on the personality traits of the candidates, "male" traits are generally emphasized—but significantly less so when discussing the traits of female candidates (Kahn, 1993:496–97). In short, gender bias in news coverage of the campaign may wipe out any advantage a woman may gain by appealing to popular stereotypes in her political advertising.

Nevertheless, studies of political advertising have found both differences and similarities with respect to male and female candidates. Generally, the differences between the videostyles of men and women candidates have been attributed either to stereotypes rooted in gender-role socialization or to a candidate's status as incumbent or challenger. Since we expect to find differences, discovering them and explaining them may hold little intellectual appeal.

Explaining the similarities found within the videostyles of male and female candidates, however, is a more tricky, though more engaging, puzzle. On the one hand, we could argue that the demands of candidacy, the strategic situation faced by a candidate, are similar for any incumbent or challenger. In this case, the advertising strategies of men and women are alike because they have to achieve the same end—namely, creating a comparative advantage. That is, any candidate must undermine an opponent's support while simultaneously giving voters a positive reason to support himself or herself.

On the other hand, the videostyles of men and women may be similar because political discourse has been previously structured by male experience. If the sphere of electoral politics has been occupied almost exclusively by men, we should not be surprised if the spot ad appears as "a male-dominant structure" (Kern and Edley, 1994:80). Taking this view of political discourse seriously may well require that students of politics alter their conceptions and approaches. For example, if we begin to view the media campaign not as a war but as a courtship (Nesbit, 1988:12–15), then we will have to pay less attention to attack and comparative advantage and pay more attention to attraction and relationship.

Or, if we conceive of campaigns as involving contrasting narratives (Whillock, 1991:141–43), then we should begin to inquire into the types of stories candidates tell the electorate, as well as the conditions under which voters will or will not accept them. Undoubtedly, such an inquiry would focus on the basic elements of ads—namely, signs. In this vein, as Frank Biocca (1991:18) suggests, "we might look at how these elements are used to generate meaning within the context of communication (semiotic) codes, discourses (discursive structures), and semantic frames (overarching topical, schematic, or rhetorical structures)." A semiological approach, then, would emphasize that political ads do not contain or even transmit meaning, so much as they evoke it from their viewers.

In summary, this review of gender-related research suggests that the study of political advertising should begin to augment its current focus. At the moment, we are in a stage that focuses on demonstrating the existence of gender differences in the use of political ads. Research in this vein has produced evidence of both differences and similarities in the ways men and women running for office use the 30-second spot. Certainly, we should expect to produce further research that crystallizes and solidifies whatever conclusions have been drawn in this area. However, scholars should not rest there.

One track that might be pursued would be to bring some order to the classification of political advertisements. Indeed, there are almost as many typologies of ads as there are researchers who have studied them and perhaps as many as the consultants who have produced them. As Trent and Friedenberg's (1995:126–34) survey indicates, the range of typologies could be reduced to one that identifies three types—ads extolling the candidate's virtues (positive), ads attacking the opponent (negative), and ads responding to attacks (response). Even so, many researchers and consultants have developed their own unique typologies of ads within each of these broad categories. We need to make the categories more meaningful, and more uniform, by doing research that either (1) stipulates a set of categories, and further develops that set through research over time, or (2) tries to determine the relative validity of one conceptual scheme or another. Either path would allow us to develop more commensurable judgments about the presence or absence of gender influences on advertising.

A second track would take advantage of future opportunities. Currently, there are still relatively few women who have run for elective office or who occupy one. Nonetheless, as more women seek positions of power and authority, gender-related research should move beyond a simple demonstration of influences to research that would account for those influences and understand the conditions under which they operate. This would mean exploring gender influences in political advertising as they might be affected by such factors as the status of the candidate (challenger or incumbent), the level of the office sought, the party or ideology of the candidate, the type of election (primary or general), and the structure of competition (male-female, female-female, male-male). Similarly, beyond exploring how women candidates employ attack ads, we should also investigate how they typically respond to or preempt such ads (Pfau and Kenski, 1990). Ultimately, though, a thorough study of gender influences in political spots not only would help us theorize adequately about gender but, properly guided, would also help us better understand political advertising in general.

The empirical results in this chapter suggest that men and women generally adopt similar advertising strategies. Although there is some lingering evidence that women must deal with the complicated task of appearing to be strong in both traditionally masculine and feminine traits, differences in advertising styles and themes are generally small. If women and men advertise their campaigns in similar ways, and if women win as often as men, then potential women candidates need not fear that their candidacies will face impossible demands. There exists an ample variety of advertising strategies to help women win.

Appendix A

Year	Candidate	Office	Number of Spots
1994	Ann Richards*	Governor, Texas	6
	George W. Bush		4
	Kathleen Brown	Governor, California	6
	Pete Wilson*		2
	Dawn Clark Netsch	Governor, Illinois	5
	Jim Edgar*		1
	Bonnie Campbell	Governor, Iowa	5
	Terry Branstad*		1
	Ellen Sauerbrey	Governor, Maryland	1
	Parris Glendening		1
	Kay Bailey Hutchison*	Senator, Texas	2
	Robert Fisher		1
	Dianne Feinstein*	Senator, California	2
	Michael Huffington		2
	Olympia Snowe	Senator, Maine	1
	Thomas Andrews		1
1992	Lynn Yeakel	Senator, Pennsylvania	1
	Arlen Specter*		1
	Jean Lloyd-Jones	Senator, Iowa	1
	Charles Grassley*		1
1990	Dianne Feinstein	Governor, California	2
	Pete Wilson*		3
	Lynn Martin	Senator, Illinois	2
	Paul Simon*		2
	Patricia Saiki	Senator, Hawaii	4
	Daniel Akaka*		2
	Josie Heath	Senator, Colorado	2
	Hank Brown		2
	Barbara Roberts	Governor, Oregon	3
	David Frohnmayer		3

*Denotes incumbent

Appendix B

Bonnie Campbell, 1994 Iowa gubernatorial, "Friends"

Video	Audio
Black-and-white film still of Branstad	MALE VOICEOVER: "After twelve years, Terry Branstad's
Superimposed newspaper clippings with headlines: "Branstad's never sunk so low"; "Branstad charge sets new low"; "Branstad should apologize for slur"	hiding behind the death penalty and sleazy tactics to obscure his shameful record on crime.
Fade to new clip with headline: "A record 2,301 inmates are freed in Iowa"	Branstad's appointees have allowed thousands of criminals to win early release.
Close-up of jail cell with open door	One, a convicted murderer, was paroled after serving just two years of a 50-year sentence,
Superimposed clips with headlines: "Influence entwind in swift parole"; "Politics and Iowa justice"	thanks to lobbying by a friend and Branstad appointee who gave thousands to the governor's campaign.
Superimposed over jail cell image, photo of Branstad above white-on-black print: "Politics. Influence. A Killer Goes Free."	Politics. Influence. A Killer Goes Free. That's Branstad on crime."

Appendix C

Kathleen Brown, 1994 California gubernatorial, "Wilson Recession"

Video	Audio
Black-and-white film of exterior of abandoned factory building	MALE VOICEOVER: "The Wilson recession ..
Cut to film still of Wilson at podium; superimposed print: "550,000 JOBS LOST"	550,000 jobs lost—more than any other state."

Color video: Brown talks directly to camera from an office. U.S. and California flags are placed over her left shoulder.	CANDIDATE: "I'm Kathleen Brown. As your treasurer, I've managed America's largest state investment fund, and earned four billion dollars for taxpayers. With tough fiscal management, I kept California solvent through the worst economic crisis since the Great Depression."
Color print on white background: "For Governor KATHLEEN BROWN America's Best Treasurer To Revive America's Worst Economy"	MALE VOICEOVER: reads words printed on screen

Notes

1. The dominance of military metaphors for election campaigns is underscored by the inattention given to a somewhat more feminist alternative. Dorothy Nesbit (1988:12) has suggested that campaigns are best described as "a courtship process" during which "the candidates' relationship with constituents potentially passes through five relationship stages: initial attraction, building a relationship, continuation, deterioration, and ending."

2. Political ads were obtained from the Political Commercial Archive of the University of Oklahoma (tape C0315), from the Public Affairs Video Archives (tapes entitled "1990 Campaign Commercials"; "Senate Campaign Commercials," from 1992; and "1994 Campaign Commercials"), and from off-air taping of C-SPAN broadcasts ("Campaign Almanac," with 1994 air dates of Sept. 18, Sept. 25, Oct. 2, and Oct. 30). Ads from the Political Commercial Archive covered four major gubernatorial campaigns waged by women in 1994; these campaigns were selected because they were nationally prominent and because they occurred in different regions of the country. The campaigns selected from the remaining tapes were those involving a female senatorial or gubernatorial candidate, whether challenger or incumbent. For a complete listing of the candidates and races selected, see Appendix A.

4

Voter Reaction to Women Candidates

Elizabeth Adell Cook

Over the past two decades, women have increasingly sought statewide and national office, and voters in most states have had the opportunity to cast ballots for or against women candidates. How do voters react to women candidates? Three possibilities exist: voters might discriminate against women candidates, voters might discriminate in favor of women candidates, or they might be neutral between male and female candidates. If voters discriminate, they may do so only under some circumstances—for example, voters might prefer women in elections that turn on issues such as education and unemployment but men in elections that turn on military issues, or women in legislative elections but men in executive office, or women in local elections and men in national ones. Moreover, it may be that only some voters discriminate, or that different groups discriminate in different ways. Men might prefer male candidates and women female candidates, or older men and women alike might prefer male candidates while younger voters are indifferent to the sex of the candidate.

There are three methods available to discover how voters respond to women candidates. First, we can ask voters or potential voters how they feel about women candidates, in either an actual or a hypothetical election. This approach is straightforward, and has been used in surveys for several decades. For example, Gallup and the General Social Survey have asked citizens whether they would be willing to vote for a woman for president if their party nominated a qualified candidate. This approach has limitations because most voters realize that it is no longer socially acceptable to voice prejudice against women candidates. So at least some voters who would never vote for a woman candidate doubtlessly tell the interviewer that they might or would do so.

A second approach to test voter response to women candidates is to design an experiment in which subjects respond to candidates who have different sets of qualifications and differ in their sex. Because subjects are not told the purpose of the experiment, and the researcher decides what information to give to each subject, well-designed experiments can avoid some of the problems of social desirability.[1] Experiments have the advantage of allowing the researcher to control the information their subjects receive and systematically varying the conditions. Yet, experiments are artificial; rating candidates is different from following a campaign, watching advertisements and debates, and deciding which candidate to vote for. Moreover, experiments are frequently conducted on unrepresentative sets of citizens, such as college students, suggesting limits to generalizability.

A third approach to test voter reaction to women candidates is to examine the vote decisions of citizens who have voted in elections in which women candidates sought office. By using data from large surveys, researchers can hold constant a variety of factors that might influence vote decisions, such as partisanship, ideology, and incumbency status, and see how voters respond to elections with female candidates compared to those with only male candidates. This kind of analysis has the advantage of measuring behavior in the "real world."[2] This approach also has an important disadvantage, however. Elections involve real candidates, who differ from one another in qualifications, issue positions, and partisanship, and in their ability to campaign. If a woman candidate wins in a given Senate race, how do we decide if some voters supported (or opposed) her because of her sex, or because of her issue positions, or because of her party, or because she was the best candidate? There are statistical techniques that help us infer the source of vote decisions, but there is always some room for doubt.

In this chapter, all three approaches are used to assess voter response to female candidates. First, polling data are used to see whether voters voice a bias against female candidates. Second, some of the results from experiments to find out how experimental subjects respond to hypothetical male and female candidates are reviewed. Finally, data from elections from 1990, 1992, and 1994 are used to determine how voters responded to female candidates.

Theoretical Perspectives

Why might voters have a bias for or against women candidates? First, deeply held ideological views about the role of women can be operative. Some voters believe that women and men have distinct roles for which they are best suited, and that politics is a role best left to men. This belief is more common among older Americans, many of whom grew up in an era when most women stayed home to raise children while men worked to support the family, and whose own mothers grew up before women had gained the right to vote in 1920. It is also more common among conservative evangelical Protestants, who interpret the Bible as dictating sex roles. Conversely, many feminist women and men believe that women and men are equally qualified for politics, and should play an equal role in political affairs. Because women are underrepresented in political office, these voters think it is important to elect more women, and may prefer women candidates when other factors such as party and ideology are equal.

Second, some voters believe that male and female candidates bring different values with them to politics, and that one of these sets is preferable to the other. Some may fear that women lack the toughness to deal with issues such as crime and war, while others may believe that men lack the compassion to deal with the problems of poverty, and are too quick to resort to violence to deal with international and domestic disagreements. If voters are responding to the values that they impute to candidates, they may discriminate on the basis of sex in that they ascribe characteristics they like to candidates of one sex but not the other.

Third, some voters structure their politics around their gender identity, and cast their ballots accordingly. Women may believe that only another woman can adequately represent their interests. Jane Hasler Henick, vice president of the National Women's Political Caucus, has said, "A man cannot speak for a woman in Congress." By that logic, of course, a woman cannot fully represent a man either. If men and women allow their gender identity to influence their vote decisions, then men might be more willing to vote for men, and women more likely to vote for women. If women find their gender identity more salient, then they will be especially likely to vote for a woman candidate, regardless of her party or ideology.[3]

It may also be that women and men do not respond to candidate sex so much as to the party, ideology, and policy views of the candidates. Thus, a feminist woman may vote for a feminist man if he is opposed by a conservative woman, and a socially conservative woman may support a conservative man over a liberal, feminist woman. In this formulation, it is policy representation that matters, not descriptive representation. Women are more likely than men to identify as Democrats, and to take liberal positions on a variety of issues, and therefore might be expected to use these partisan and policy views in determining which candidate to support.

Do Voters Admit to Bias in Surveys?

Since 1937, surveys have asked whether Americans would vote for a woman for president. When the Gallup organization first asked the question in 1937, only one in three respondents indicated they would do so. The percentage willing to vote for a woman increased steadily over time, and by the 1970s three in four said they would vote for a woman for president. In recent years, the vast majority of respondents in public opinion polls reported that they would vote for a woman for president. In the 1993 and 1994 General Social Surveys, 92 percent of respondents indicated that they would vote for a woman for president if their party nominated one and she was qualified. Thus, although at one time Americans readily admitted that they would not vote for a woman for president, currently only a very few voice that opinion.[4]

Relatively low levels of prejudice against women candidates are reflected in other survey questions. In the 1993–94 General Social Survey, 86 percent of respondents disagreed that women should take care of running their homes and leave running the country to men, and 79 percent disagreed that most men are better suited emotionally for politics than are most women. There was no gender gap on these questions, but older respondents, those with less education, those who call themselves conservatives, and those who hold traditional religious views were more likely to express prejudice against women candidates and an unwillingness to vote for them. Even among older conservatives with a high school education or less who believe that the Bible is the literal word of God, however, 66 percent of women and 80 percent of men expressed a willingness to vote for a woman for president.[5]

These data suggest that only a minority of Americans are willing to voice prejudice against women. It is possible, too, that voters might want to elect more women because women are currently underrepresented in national and statewide office. The 1992 American National Election Study (NES) showed that 73 percent of women and 66 percent of men believed that women and men should have equal power in government, business, and industry, but that men in fact have more power.[6] These data tell us two things. First, most Americans believe that women are underrepresented in positions of power, presumably implying that more women should be elected to office. Second, women are significantly more likely than men to believe that women are underrepresented in government, business, and industry, and so might be more likely to favor electing more women.

In recent years, a few surveys have asked whether voters *prefer* women candidates. In 1992, voters were asked whether they would prefer a generic male or female candidate. Although most indicated that sex was irrelevant, more voters indicated a preference for female candidates over male candidates. Exit polls in five states with female Senate candidates in 1992 asked voters how important it was to elect more women to the Senate, and exit polls in four states with women running for either the Senate or the governorship in 1994 asked how important it was to elect more women to public office.[7] The percentages saying it was "very important" to elect more women are reported in Table 4.1. In 1992, between 31 and 44 percent of voters in each state indicated that electing more women was "very important," whereas in 1994 the percentages ranged from 24 to 35 percent.

It is unclear whether the lower values in 1994 are due to the political context (1992 was commonly called the "year of the woman," 1994 the "year of the angry white male"), the difference between the two questions asked (electing more women to the Senate or to public office), the particular female candidates who were running in each state in each year, or the states in which the questions were asked. The only state for which data are available for both 1992 and 1994 is Illinois. In 1992 when Democrat Carol Moseley-Braun was elected to the Senate, 38 percent of those surveyed in the exit poll indicated that it was very important to elect more women to the Senate. In 1994, when

TABLE 4.1
Percentage Saying It Is Very Important to Elect More Women[*]

	Total	Men	Women	Gap
1992				
California	41	32	51	19
Illinois	38	30	46	16
Missouri	31	25	36	11
Pennsylvania	34	22	46	24
Washington	44	30	56	26
1994				
Illinois	27	16	38	22
Iowa	31	21	39	18
Maine	35	25	45	20
Minnesota	24	17	31	14

[*]In 1992 voters were asked about electing more women to the Senate and in 1994 they were asked about electing more women to public office.

Democrat Dawn Clark Netsch lost her bid for governor, 27 percent of those surveyed in the Illinois exit poll indicated that it was very important to elect more women to public office.

Although there is no gender gap in prejudice against women candidates, there is a gender gap in the belief that it is important to elect more women. In both 1992 and 1994, in each state, women were more likely than men to indicate that it is important to elect more women. The gap ranged from 11 percentage points to 26 percentage points. Statistical analysis shows that women, Democrats, and better educated voters were more likely to think that electing women is very important.

Although some voters, in particular female voters, want to see more women elected to office, other issues often take precedence. In several states, voters were presented with a list of eight or nine issues and asked to select the two issues that mattered most in their vote for governor or U.S. senator. In each state with a female candidate running for office, candidate's sex was one of the issues listed. In Maine's Senate election, for example, the issues listed included health care, crime, taxes, and the need for the candidate to put Maine's interests first. In each case, sex of candidate was selected by fewer voters than *all* of the other options. Thus, although many voters would like to see more women elected to office, they are unlikely to base their vote primarily on candidate's sex.

Evidence of the role of sex in a real election in Maine illustrates this point. In 1994 Olympia Snowe was the Republican nominee for the Senate and she won the election with 60 percent of the vote. However, those who said it was very important to elect more women to public office were less likely to vote for her than those who said it was somewhat important or not important.

This paradox occurred because Democrats were more likely to indicate that electing woman was important but less likely to vote for Republican Snowe, suggesting that for many voters electing more women is important when all things are equal, but all things are seldom equal.[8]

The evidence from survey data is that a minority of Americans are willing to admit to prejudice against women candidates, and a minority of voters would like to see more women elected. Very few voters, however, indicate that the sex of the candidate is an important issue in deciding how to vote.

Results from Experiments

Although most voters may believe that they do not discriminate against women candidates, it is nonetheless possible that women are disadvantaged by the electorate. Voters may be willing to vote for a woman candidate whom they view as equally qualified as a man, but when they assess women candidates they may rate them more negatively than men. In this way, women may be disadvantaged in elections—because they are stereotyped by voters as failing to possess certain desirable qualities.

American elections present voters with a substantial information-gathering chore. Although in most democracies voters can infer a candidate's positions quite accurately from her or his party, in the United States each candidate takes a somewhat different set of positions, and because elected officials are not bound to follow the party line, their policy preferences and personalities are important determinants of job performance. Faced with the difficult task of determining the positions and qualifications of many candidates for many different offices, most voters rely on heuristics—using stereotypical images of Democrats and Republicans, men and women, and blacks and whites (Rahn, 1993).

Experiments allow researchers to investigate the nature and effects of gender stereotyping. There is considerable evidence now that voters do evaluate male and female candidates differently. Women are perceived as more compassionate, nurturant, and oriented toward people, and are thought to be better than men in dealing with issues of poverty, education, and the needs of the aged, while men are perceived as tougher, more assertive, more active, and more self-confident, and better at handling the problems of crime and international conflict (Huddy and Terkildsen, 1993a, 1993b; see also Sapiro, 1981).

Moreover, at least some voters rate candidates in part based on whether they possess stereotypically masculine and feminine traits. Male voters appear to devalue "feminine" traits, and may therefore be less likely to vote for women candidates (Huddy and Terkildsen, 1993a). Of course, female candidates frequently emphasize their masculine traits during their campaigns, in part to persuade male voters that they are not "typical" women (Williams, 1994). Yet research shows that many subjects assign women candidates "feminine" traits regardless of the information they receive in an experiment, and by extension from a campaign. Moreover, many challengers cannot raise enough money to fully introduce themselves to voters, and therefore are more likely to be judged according to gender stereotypes.

This does not automatically translate into a disadvantage for women candidates. Alexander and Andersen (1993) report that voters with egalitarian gender role attitudes evaluated women candidates as possessing both masculine and feminine traits. Kahn (1994b) reported that sex stereotypes produced more positive evaluations of female candidates.

In elections in which voters are most concerned with poverty, unemployment, education, and other domestic issues, gender stereotypes may benefit women. In elections in which voters are concerned with war and peace, or stopping a domestic crime wave, gender stereotypes may work to the detriment of women candidates.

Until quite recently, it appears that women candidates have perceived their sex as a handicap. Authors Witt, Paget, and Mathews (1994) have argued that women candidates used to avoid "running as women." Because being female was considered such a liability, candidates made every effort to minimize and downplay their sex. Geraldine Ferraro, the Democratic vice presidential nominee in 1984, found it necessary to emphasize her toughness. Dianne Feinstein, in her 1990 bid for the California governorship, similarly emphasized her tough position on crime. In contrast, in 1992, conditions seemed to favor female candidates, and they took advantage of this situation by "running as women"—that is, by embracing some of the traditional stereotypes voters have of female candidates. For example, female candidates are perceived as better than men on compassion issues, like education and spending on the poor. In more recent years, female candidates have been less likely to "run away" from being female. In particular, in 1992, Patty Murray, the Democratic Senate nominee from Washington State, embraced the label with which she had been pejoratively dismissed earlier in her political career: "just a mom in tennis shoes."

Do Voters Support Women Candidates?

Survey questions and experiments can tell us much about how citizens think or respond in hypothetical circumstances, but the only votes that count are cast in real elections. In these elections, women candidates have become increasingly successful over time. In this section we explore the way that men and women have responded differently to women candidates in elections for governor, for U.S. Senate, and for U.S. House.[9]

Table 4.2 shows the gender gap in all gubernatorial elections in 1990, 1992, and 1994 for which exit poll data are available. Races with Democratic women candidates are indicated by bold typeface, and those with Republican women are indicated by italics. For each election, four columns of data are presented. The first column shows the overall difference in the percentage of women and men voting for the Democratic candidate. A positive gender gap means that women were more likely than men to vote for the Democrat; negative scores mean that women were more likely to vote for the Republican. Because partisanship is usually the single best predictor of votes, and women are more likely than men to be Democrats, it is important to control for party identification. The next three columns present gender differences among self-identified Democrats, Independents, and Republicans.

This table allows us to compare three types of elections. The most common situation is an election involving two male candidates for governor. If both candidates are male, the sex of the candidate is irrelevant. Thus, this serves as our baseline for comparison. We can compare elections with a female Democrat and those with a female Republican to elections involving only male candidates to see how they differ.[10]

In this table and in Table 4.3, the total gender gap is almost always positive—that is, overall, women are more likely to vote Democratic than men. Women are more likely than men to identify as Democrats and vote for Democratic candidates, and this gap has been increasing (Bendyna and Lake, 1994; Cook, 1994; Wilcox, 1996).

With so few women candidates running in these elections, it is difficult to identify any definitive trends, but it is possible to draw a few tentative conclusions. First, of the four elections that featured a Republican woman candidate, in only one case was any subset of female voters significantly more likely than men to support the woman candidate: in Wyoming in 1990, Democratic women were significantly more likely than men to vote for the Republican woman candidate. In contrast, in Maryland in 1990, Independent women were more likely than men to vote for the Democratic male candidate instead of the Republican woman. With the exception of Maryland, Republican women have generally attracted a slightly higher percentage of women's votes than men's, although women preferred Democrats to Republicans in almost every gubernatorial election that featured two male candidates.

Second, in several races with Democratic women candidates, independent women were significantly more likely than men to vote for the female candidate. In California and Texas this occurred in both 1990 and 1994, and in Colorado and Wyoming it occurred in 1994. In some elections, Democratic women candidates won disproportionate numbers of votes from Republican women as well (e.g., Texas, 1990; California, 1994).

Third, the average gender gap among Independents was more than twice as high when a Democratic woman was running (12.6 percent) as when two male candidates were running (5.4 percent). This difference is hard to interpret since there were only nine Democratic women candidates in these years, and several of these elections involved issues that politicized gender. Moreover, there were a number of all-male elections with substantial gender gaps, which in some cases were larger than in those states with women candidates. Nonetheless, women Independents were more likely to vote Democratic relative to their male counterparts when the Democratic candidate was female than when both candidates were male.

TABLE 4.2
Gender Gap in Voting for Democratic Candidate in Gubernatorial Elections, Total and by Party[*]

	1990				1992				1994			
	Total	Democrat	Independent	Republican	Total	Democrat	Independent	Republican	Total	Democrat	Independent	Republican
Alabama	4	5	4	-3					7	7	1	4
Arizona	4	-6	9	3					8	1	14	5
Arkansas	5	-1	5	5					14	7	15	12
California	**13**	**5**	**16**	7					**11**	**3**	**18**	**3**
Colorado	5	-3	4	2					10	-1	12	12
Connecticut	6	-5	2	4								
Delaware					7	2	14	2				
Florida	1	0	-2	4					9	-1	19	3
Georgia	8	1	5	4					2	2	5	-2
Idaho	6	-2	11	3					9	-6	16	2
Illinois	-3	-4	-7	-1					**5**	**0**	**9**	**-3**
Indiana					2	5	4	-1				
Iowa	-1	-3	-3	-4					**4**	**-8**	**3**	**2**
Kansas	3	-4	-3	-4					14	-3	5	11
Maine	3	-4	3	1								
Maryland	7	5	-8	8					*13*	*5*	*10*	*4*
Massachusetts	1	7	2	3					1	-11	2	0
Michigan	8	2	13	3					15	6	13	2
Minnesota									6	2	2	1
Missouri					0	-1	-7	3				
Montana					4	-10	17	-7				

State												
Nebraska	#0	−7	−5	3					6	2	16	1
Nevada	5	−5	5	12					4	0	−3	3
New Hampshire					9	**12**	**2**					
New Mexico	1	−3	−2	3	−1				7	1	11	−2
New York	13	2	21	10					7	0	−2	2
North Carolina					6	1						
North Dakota					1	−12						
Ohio	3	4	−1	6					1	−4	0	2
Oklahoma	7	6	16	2					7	−4	20	0
Oregon									11	4	12	5
Pennsylvania	*−1*	*5*	*−9*	*0*	*−3*				5	−4	2	5
Rhode Island					*0*	*0*						
South Carolina	2	−3	−11	3	0				0	−14	−5	1
South Dakota	−11	−6	−27	−7								
Tennessee	7	3	18	−2	−2				6	6	−6	8
Texas	**15**	**10**	**17**	**10**					**#9**	**0**	**24**	**3**
Utah					−2	12	−5					
Vermont	9	0	11	11	6	3	6					
Washington					7	0	5	4				
West Virginia					6	5	−1					
Wisconsin	6	1	2	3					5	−9	10	3
Wyoming	*−4*	*−18*	*−4*	*2*					**8**	**0**	**11**	**3**

* # indicates woman is incumbent. **Bold** indicates Democratic candidate is female. *Italics* indicate Republican candidate is female.

Source: Voter Research and Survey Exit Polls for 1990 and 1992; Voter News Service Exit Polls for 1994.

TABLE 4.3
Gender Gap in Voting for Democratic Candidate in Senate Elections, Total and by Party*

	1990				1992				1994			
	Total	Democrat	Independent	Republican	Total	Democrat	Independent	Republican	Total	Democrat	Independent	Republican
Alabama	7	2	7	2	6	5	-9	8				
Arkansas					7	5	11	-3				
Arizona					2	-9	19	0	9	2	19	5
Alaska					1	-3	13	-4				
California												
Full					14	11	23	6	#14	5	11	9
Short					14	4	21	9				
Colorado	8	5	4	0	5	-1	8	-1	10	2	12	0
Connecticut					3	-1	-1	6	0	0	5	-8
Delaware	8	0	10	3					2	-2	-8	0
Florida					2	-1	10	-2				
Georgia					6	6	-2	2				
Hawaii	0	-3	-2	-3	0	9	-3	-12				
Idaho	1	-2	-3	0	4	-8	2	4				
Illinois	4	-1	-5	4	-7	0	-2	9				
Indiana	0	-3	-2	5	0	-2	7	-1				
Iowa	4	-4	10	4	12	7	10	8				
Kansas	#-10	-7	-23	-4	6	8	0	4				
Kentucky	3	-2	-7	2	0	2	1	3				
Maine	4	-2	0	8					1	-5	-5	2
Maryland					10	1	9	9	13	6	13	2
Massachusetts									10	5	2	4
Michigan									14	0	8	2
Minnesota	2	-7	4	1					11	4	19	-1
Missouri					9	8	13	3	9	4	3	6
Montana									4	0	-3	4

State								
Nebraska	#0				6	2	16	1
Nevada					11	7	5	6
New Hampshire	5	-4	7	0				
New Mexico	-1		-6	1	9	3	11	5
New York					4	-2	-3	*-1*
North Carolina	11	8	10	2				
North Dakota								
Ohio	4	1	19	2	4	5	0	0
Oklahoma					6	1	-4	*-1*
Oregon	4	3	17	-9				
Pennsylvania	4				4	-1	7	3
Rhode Island	*-1*	-5	*-1*	6				
South Carolina	1	-4	-3	0				
South Dakota	-3	1	-19	-2				
Tennessee								
Full	10	3	16	4	9	2	1	4
Short	5	-3	3	1	7	2	*-1*	1
Texas					#1	*-1*	*1*	*-3*
Utah								
Vermont								
Virginia	13	9	11	15	10	1	14	0
Washington					12	9	13	5
West Virginia								
Wisconsin		0			8	-1	7	4
Wyoming	1	0	**-14**	1	8	1	9	5

* # indicates woman is incumbent. **Bold** indicates Democratic candidate is female. *Italics* indicate Republican candidate is female.

Source: Voter Research and Survey Exit Polls for 1990 and 1992; Voter News Service Exit Polls for 1994.

Table 4.3 presents similar information for Senate elections from 1990, 1992, and 1994. With so few women candidates, it is difficult to identify clear trends, but some of the same patterns found in Tables 4.1 and 4.2 are evident here. Senate elections do appear to differ from gubernatorial elections in that female Republican Senate candidates do better among male voters than among female voters. Of the ten Republican women candidates in this table, only one—Nancy Kassebaum in 1990—attracted significantly more votes from women than from men. Kassebaum drew heavily from middle-aged and older Independent women, but among the youngest voters, women were somewhat more likely than men to support her Democratic male challenger. In most other states with Republican women candidates, the gender gap was positive, indicating that women were more likely than men to vote for the Democratic man over the Republican woman. Indeed, in some states (e.g., New Jersey in 1990) women's votes were the critical element in defeating a Republican woman candidate.

As we saw earlier for gubernatorial elections, in a number of states with Democratic women U.S. Senate candidates, there were large gender gaps, especially among Independent voters. In 1992, the gender gap was large and statistically significant among Independent voters in Arkansas, in Iowa, and for both California seats. This same pattern held in California and Minnesota in 1994. The average gender gap was higher over this period when a Democratic woman ran (8.9 percent) than when two male candidates ran (5.6 percent), but once again there were a number of all-male contests with larger gender gaps than those in many states with women running.

In order to study the gender gap in House races, we have combined data from the 1990, 1992, and 1994 National Election Studies (NES).[11] The overall gender gap in races with two male candidates and those with Democratic women or Republican women is shown in the top of Table 4.4.[12] The gender gap was positive in each cell—suggesting that women were more likely than men to vote for the Democrat in each type of race. The gender gap was largest when a Democratic woman sought election, and smallest when a Republican woman ran against a Democratic man.

Although there are only a very limited number of variables available across the state exit polls for the governor and Senate elections that can help explain the gender gap, use of the NES for House elections allows multivariate analysis. This enables us to hold constant a number of factors, including partisanship, ideology, religious views, attitudes toward feminism, and whether the woman candidate was an incumbent, running in an open-seat, or a challenger. Table 4.4 shows the results of the best-fitting models for races with Democratic women and with Republican women.[13]

In this table, positive coefficients indicate that the variable was associated with increased voting for the Democratic candidate, not the female candidate. There are some similarities and differences in these equations. First, partisanship, ideology, and candidate status were strong predictors for races involving both Democratic and Republican women. Women and men were both more

TABLE 4.4
Voting in House Races, 1990–1994

	Two Men	Democratic Woman	Republican Woman
Gender gap	6	11	2

	Democratic Women Candidates	Republican Women Candidates
Partisanship	.57**	.92*
Ideology	.39**	.92*
Affect, women's movement	.05**	.03
Belief in Bible	−.45*	−.21
Incumbent	1.70**	−5.10**
Open seat	1.26**	−2.76**
Sex	.18	−1.20*
Constant	−1.26	12.11**
Model chi square	148.78**	111.54**
−2 log likelihood	198.33	77.70
Percentage predicted correctly	85%	87%
Democratic ballots	75%	87%
Republican ballots	90%	88%
Number of races	269	137

$*p \leq .05$; $**p \leq .01$. Entries are unstandardized logistic regression coefficients.

likely to vote for candidates who shared their party and ideology, and also more likely to vote for incumbents rather than challengers.

Second, gender and feminism seem to have different impacts for voters in races involving these two sets of candidates. When Democratic women seek office, it is feminism, not voter sex, that influences vote. Feminist men and women are more likely to vote for the Democratic woman, even after holding constant their ideology and partisanship. When Republican women seek office, however, women voters are more likely than male voters to support the Republican candidate, once partisanship, ideology, and candidate status are held constant. That is, Republican women candidates for the House of Representatives attract more women's than men's votes from those who do not share their partisanship and ideology.

Interpreting the Evidence: Voting for Women Candidates

What can we conclude from the data presented here? First, partisanship is a better predictor of votes in races featuring women candidates than the sex of the voter. Most voters, women and men alike, support the candidate of their party, regardless of the sex of the candidates. This is true even in elections with large gender gaps. In Texas in 1990, for example, when Republican Clayton Williams angered women with a series of offensive comments about rape, 75 percent of Republican women voted for him against Democrat Ann Richards. Of course, 85 percent of Republican men voted for Williams, so there was a substantial gender gap in Texas. Overall, women are more likely than men to vote for liberal Democrats, whether the candidate is male or female.

Second, when Republican women run for the Senate, they attract more votes from men than from women. When they run for the governorship, however, they attract more votes from women than do their male Republican counterparts, and when they run for the House they attract significantly more votes from women than from men. For each of these generalizations there are exceptions, but the difference is striking. How might we explain this pattern? First, it may be an artifact. There have been few elections in which Republican women ran for the governorship, and the states from which they have run have been small and homogeneous. Second, it may be that House and gubernatorial races focus more on competence, management skills, and ability to provide benefits for the district, while Senate elections focus more on general ideology. When citizens consider a vote for the Senate, their partisan and ideological beliefs are activated, but when they consider a vote for the governorship, they may want someone who will manage the state's economy and programs efficiently. And when they consider a vote for the House they may vote for someone who will take care of their narrow geographic district. Party and ideology may lead women to choose liberal Democratic men over more conservative Republican women in Senate races, but in less ideological races the appeal of gender identity may counter some of the "normal" partisan and ideological gender gap.

Third, it appears that the gender gap is larger when Democratic women run against Republican men than when both candidates are men—at least since 1992. Whether this reflects a positive bias by women voters or a negative one by men cannot be determined by these data. In a careful analysis of voting in 1992, Plutzer and Zipp (1996) concluded that both factors were at work, with men less likely to vote for some women candidates and women more likely to vote for a slightly different set of candidates. Presumably, in these elections, gender identity interacts with candidate party and ideology to widen the differences in voting between men and women. The gender gap is not large in all races with Democratic women, and is quite large in some races between two men.

Fourth, the gender gap is larger in elections in which the context of the election activates basic gender beliefs and identities. The gender gap was large in a number of races in 1992 when the media and candidates focused heavily on gender issues, in California in 1990 and 1992 when two women ran at the top of the ticket, and in Texas in 1990 when Ann Richards beat Clayton Williams. The gender gap in Texas was smaller in 1994 when Republican George Bush Jr. avoided the obvious sexism of the Williams campaign.

Fifth, the gender gap varies across states. For example, California, Maryland, New York, North Carolina, and Oregon each had large gender gaps in most elections. Note, however, that in South Dakota the gender gap was negative in all three elections in these two tables—that is, women were more likely to vote for the Republican than were men, regardless of the sex of the candidate. In all three years, women in South Dakota were also more likely than men to identify as Republicans, suggesting that there may be important local and regional contexts that affect the gender gap.

Conclusions

Men win many more elections in America than women, but this is not due to voter bias. There are more men in office for two reasons. First, most of the candidates for office are male. It is impossible to elect a woman to a given office if no woman runs. Second, most incumbents are men and incumbents usually win reelection. In fact, as Georgia Duerst-Lahti notes in Chapter 1 of this volume, when incumbency is taken into account, women candidates are just as successful as men candidates.

This does not mean that no voters are biased. Survey data show that as many as one in five of voters agree that women are less well suited to politics than men. Experimental data show that many potential voters want candidates to display "masculine" traits such as toughness and assertiveness, and that at least some men are less likely to support candidates with "feminine" traits such as empathy and compassion. Further, some voters will attribute masculine traits to male candidates and feminine ones to female candidates. Because many voters use gender role stereotypes as heuristic devices to help them assess candidates, women are clearly disadvantaged among some voters.

On the other hand, some voters are especially supportive of women candidates. A significant portion of the public thinks that women should play an equal role in politics, but that politics today is dominated by men. Moreover, a significant minority of voters believe that it is important to elect more women to office. Thus some voters appear to be biased against women candidates, while others are biased in their favor.

In almost all cases, those voters who display a gender preference also consider other factors in making their vote decisions. Voters who want their candidates to be aggressive and tough will vote for women candidates who fit that description, and most of those who want to see more women in office will vote for a man over his female opponent if he better fits their partisan and ideological views. Thus, although sex of the candidate is a factor, incumbency, partisanship, and ideology drive most vote decisions.

Notes

1. However, experimental subjects do try to please the experimenter, and these "demand characteristics" make careful attention to the design of the experiment critical.
2. Or, rather, reported behavior. In a related area, there is evidence that voters lie in exit polls about their votes when one candidate is black and the other white.

3. Identity politics is usually focused on groups which are disadvantaged in power and status, and we might therefore expect women to find their gender identity more salient than men.

4. Similar results obtain when Americans are asked about voting for a woman for Congress.

5. Source: General Social Survey data, 1993 through 1994.

6. Data from the National Election Studies were made available by the Inter-University Consortium for Political and Social Research.

7. Exit poll data for 1990 and 1992 are from Voter Research and Surveys (VRS). Exit poll data for 1994 are from Voter News Service. These data were made available by the Inter-University Consortium for Political and Social Research, University of Michigan.

8. In the other states in 1994 the female candidate was a Democrat, and thus partisanship and gender preference overlapped. Those who indicated that it was important to elect a woman were more likely to vote for the female Democratic candidate.

9. Lists of female candidates for governor, U.S. Senate, and U.S. House were made available by the Center for the American Woman and Politics. My thanks to Gilda Morales for her assistance with this matter.

10. There were no elections involving both a Democratic and a Republican woman for governor or the U.S. Senate during this time period. This analysis focuses on the two-party vote. In Maine in 1994 a Republican woman did run for governor, but since an independent (man) won the election this race is excluded from the analysis.

11. The NES does not conduct surveys in every congressional district, but instead surveys from a multi-area probability sample. In such a sample, there will be no respondents from many congressional districts and there will be several respondents from others. The districts that do end up being represented in the sample do not constitute a random sample of congressional districts, so all inferences must be tentative. Nonetheless, we can examine the sources of voting in elections with women candidates if we hold constant a variety of factors.

12. We do not show those few respondents who voted in races where two women candidates ran against each other. The number of cases was too small to have confidence in the estimates.

13. A number of models were estimated, with generally similar results. Age, race, education, and income were not significant in any equation, so we do not include them in the final equations. Elections with two women candidates are excluded from these equations.

5

Are All Women State Legislators Alike?

KATHLEEN DOLAN AND LYNNE E. FORD

On August 26, 1995, the United States celebrated the 75th anniversary of women's suffrage. A look back at the expectations of both supporters and opponents of women's suffrage is illuminating with respect to how we study and understand the role women play in politics today. Both the suffragists and the antisuffragists overestimated the impact women's votes would have on policy and the political process. Those opposed to woman's suffrage, particularly those worried about the growing sentiment in favor of prohibition, argued that a woman's vote would upset the stability of society and the existing political order (Matthews, 1992; Ryan, 1992). The suffragists, as Mother Jones once observed, expected that "kingdom come would follow the enfranchisement of women" (quoted in Woloch, 1984:355). Neither prediction came true.

To the dismay of suffrage leaders and the relief of sitting lawmakers, the removal of legal barriers to women's political participation did not result in great or immediate change. Women did not flood the ballot boxes with demands for social change, nor did they appear in large numbers on the ballots as candidates. The mistaken presumption by both groups was that all women would vote, they would vote as a bloc, and they would vote differently than men. The underlying assumption, of course, is that all women share like goals and policy priorities that differ substantively from those of men, thus rendering them one homogenous and predictable political entity.

Similar expectations and assumptions have governed research on women in elective politics. Once there were enough women elected to office to allow for scholarly attention, the first question was, "How do women differ from their male colleagues as candidates and as lawmakers?" As a result, very little recent attention has been paid to examining how women might differ from one another in their backgrounds, their political experience, their ambition for higher office, and their political behavior once in office.

In this chapter we review the research literature on two important questions in research on women in public office. First, what are the characteristics of those women who win seats in legislatures? Second, how do women behave and what policy priorities do they pursue once in office? Next, we offer an original analysis of women serving in the 1992 state legislatures. Using an original data set collected from surveys of women serving in state legislatures in 1992, we explore the diversity among women in their backgrounds, preparation for political office, attitudes, legislative behavior, and willingness to encourage other women to enter politics. This approach offers us a more complete picture of the representation women provide in U.S. state legislatures.

Women in Elective Office: Seventy-five Years of "Progress"?

Ratification of women's suffrage was not followed by widespread voting by women or policy solutions to problems women in society faced. Several theories have been advanced to explain the lack of impact, including the question of whether women might have to hold office themselves in order to enact policies favorable to women (Hansen, 1995:3). However, not until the National Women's Political Caucus was established in 1971 was an explicit strategy of electing women to "act for" women's interests pursued (Mandel, 1981). Women have, therefore, entered political office slowly. Only in the past 25 years have women occupied elective office in significant enough numbers to allow for an evaluation of whether they exert a particularized influence. By the 75th anniversary of suffrage there was no level of government at which the number of women serving approached parity with men (although there have been a few city councils and boards of supervisors on which women's numbers have been equal to men or have surpassed them).

Women have made the greatest electoral gains, however, at the state legislative level, and the majority of research concentrates on women serving in statehouses (see, for example, Carroll, 1994; Diamond, 1977; Kirkpatrick, 1974; Thomas, 1994a). As women won an increasing number of seats during the 1970s, research confirmed the importance of state legislatures to women's representation in politics for several reasons. First, evidence shows that service in the state legislature functions as a key entry point to higher office; the rate of gains for women at the state level has an impact on the number of women serving in the national legislature and executive positions nationwide (Darcy, Welch, and Clark, 1994). Of the 47 women currently serving in the U.S. House of Representatives, 20 served in their state legislatures prior to being elected to Congress (CAWP, 1995b, also 1995a).

State legislatures hold particular importance for women from a policy perspective as well; many of the issues of direct concern to women are decided at the state level. The Equal Rights Amendment, issues of pay equity, spousal retirement benefits, teen pregnancy, women's health concerns, maternity leave issues, and workplace climate concerns have all received direct attention at the state level (Darcy, Welch, and Clark, 1994). So, although women do not yet constitute a majority in any state legislature, the 20 percent share of seats across the nation (compared to their 10 percent share of Congress) means that their influence is significant in both setting the agendas and promoting legislation supportive of women's rights.

Women State Legislators: A Portrait of Diversity across Three Decades

When scholars first began to study women elected to the state legislatures, they compared their characteristics, motivations for seeking the office, and legislative behaviors to those of their male colleagues (Werner, 1968). These researchers found that women elected through the early 1970s had less education and were older than their male colleagues, less likely to be married, less likely to have small children at home, and unlikely to have pursued a professional career outside the legislature. They were also more likely than men to be motivated to seek public office by civic concerns and the desire to make life better for others (whereas men were more likely to have pursued politics as a career choice), they were unlikely to have been tapped for the seat by local party elites (even though they may have worked for years within the party ranks), and they expressed little desire to pursue higher office or a full-time career in politics (see, for example, Nechemias, 1985, 1987; Rule, 1981). While women were about equally as likely as men to have held a political office prior to their election to the legislature, their experience was most likely a seat on the school board, whereas their male colleague was most likely to have served on the city council (Diamond, 1977). These early women legislators followed a rather passive path in office. Very rarely could a woman of this era plan for a career in politics and undertake the necessary preparation for success.

Once inside the door of the legislature, differences between men and women persisted. Women elected in the 1970s tended to serve on committees dealing with traditional "women's issues" like education and social welfare. Either by choice or by discrimination, women rarely served on finance, budget, or taxation committees (Diamond, 1977; Thomas and Welch, 1991). Women legislators traditionally spent more time on constituent service and less on legislative activities such as committee hearings and meetings with lobbyists (Diamond, 1977; Thomas, 1994a). Evidence suggests that women and men of the 1970s took different policy positions as well. Women were more likely to support day care for all and liberal abortion-rights laws than their male colleagues (Thomas, 1994a). On roll call votes, women voted in a more liberal direction than men at both the state and national level, but their numbers were so small that their influence was decidedly limited (Mezey, 1978b; Sapiro, 1981; Thomas, 1994a). Despite this distinctiveness, there is no evidence that women had different priorities than their male colleagues.

As the career paths and socioeconomic characteristics of men and women in society at large converged in the 1980s, women's "effective political opportunity" (Gertzog, 1995; Seligman et al., 1974) also increased, resulting in more women being elected to office (Darcy, Welch, and Clark, 1994; Gertzog, 1995). Effective political opportunity refers to the informal social, economic, vocational, and political qualifications that make election to office practically (as opposed to legally) possible (Gertzog, 1995:50).

Although women serving in the 1980s were just as likely as their male colleagues to have a college degree, male state legislators were significantly more likely to have gone beyond the baccalaureate degree (Thomas, 1994a). Advanced degrees usually translate into professional careers that provide the resources and flexibility to seek political office, and women still lagged behind men in the vocations most likely to precede a political career.

While women in the 1980s came from a more diverse set of careers than the women in the 1970s, 41 percent still came to office from the traditional occupations of homemaker, clerical or sales work, and education; 25 percent came from business or management; and only 15 percent came from professional occupations (Thomas, 1994a:45). For comparison, in 1994 women made up only 19 percent of practicing attorneys, 11 percent of active military personnel, and just 3 percent of management in the thousand largest U.S. corporations (D'Amico, 1995).

Women elected in the 1980s and 1990s were still more likely to be older than their male colleagues. Males in the 1990s are, on average, four years younger than women when first elected to the state legislature and twice as likely to have young children at home (Dodson, 1994). While women are still more likely to postpone a political career until their family responsibilities have lessened, more are seeking office at all points in the life cycle. Recent evidence suggests that contemporary women legislators struggle with finding a balance between personal and professional lives (Dodson, 1994). Whereas women elected in the 1970s had, for the most part, atypical background characteristics, women elected today reflect the myriad of experiences, problems, and choices facing women throughout society. Women are also coming to office with a wider variety of officeholding experience and are equally as ambitious as men (for more information about ambition levels, see Carey, Niemi, and Powell's chapter in this volume).

Women state legislators in the 1990s differ in other significant ways from both the women serving in the 1970s and 1980s and their contemporary male colleagues. Women continue to differ from men in how they view their legislative role, their ideological identification, and their attitudes on issues, policy priorities, and policy-making approaches. For example, Thomas (1994a) found that women state legislators saw themselves as harder working than their male counterparts, more attentive to legislative detail, and more attuned to constituency needs. She also found, like many others including Carey, Niemi, and Powell in this volume, that women are ideologically more liberal than men. Finally, Thomas found that women of the more recent era are represented on the full range of committees rather than being restricted to traditional choices.

Existing research also finds that a higher percentage of women than men spend time promoting passage of "women's rights" bills and that women are more likely to list "women's distinctive concerns"—for example, health care, welfare, and education—when asked to name their top legislative priority (Mandel and Dodson, 1992; Saint-Germain, 1989; Thomas and Welch, 1991; Thomas, 1994a). Further, women who sponsored and carried the most legislation affecting women and children were those with close ties to organized women's groups (Witt, Paget, and Matthews, 1994). To many interested in the promotion of women's rights, this suggests that as the numbers of women serving at all levels increase, the attention devoted to policy of direct concern to women will also increase.

There is a variety of evidence to support the "critical mass" thesis—that women act more distinctively once their numbers reach a certain threshold. Hansen (1995) investigated the representation of women's interests by examining both the percentage of women legislators and a variety of characteristics of the states themselves. Although she finds that states' wealth, political capacity, history of adopting liberal policies, and social diversity are all positive indicators of a record of women's rights policy, the election of women exerts a much stronger influence. Perhaps the most direct evidence, however, comes from Thomas's (1994a) study of women and men in 12 state legislatures. In states where the proportion of women in the legislature falls below 15 percent, women felt constrained and reluctant to take a high profile on women's issues. In states where the proportion of women reached or surpassed 20 percent, however, women legislators openly gave priority to bills dealing with issues of women, children, and the family and were more successful in introducing, monitoring, and passing distinctive legislation than were their male colleagues (Thomas, 1994a).

The presence of an organized women's caucus also exerts a positive influence on the passage of legislation dealing with women, children, and the family (Thomas, 1991b). In the absence of proportionately high numbers, however, women may not feel comfortable forming a formal women's caucus (Witt et al., 1994). In 1994, only 17 states reported having organized women's caucuses and many of those met infrequently or informally (NCSL, 1994). A feminist orientation among women in the legislature appears important both to whether a women's caucus is formed (Witt et al., 1994) and to the vigor with which women support distinctive legislation in the absence of a critical mass (Becker, 1989). Support for a feminist ideology as a predictor of support for women's rights legislation also extends to men and explains legislative success on issues of child care, health care, and education even in the absence of gender parity (Witt et al., 1994:275).

There is increasing evidence that women approach public policy making differently than their male colleagues. Just as their leadership styles tend to be more consensual, with an emphasis on cooperation, consensus-building, and process (Jewell and Whicker, 1993; and Whicker and Jewell in this volume), women see the roots of societal problems connected and interactive with social forces larger than the individual. Male legislators are more instrumental in their approach to policy making, focusing—with regard to crime, for example—on the individual, the crime itself, and discrete solutions (Kathlene, 1995a:721; and Kathlene chapter in this volume).

Current Research on Women Legislators

The 1990s are a critical period in which to explore the diversity among women themselves, because there are a number of distinct cohorts of women elected for the first time over the course of three decades serving simultaneously in today's legislatures. The states and legislative institutions are in a period of transition as well. Many state legislatures are meeting for longer periods, increasing legislators' salaries, and professionalizing both the institution and constituent services. As a result of Republican gains in the 1994 midterm elections and the emphasis in the Contract with America on devolution of governmental power to the states, social and economic policy leadership may be more likely to come from the states than in the past. All of this suggests that, at the same time that the proportion of women serving in the states is increasing most significantly, their opportunities to exert influence both within the institution and in setting the agenda for the formation of public policy are greater than ever before. It is important, therefore, to explore the diversity in characteristics and behavior of contemporary women serving in the 50 states.

Research done over the last 25 years has given us a wealth of information about women state legislators. These projects, while examining a range of important topics, share a common focus: that of comparing women to men. This comparison with men is appropriate when research seeks to determine how gender influences attitudes or activities. But, one unintended consequence of this approach is a tendency to generalize about women. We talk about women being "more likely than men to believe x" or "less likely to take part in y" without having a full understanding of the diversity among women. As a result, we know how many there are, we know how they differ from their male colleagues, but we know less about the diversity among them.

With these concerns in mind, we developed a research project that would allow us to get an idea of what women state legislators in the 1990s are like. The data used to create this contemporary portrait come from an original mail survey of the 1,373 women serving as state legislators in all 50 states during the 1992 legislative session. The survey asked women for detailed information about their political, professional, and legislative careers. Surveys were returned from all 50 states, and the number of surveys received from each state is strongly related to the number of women legislators serving in that state (R = .95). There were 627 usable surveys returned, for a response rate of 46 percent. The women state legislators who responded to the survey closely match the population of women state legislators on such characteristics as political party, chamber of service, and race.[1] Because of this, we feel confident about our ability to draw an accurate portrait of the contemporary woman state legislator.

Personal, Professional, and Political Diversity

Recent research indicates that there has been substantial diversity among women state legislators over time with regard to their personal and political backgrounds and legislative experiences. For example, contemporary women state legislators are more well educated, more professional in their occupational attainment, and more likely to be involved in a wider range of political and legislative activities that those women who served in earlier times (Dolan and Ford, forthcoming). If we have evidence that women state legislators are changing, it makes sense to examine the context and consequences of these changes. Using the data from our survey of women state legislators, we illustrate the demographic and political diversity among women and then explore one possible source of the differences.

The data in Table 5.1 reveal that the women state legislators in our sample are an accomplished, active group of women who bring a tremendous range of experiences and attitudes to their positions. They have high levels of educational attainment (fully 59 percent have had graduate-level training) and have put their education to use by pursuing an impressive array of careers outside the home. These woman are also likely to be balancing marital, family, and professional obligations, much like the majority of women as a whole. Seventy-two percent are married and 80 percent are parents.

The political backgrounds and attitudes about politics displayed by our respondents are also marked by great diversity, a reality quite different from the image imparted by their comparison to men. The majority of our respondents (68 percent) had officeholding experience before their election to the legislature, with one-third of them having held two or more offices. Yet a substantial minority began their elected careers at the state legislative level. Our respondents exhibit strong political motivations for office, being much more likely to express an ambition-based motivation (such as they were recruited to run, wanted to enter politics, or had previous political experience), as opposed to the more traditional civic-oriented reasons (wanted to help community, liked idea of public service). At the same time, these women legislators are evenly split in their attitudes about a long-term future in politics. A significant portion consider politics a career and plan to seek higher office. Of course, there is an equally large group without such ambition and about one-fifth of the sample that is still undecided in their level of commitment to a future in politics.

Activities Once in Office

Past research found women to be more concerned than men with issues having an impact on the lives of women and in areas of traditional concern to women, such as children, welfare, and education (Welch and Thomas, 1991; Thomas,

TABLE 5.1

Demographic and Political Characteristics of Women State Legislators, 1992

Education Attainment		Committee Assignments	
High school	4.0%	Women's issues	51.0%
Some college	18.2	Health/welfare	40.0
B.A. degree	21.2	Education	36.3
Post-graduate work	14.9	Finance	35.0
Master's/Ph.D.	32.1	Business	46.3
Law degree	7.8		
Marital Status		Legislative Priorities	
Single	6.5%	Women's issues	38.2%
Married	72.4	Children/family	30.1
Divorced	11.5	Health	10.2
Widowed	9.6	Education	23.2
		Business	21.1
Children		Mentoring Women	
None	17.3%	Individuals	75.3%
Ages 1–5	76.6	Speak to groups	55.3
Ages 6–10	3.3	Target young women	52.6
Ages 11–18	20.1		
Previous Office		Ideology	
None	32.5%	Very conservative	2.4%
One	30.0	Conservative	20.7
Two	16.4	Moderate	40.1
Three	10.2	Liberal	29.4
Four	6.1	Very liberal	7.4
Five	4.8		
Political Motivation		Politics a Career?	
Ambition	74.5%	Yes	40.3%
Civic	25.5	Unsure	13.9
		No	45.8
Higher Office?			
Yes	42.0%		
Unsure	20.3		
No	37.8		

Note: N = 627. Percentages in all categories do not equal 100%.

1994a). Nevertheless, researchers have found that women are interested and active in a wide range of areas. Our data suggest that this trend has continued.

With regard to committee assignments, our respondents do focus much of their legislative activity on women's issues—for example, women's health, domestic violence, pay equity—and other issues of traditional concern to women such as children, education, and welfare. Yet almost half were members of committees such as Appropriations, Banking, Finance, and Industry and Labor. This finding signals women's extensive involvement in issue areas generally thought of as "nontraditional." This same diversity of interests is reflected in their self-described legislative priorities. We asked legislators to identify their top three legislative priorities during the most recent legislative session. Here, 38 percent of the sample identified a legislative priority that we classified as being related to women's interests. Among the most frequently offered of these priorities were issues related to child care, families, and women's health. Yet, alongside these priorities, a large number of respondents listed concerns about economic development, substance abuse, labor issues, and agricultural and environmental issues. These data indicate that our respondents are sensitive to the needs of women and that they pay considerable attention to the so-called women's issues. However, it would be misleading to suggest that women legislators are solely devoted to the needs of their descriptive constituencies.

One of the important ingredients for increasing the number of women in elective office is the presence of a body of women who can serve as role models and examples for other women to emulate. Research that finds, for example, a relationship between women's presence in state legislatures and the existence of a formal women's caucus works from such an assumption (Thomas, 1991b). Yet very little attention has been paid to the potential for mentoring that is created when successful women legislators encourage other women to join the political process. We examined this potential by asking women legislators about their efforts to act as political mentors for other women.

As the data in Table 5.1 indicate, our respondents are involved in several activities aimed at bringing women into politics, although this activity is by no means universal. A majority of these women are frequently involved in encouraging individual women to become active (75 percent) or in speaking to groups of women about the importance of their involvement (55 percent). So, while women legislators have influenced legislative outputs through their work on an expanded set of issue areas, they are also active in influencing potential inputs—by serving as role models and active mentors for other women who may be considering political careers of their own. These mentoring activities may be an important attempt to change the reality of women's underrepresentation in politics in general and elective office specifically.

A Closer Look

To this point the data have supported our major contention: studying women legislators themselves, without comparing them to men, is crucial to gaining a fuller picture and a more complete understanding of the role these women play in our political system. Research on women state legislators generally attributes their professional, political, and policy differences from men to the different personal attributes, life experiences, and perspectives that women bring to office (Mandel and Dodson, 1992; Thomas, 1994a; Dodson, 1994). It is logical to assume that if men's and women's lives are different, their perspectives and actions will be different as well. We would suggest that the same idea can be applied to women legislators. If there is diversity among women, isn't it likely to be driven by the differing personal attributes and life experiences they bring to office? Such an assumption receives support from research that cautions us against treating women as an "undifferentiated group" with one voice (Conover, 1988; Kelly, Saint-Germain, and Horn, 1991). Conover's work is particularly relevant. In trying to account for the gender gap in attitudes at the mass level, Conover concludes that one value in particular drives much of the gender gap and much of the difference in attitudes among women themselves—the presence of a feminist identity. For Conover, a feminist identity is the "mechanism" that enables women to make their distinctive mark on politics. We would suggest that a feminist identity may also be a useful value in differentiating among women themselves. It may be that women who possess a feminist identity are different from those who do not—different in their backgrounds, experiences, and activities in office. If feminist and nonfeminist women are different, this awareness will be important in helping us determine the impact women's actions and attitudes will have on the political and policy life of state legislatures.

To determine whether or not our respondents possessed a feminist identity, we asked them how often they identified themselves as feminist—frequently, sometimes, or never. There was considerable variation among our respondents: 42 percent said they never identify themselves as feminists, 27 percent said they did so sometimes, and 31 percent said they frequently refer to themselves as feminists. The analysis that follows is conducted on a variable that considers women who frequently or sometimes call themselves feminists to be in possession of a feminist identity. The analysis proceeds in two steps. First, we examine differences in demographic, political, and legislative variables of respondents with a feminist identity and those without. Then we look more closely at the importance of a feminist identity to one set of variables, mentoring activities towards women. For this purpose, an analysis of variance (ANOVA) of the difference of means for each group is employed. This technique allows us to determine whether the difference between the mean values for the two groups on a particular variable is statistically significant. Table 5.2 presents the means for each variable for feminists and nonfeminists.

Feminists and Nonfeminists

Clearly, there are several significant differences between feminists and nonfeminists in our sample. With regard to their personal characteristics, feminist women legislators are more likely to be college graduates, less likely to be married, and less likely to come from southern states. They are also less likely

TABLE 5.2
Mean Personal, Political, and Legislative Differences among Feminist and
Nonfeminist Women State Legislators

	Feminists	Nonfeminists	F
Personal			
College education	81%	62	24.321**
Marital status—single	10	2	12.335**
From a southern state	9	16	8.240**
Children	78	88	8.449**
Minor children	44	28	3.767*
Ideology—liberal	52	14	106.670**
Political			
Democrat	74	39	77.364**
Previous office	67	70	1.018
Civic motivation	29	38	5.191*
Think of politics as a career	43	21	11.541**
Run for higher office	41	35	2.157
Legislative			
Committee assignments[1]	22	19	1.782
Legislative priorities[2]	21	15	7.588**
Mentoring behaviors	89	68	41.919**
Most Important Problem			
Personal autonomy	75	58	19.499**
Job/economic	76	62	13.185**
Education	25	27	.387

[1]Committee assignment variable is a measure of the number of assignments to women's committees a
respondent held divided by her total number of assignments.
[2]This variable measures the number of priorities related to women's issues divided by the total number of
priorities listed.
*p>.05.
**p>.01.

to have children than their nonfeminist colleagues, although among those
respondents with children, feminists are significantly more likely to have minor
children than nonfeminists. Feminists are also more likely to describe their
political ideology as liberal.

Significant differences are also evident with regard to political variables.
Not surprisingly, feminist women are more likely to be Democrats than are
nonfeminists. Neither group was more likely to have previous political experience, although feminist women were less likely to express civic-oriented motivations for their involvement in politics. Interestingly, while feminist women
are significantly more likely than nonfeminists to think about politics as a
career, they are no more likely to express a definite plan to seek higher office.

Finally, a feminist identity helps us differentiate among women when
we turn to legislative activities. The only measure for which there was not a

significant difference between feminist and nonfeminist activity in the legislative setting was service on committees with jurisdiction over issues of concern to women such as children and family issues, education, and health and welfare. Beyond this, feminist women are more likely to include women's issues among their legislative priorities and to engage in the mentoring activities targeted at bringing more women into the political arena. Feminist women also responded differently when we asked them to identify the most important problems facing women in the U.S. They were significantly more likely than their nonfeminist colleagues to say that the greatest challenges to women were in the area of personal autonomy: issues such as physical abuse, reproductive rights, health care, child support, and balancing career and family.

Mentoring Women

To this point, our examination of feminist identity among women state legislators has offered preliminary support for the hypothesis that feminists and nonfeminists will come to the legislature with different characteristics and pursue different activities once there. But before we can speak definitively about the role of a feminist identity in shaping women state legislators' actions, we have to consider the influence of other variables. To do this, we conduct further analysis on the variables measuring the degree to which respondents are involved in mentoring activities. Regression analysis is used to control for the effects of important personal and political variables that might have an impact on whether a woman is involved in mentoring other women, including years of service in the legislature, political party, ideology, education, region of the country, marital status, age, and number of children.

Table 5.3 presents the estimates for feminist identity in the regression model with the control variables. Possessing a feminist identity is positively and significantly related to taking part in activities designed to bring more women into politics. In fact, feminist identity is the strongest variable in the model. Feminist women, therefore, are more likely to encourage individual women to become active in politics, to speak to groups of women about getting involved in the political process, and to specifically target young women for further involvement in political life.

This finding lends support to the hypothesis that differences among women state legislators matter. Here, the possession of a feminist identity leads to a distinctive behavioral outcome with regard to mentoring. Identifying those differences among women may help predict the impact women will have on politics in the future. If a feminist identity serves to structure the attitudes or behaviors of women officeholders, then we get a better sense of what the election of an increased number of feminists, or nonfeminists, will mean to politics and to our political institutions.

Conclusions

Upon winning the vote in 1920, women neither entered the electorate in large numbers nor exerted the powerful force for social change that some

TABLE 5.3
Multivariate Analysis of Mentoring Behaviors of Women State Legislators

	Mentoring Behaviors	
Variable	*b*	*t*
Feminist identity	0.515**	3.548
Tenure in legislature	0.023†	1.744
Political party	0.083	.541
Ideology	0.236	1.488
Education	0.319	2.135
Age	−0.001	−.214
Marital status	−0.007	−.048
Number of children	0.039	.205
From the South	0.241	1.244

Note: $N = 459$; $R^2 = .10$.
Variable codes: tenure (in years), political party (Democrat = 1, Other = 0), ideology (liberal = 1, other = 0), education (college graduate = 1, other = 0), age (in years), marital status (married = 1, other = 0), South (South = 1, other = 0).
*$p > .05$.
†$p > .10$.
**$p > .01$.

expected and others feared. The underlying assumption then, and in much of the research on women now, is that women are like one another and inherently different from the men who previously dominated the public sphere and represented the interests of all citizens. The question of whether women are fundamentally different from men is one that has divided feminists from nonfeminists and feminists from one another since 1790 when Mary Wollstonecraft (1975:259) knew she would "excite laughter, by dropping a hint . . . that women ought to have representatives, instead of being arbitrarily governed without having any direct share allowed to them in the deliberations of government." For democratic theorists, it is a vexing issue that calls into question the very validity of representative democracy when one sex so thoroughly and completely dominates the representational function for all. It may have more to do with the historical division of the public and private spheres than with the nature of the sexes or with theories of democratic representation, but the question remains nonetheless: Do women serving in state legislatures make a difference? In other words, do they act differently than men in state legislatures? Women legislators do still differ from men in a number of ways that have been consistently confirmed through research.

To stop with this question alone, however, ignores the rich diversity among women themselves. The evidence presented in this chapter confirms that women are, in many ways, as different from one another as they are from their male colleagues. We should no more expect women to behave as one homogenous and predictable group than we would expect all men to behave alike. There is a legitimate and productive path for future researchers to explore in examining the diversity of experience and behavior among women themselves. Further, fully exploring the nature of women's influence and representation in state legislatures is critical if we are to accurately predict the impact and understand the significance of their actions in the future.

Notes

1. The following is a comparison of characteristics of the population of women state legislators serving in 1992 and those who responded to our survey:

	Population	Sample
Party		
Democrat	60%	59
Republican	39	40
Independent	1	1
Chamber		
Upper	22	26
Lower	78	74
Race		
White	88	92
African American	9	5
Other races	3	3

6

Are Women State Legislators Different?

JOHN M. CAREY, RICHARD G. NIEMI,
AND LYNDA W. POWELL

Women state legislators are different from their male counterparts in important ways, and the nature of those differences has changed over time. As recently as the early 1980s, women state legislators were a small group and they were marginalized within legislatures. By the late 1980s and early 1990s, the presence of an increased number of women had institutional consequences. Rather than being marginalized, women were equally as effective as men at securing passage of legislation on their priority issues (Thomas, 1994a).

As the number of women in state legislatures has quintupled over the past three decades, academic research has provided an increasingly clear picture of what this population is like and how it has evolved (see especially Darcy, Welch, and Clark 1994; Thomas 1994a). Because the characteristics and status of women state legislators changed rapidly during the 1970s and 1980s, it is useful to look at women in state legislatures in the 1990s. In this chapter we present data from all 50 states collected during 1995. These data show that the changes have continued, leading to differences from even assessments made during the late 1980s.

Overall, we demonstrate that there are important differences between men and women with respect to their levels of political ambition and professionalization, their legislative activities, and their policy positions and ideology. Having provided a detailed portrait of women state legislators, we conclude by postulating that changes in the nature of women's representation over the past two decades seem to be running counter to changes in the nature of the electoral environment in the 1990s. Whether women continue to make progress on par with recent years depends a great deal on whether or not the electoral environment of the 1990s continues in the same direction or changes course.

Our study of state legislators was conducted in the spring of 1995. We mailed surveys to all members of the upper houses (including the single chamber in Nebraska) and to roughly three-quarters of the members of the lower houses in all 50 states.[1] In addition, we surveyed all former legislators who last served in 1993 or 1994 for whom the National Council of State Legislatures had valid addresses. The data are weighted here both to correct for the differential probability of selection in the lower chambers and to correct for differential response rates.[2]

With the weights, the sample is representative of the population of all state legislators, where each legislator is counted equally. This means, for example, that New Hampshire (an extreme outlier, with over 400 members in its lower house) contributes more than the representation of California, Texas, and New York combined. From the perspective employed in this chapter, this is exactly as it should be, inasmuch as each state contributes to the sample in proportion to the size of its legislature. We shall, of course, control for chamber size in all multivariate analysis.

Personal Professionalization

Studies of women legislators in the 1980s noted that the "professionalization gap"—the degree to which men were more ambitious and experienced and mobilized greater resources than women—was shrinking. By the time of our survey in 1995 these changes had continued, so much so that women appear to have overtaken men and now have career outlooks that are *more* professional than those of male legislators. Consider a variety of indicators related to officeholding (Table 6.1). The differences are nowhere great, but in four of the five instances the advantage goes to women. The biggest margin occurs on how legislators see themselves: women are 38 percent more likely than men to think of politics as a career. Moreover, their plans for the future match their feelings. Women are more likely to aspire to legislative careers, with a greater proportion of all women legislators saying they definitely plan to seek reelection to their current chamber and more women than men in the lower houses saying they would seek election to the upper house. There was virtually no sex difference on intentions to seek nonlegislative office or on levels of previous experience in elected office.

In interpreting these data, it is important to keep in mind that simple percentage differences can be misleading. For example, if women were systematically more likely to be elected to professionalized legislatures, and if members of such chambers were more likely to consider politics as a career, then the relationship between gender and careerism might be driven entirely by the sorts of legislatures in which women tend to serve. Accordingly, we attempted to isolate the effects of sex by controlling for a number of other personal and contextual variables that might also affect careerism, including the tenure and age of the legislator, the professionalization of the legislature, and the population and competitiveness of the legislative district. Not surprisingly, the more highly professionalized the legislature (higher salaries, more

TABLE 6.1
Career Characteristics of Female and Male State Legislators

	Percentage of	
	Women	Men
Thinks of politics as a career	29	21
Definitely plans to seek reelection	48	43
Will seek move to state senate[a]	28	25
May seek other elective office[b]	55	54
Previous offices held[c]	35	36

Note: The (unweighted) numbers of women and men in the survey were 550 and 2,558, respectively. *N*s in a given table will vary slightly due to missing data.
[a]State lower-house members only.
[b]Congress, statewide office, or local office.
[c]Local/county, judgeship, other state legislative chamber, statewide office, political party office.

days in session, larger staffs), the more likely members are to consider politics a career. Similarly, members who have served more terms are more likely to take this perspective. On the other hand, the greater a legislator's age, the less likely he or she is to consider politics a career, all else constant. Most important for our purposes, however, the impact of gender on careerism not only *persists* when all these variables are included in a regression equation, it *increases*.[3] That is, the difference shown in Table 6.1, indicating that women are more career-oriented than men, is greater once a host of other variables that also affect careerism are controlled.

If increased professionalization is more than just a matter of ambition and self-identification, it ought to be evident in women legislators' campaigns. Table 6.2 shows that, consistent with research from the mid-1970s (Darcy, Welch, and Clark 1994:63–73), women candidates were opposed in primaries and general elections just as frequently as men. Women now in the state legislatures have not had to depend on favorable circumstances, such as uncontested elections, to win a seat. Moreover, successful women candidates were substantially more likely than men to have established a formal campaign headquarters in their most recent election (though more often than with men it was in their home). They were also more likely than men to have hired a campaign manager rather than organizing the effort themselves or relying entirely on volunteers. Thus, there is substance, in the form of tangible political resources, behind the increasingly professional outlooks of women state legislators.[4]

In addition to being descriptively important, the picture of women as even more professionalized than men serves to clarify what has been something of a puzzle regarding the growth of women's representation in state legislatures. Consider the following: women grew from 4 percent of state legislators in 1969 to over 20 percent in 1993. During this period, however, state legislatures and legislative elections underwent significant changes that

TABLE 6.2
Campaign Characteristics of Female and Male State Legislators

| | Percentage of | |
	Women	Men
Was opposed in last primary election	37	35
Was opposed in last general election	73	73
Had campaign headquarters in most recent election[a]	76	67
Had campaign manager in most recent election[b]	72	63

[a]In candidate's home, friend's home, donated office space, or rented office space.
[b]Part-time volunteer, part-time paid, full-time volunteer, or full-time paid.

might have been expected to *impede* women's success. For example, although women consistently fare better in multimember than in single-member district elections (Rule, 1993), the proportion of state legislative seats filled in multimember contests has *decreased* substantially over this period (Niemi, Jackman, and Winsky, 1991). In addition, as many state legislatures have professionalized since the 1970s, increasing staff, salary, and session length, the attractiveness of state legislative seats has grown, reducing turnover and requiring candidates to have more political resources and experience.

Thomas (1994b:145–46) notes the apparent paradox between these trends and the increasing ability of women to compete in this environment, but does not offer an explanation. Acknowledging, however, that women themselves have become more highly professional, such that they are now more professionalized than men state legislators, resolves the paradox. It is no longer the case that a group of amateur women are competing for space alongside much more professionalized men. Instead, women to a large extent epitomize the kind of individual that has thrived in state legislators in recent decades. What this trend implies for women's electoral fortunes in the second half of the 1990s, however, is another question, and one to which we return after we discuss gender differences in legislative activities and ideology.

Legislative Activities

Feminist theorists and women legislators alike suggest that women view power and process differently from men. Women, it is said, tend to favor cooperation rather than confrontation and think of power as a way of benefiting everyone rather than some at the expense of others. As a consequence, Thomas (1994a:108–12, 141–42) suggests, increased representation of women could spur procedural changes within state legislatures away from confrontation and toward more bargaining and accommodation. Although it is not clear precisely what procedural changes such a transformation would entail, our survey results show that gender matters to legislative style. We asked legislators how much time they spent on a variety of activities. Women said they spent more time on every one of the eight items we inquired about. Moreover, the magnitudes of the differences are consistent with and amplify what others have reported about differing styles of women and men.

Consider, for example, their relationships with their constituents. Women report spending substantially more time than men "keeping in touch" with constituents, an activity that presumably fosters mutual understanding and a cooperative outlook. They also report devoting more effort than men to helping constituents with their problems, again suggesting a caring outlook (Table 6.3). Conversely, consider some activities that are considered inherently confrontational. Battles over budgetary resources are frequently thought of as zero-sum affairs, dividing up a fixed pie, so that one legislator's gain is necessarily another's loss. On "making sure that my district gets its fair share of projects," women differ only negligibly from men. Neither is there a significant difference in the amount of time women and men report for engaging in campaigning and fund-raising, activities that require them to promote their own qualifications and interests at the expense of others.

Within the legislature, women report more time spent than men for engaging in coalition-building, both within and across parties. They also report more time studying proposed legislation, but no difference in time spent introducing new legislation.[5] Such results paint a portrait of women as more committed team players than men. They report more engagement in activities that contribute to the collective performance of their institutions and appear no different from men on activities that are more likely to generate individual recognition.

TABLE 6.3
Time Spent on Legislative Activities by Female and Male State Legislators

Activity (percent spending a great deal of time)[a]	Women	Men
Keeping in touch with constituents	55	39
Helping constituents with problems	48	41
Getting fair share of projects for district	22	20
Campaigning/fund-raising	7	5
Building within-party coalitions	14	8
Building across-party coalitions	13	9
Studying proposed legislation	40	26
Developing new legislation	21	17
Primarily concerned with needs of district (percent)[b]	32	37
Follow district preferences (percent)[c]	20	29

[a]Question: How much time do you spend on each of the following activities?
[b]Question: Do you feel you should be primarily concerned with looking after the needs of your district or the needs of the state as a whole?
[c]Question: When there is a conflict between what you feel is best and what you think the people in your district want, do you think you should follow your own conscience or follow what the people in your district want?

It is important to underscore that the gender differences are not simply products of seniority of individual legislators or characteristics of the legislatures in which women serve. That is, the differences are generally even stronger in a multivariate model controlling for professionalization of the legislature, size of the legislature, tenure of the legislator, and a variety of other characteristics that affect how legislators spend their time. For keeping in touch with constituents, helping constituents with problems, and building within- and across-party coalitions, the difference between women and men is larger after one controls for these additional factors. For studying proposed legislation, the difference is reduced only marginally. And all of these differences remain statistically significant. On the others—getting a fair share for one's district, campaigning/fund-raising, and developing new legislation—differences are not significant with or without the controls.

A related set of differences shows up on other items in our survey. When asked whether they should be primarily concerned with the needs of their own district or the interest of the state as a whole, women were more likely than men to indicate that one should favor the state as a whole. On the other hand, if the conflict exists between district interests and the legislator's own conscience, women were more likely to indicate that they should follow their conscience. As with time spent on legislative activities, these differences are robust in multivariate tests.

Based on their proclivity toward state over district interests, we might well expect a legislature with a greater proportion of women to be substantially better suited to compromise and accommodation on issues that are geographically divisive. On the other hand, it is not clear whether a stronger commitment to conscience over district particularism should make women legislators more amenable, or less, to compromise. At any rate, the survey responses suggest that both in their behavior and in their attitudes, women and men reveal differences in their approach to legislative tasks. And overall, the approach of women legislators appears to be more conducive to cooperation than that of men.

Ideology

Studies of women in Congress and in state legislatures have almost without exception found that women are more liberal than men on an assortment of issues (Thomas 1994a:58, 63). Our survey confirms this observation with respect to a number of particularly contentious policy questions. Gender differences are somewhat more pronounced on social than on fiscal policy, but they are substantial across the board. Women are far more likely than men to oppose the death penalty and mandatory prayer in schools and to support the right to abortion; they are also more likely to oppose tax cuts if they will require cuts in government spending (Table 6.4). Overall, as summarized by their self-placement on a seven-point liberal/conservative scale, women were far apart from men—even more so than in Thomas's twelve-state survey in the late 1980s (Thomas 1994a:64).

TABLE 6.4
Attitudes/Ideology of Female and Male State Legislators

Issue	Women	Men
Abolish the death penalty (percent agree)	35	19
Mandatory prayer in public schools (percent disagree)	73	56
Cut taxes at expense of government programs (percent disagree)	49	38
Respect woman's right to legal abortion (percent agree)	76	52
Ideology (self-placement on seven-point scale)		
Extremely liberal	4	2
Liberal	20	8
Slightly liberal	15	9
Moderate	24	20
Slightly conservative	15	21
Conservative	20	36
Extremely conservative	2	5

As before, of course, percentage scores on issue positions create the risk of misunderstanding the sources of gender differences. For example, if women are substantially more likely than men to be Democrats, and Democrats are systematically more liberal than Republicans, the difference between women and men may be simply a function of partisanship. Alternatively, if legislators in states with higher proportions of women are systematically more liberal than the national average, this too could account for the male-female differences; in particular, the low proportions of women in a number of southern legislatures (especially Alabama, Louisiana, and Mississippi) might suggest that gender difference could be an artifact of region. Or it may simply be the case that women are systematically elected from more liberal districts within states. Of course the ideological difference between sexes would be relevant even if it were driven entirely by partisanship, region, or district liberalism, but our interpretation of it would change in that we would attribute the difference to the willingness of voters in some states, parties, or constituencies to elect women candidates. On the other hand, if the gender difference is robust even when these factors are held constant, then we can more confidently attribute the difference to gender as such.

To untangle this problem, we used a multivariate statistical technique called regression to compare legislators' opinions on each of the issues in Table 6.4 (as well as their liberal/conservative scores) based on three dichotomous variables indicating whether the legislator was a Republican woman, a Republican man, or a Democratic woman, on a series of state variables, and on a variety of characteristics describing each legislative district.[6] The partisanship/gender variables indicate the extent to which each category of legislator is systematically more liberal (negative coefficient) or more conservative (positive coefficient) than the residual category (Democratic men). The state variables assess differences in ideology among legislators in each state, ensuring that we have not overlooked some systematic regional or state-by-state pattern of difference between the sexes. And the district-level variables help ensure that the gender difference is not only due to the fact that women are routinely elected from more liberal districts.

Even relative to their constituents, women legislators are more liberal than men. We present the results in Table 6.5, leaving out the long list of state and district coefficients since they are not of interest in and of themselves. What *is* of interest is that the ideological difference between men and women clearly persists, even after controlling for state, party, and district characteristics. Democratic women are substantially more liberal than Democratic men on average—by a quarter point or more (out of five) on each of the specific issues and by two-thirds of a point on the seven-point liberal/conservative scale. Republicans of both sexes are more conservative than Democratic men, but the difference is more pronounced for Republican men than women. In short, women state legislators are more liberal than male legislators within both parties, and this is true even when one controls for differing levels of liberalism/conservatism across the 50 states and for district demographics.

An even sharper picture of gender differences emerges from a comparison of women's and men's primary bases of financial, organizational, and electoral support. We presented legislators with a list of organized groups and asked them to identify those that actively supported them in their last campaign. The results are in Table 6.6, where the groups are ranked according to the difference between the percentage of women and men who identified the group as providing strong support. Not surprisingly, groups organized explicitly around women's issues were the most disproportionately likely to be identified by women legislators as supporters. At the other extreme, a number of groups, including gun owners, businesses, and pro-life supporters gave their support most disproportionately to male legislators. Between these two ends of the spectrum, Table 6.6 shows the groups in descending order of their support for women versus men candidates.

TABLE 6.5
Attitudes/Ideology of Female and Male State Legislators, Controlling for Party, State, and District Characteristics

Variable	Death Penalty	School Prayer	Cut Taxes	Legal Abortion	Liberalism Conservatism
Democratic women	−.62 (.09)	−.32 (.08)	−.23 (.08)	−.50 (.10)	−.68 (.07)
Republican women	.71 (.10)	.58 (.10)	1.57 (.09)	.64 (.11)	1.37 (.08)
Republican men	.94 (.06)	.81 (.06)	1.67 (.06)	1.18 (.07)	1.60 (.05)

Note: The coefficients indicate scores relative to Democratic men (negative coefficients indicate greater liberalism). Not shown are the constant or the coefficients for 49 states (New York was the excluded state) and for the eleven district-level characteristics described in note 6. Standard errors are in parentheses.

TABLE 6.6
Groups Supporting Female and Male State Legislators

Group	Percentage with strong group support[a]		
	Women	Men	Difference
Women's groups	73	30	+43
Pro-choice	63	29	+34
Environmental	45	26	+19
Labor/union	49	39	+10
Gun control	14	7	+7
Pro-term limits	10	15	−5
Christian Coalition	16	27	−11
Tax relief	33	45	−12
Farmers	30	45	−15
Pro-life	21	37	−16
Business	57	74	−17
Gun owners	29	48	−19

[a]Question wording: In your last election, what groups did you regard as among your strongest supporters?

We can use these data about support groups to explore further one of our earlier speculations about the changing electoral environment for women state legislative candidates. To do so, we first divide the groups into those that are more likely to support women legislators than men and those that are more likely to support men than women. Next, we plot the likelihood that these groups were supporters of legislators (without regard to sex) who were elected for the first time in 1994, 1992, 1990, or 1988 and before.

The results are striking. Among the groups more disposed toward women candidates, four out of five have declined in significance among the newer cohorts (or at least the newest cohort) of legislators (Figure 6.1a). Whereas labor unions were identified as supporters of almost half of all legislators elected in 1988 or earlier, they are among the electoral coalition of only 35 percent of those elected for the first time in 1994. Reliance on women's groups has dropped from 39 percent to 35 percent of new legislators; reliance on pro-choice groups from 36 percent to around 30 percent. Among those groups disposed toward women candidates, only gun control organizations show no decline over time, but this was the group identified by our survey respondents as least often supporting legislators over all time periods.

Among the groups disposed toward male candidates, the changes are even more impressive (Figure 6.1b). Whereas less than 40 percent of legislators first elected in 1988 or earlier are likely to identify gun owners as supporters, nearly half of those first elected in 1994 do. Pro-life groups and the Christian Coalition are also more likely to be identified as key supporters of newer legislators; and the trend is even sharper among business groups, tax relief groups, and term limits organizations. In short, aside from farmers, every

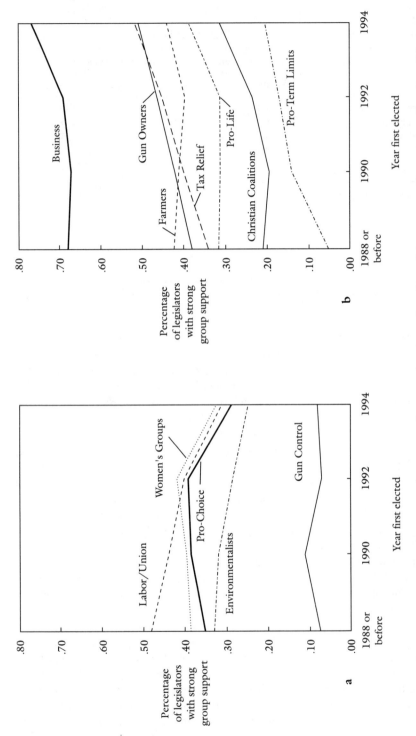

Figure 6.1. Percentage of state legislatures receiving support from various groups, by cohort: (a) groups more supportive of women, (b) groups more supportive of men.

one of the seven groups that our survey indicates is more likely to support male than female legislators is also more likely to be identified as a key support group by newer legislators than by those elected longer ago.

Once again, of course, we need to be cautious in interpreting these data, given the extent to which they may be driven by partisan shifts. The same groups that are more likely to support men than women are also more likely to support Republicans than Democrats, and Republicans have made gains in state legislative elections, most notably in 1994. Thus it is worthwhile to consider whether the trends in Figure 6.1 reflect partisan changes that may have only a spurious relationship to gender. It turns out that there are both partisan and gender implications. Most important from our perspective here is that gender differences exist above and beyond party differences. If the data in Figure 6.1 are broken down by party and sex, the groups that are more likely to support women than men generally also prove more likely to support women than men candidates *within* each party. These within-party differences are more pronounced for groups organized around social issues than for those organized around economic issues.

It would consume too much space to present the data for each group over time, but two examples will suffice. Figure 6.2a plots the proportion of legislators, broken down by party and sex as well as by cohort, who relied for support on pro-life groups. Among all cohorts Republican men were most likely to report pro-life support, followed by Republican women, Democratic men, and Democratic women, respectively. In this instance, the difference between women and men is as notable as that between parties. The pattern is similar for support from gun owners and the Christian Coalition, and identical but inverted in the cases of pro-choice and women's groups.

As noted, gender differences within each party are generally less pronounced on economic than on social issues. Figure 6.2b, for example, plots differences in level of support from tax relief groups. Republicans are more likely to receive support than Democrats, and men more than women within each party, but the gender gap is much smaller than in the pro-life example. The pattern of labor union support is similar, but inverted.

Finally, in some other cases, gender differences appear to be exclusive to Democrats. For example, Republican women and men are about equally likely to report support from farmers and business groups and are more likely to receive such support than Democrats, but Democratic women are substantially less likely to receive such support than Democratic men.

What is clear is that women and men legislators within each party have different bases of support. The way this relates to the question discussed earlier is that as Republicans have gained in state legislatures in the 1990s, the configuration of support groups that are flexing their electoral muscles (pro–term limits, Christian Coalition, pro-life, gun owners) are those more disposed toward Republican men than Republican women. The pattern is even more pronounced for Democrats; as Democrats have lost ground, the environment has grown disproportionately bleak for Democratic women (through lower

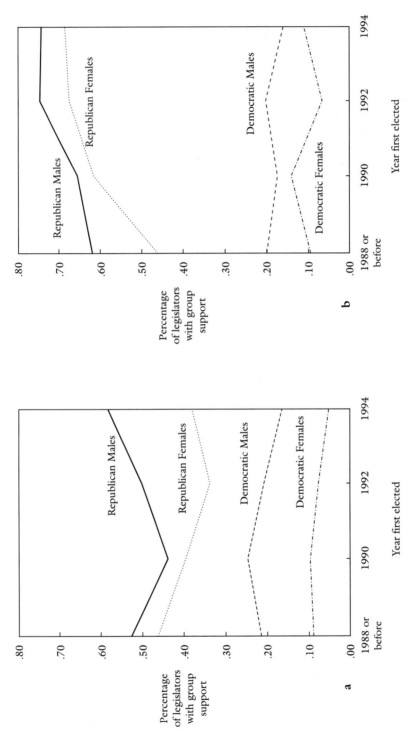

Figure 6.2. Percentage of state legislatures receiving support from selected groups, by party, gender, and cohort: (a) pro-life groups, (b) tax relief groups.

support from environmental, labor, and gun control groups). These data suggest that the electoral tides of the early 1990s may be shifting to the disadvantage of women state legislative candidates.

Of course, if women adapt to these changes in the electoral environment, then the trends may not diminish the prospects for women candidates. As we noted above, the ability of women state legislators to adapt to the increasingly professionalized environment of the 1970s and 1980s was instrumental to the gains in women's representation. It is worth asking, then, whether there are signs that women candidates are responding to changes in the electoral environment of the 1990s. If we take increasing conservatism to be the most fundamental of these changes, then the answer is no. Figure 6.3 shows, by cohort, mean scores on the seven-point ideology scale of female and male legislators from each party. If women candidates were systematically adapting to the new environment, then we would expect the newer cohorts to be more conservative, possibly narrowing the ideology gap between female and male candidates within each party. In neither party is there evidence of consistent changes. In both parties, there appears to have been a narrowing of the ideology gap through the 1992 electoral cycle, but for the 1994 cycle the gaps widened. In neither party are the movements of substantial magnitude.

In short, new women legislators have not become substantially more conservative, and in each party they have remained consistently more liberal than their male counterparts in the early 1990s. Combining these observations with the trends we observed in the nature of support coalitions for new legislators suggests that up to now there has been no discernible adaptation to recent changes in the electoral environment by female state legislative candidates. The kinds of electoral coalitions that drove the impressive gains for women candidates in the 1980s, and continue to maintain women incumbents in office, are less viable in the mid-1990s as vehicles for first-time legislative candidates. Though women have been successful in the 1990s as never before, these changes in the electoral environment may slow what has been a rapid and continuous growth over the past 20 years.

Conclusion

The short answer to the question posed in this chapter is that, yes, women state legislators are systematically different from men. In some ways these differences are consistent with the picture of women legislators portrayed in the extant literature on the subject, whereas in other ways the gender comparison by the mid-1990s had changed over time. The survey and electoral data presented here, drawn from thousands of current and former legislators from every state, are of sufficient scope that we are able to illustrate the differences between female and male legislators in keener detail than previous studies have. In particular, these data allow us to control for a range of variables that shape legislators' attitudes and behavior, so that the independent effects of gender can be confirmed and specified in multivariate analysis.

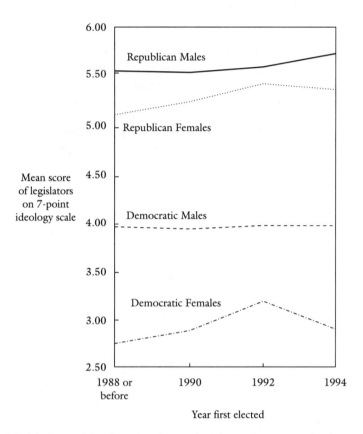

Figure 6.3. Ideology of female and male state legislators, by party and cohort.

One interesting result of this analysis is that women state legislators are more professionalized and ambitious than men. The professionalization gap between women and men noted in previous literature on the subject, which was being erased by the 1980s, has reappeared in reverse in the 1990s. Women are more likely to consider politics a career and are more likely to have run highly organized campaigns for state legislative election.

Another result, more in keeping with previous research, is that women legislators engage in a different mix of legislative activities than men. First, women report spending more time on *all* the activities about which we asked, but the gender differences are most pronounced with respect to activities that involve communication and compromise. Women spend more time than men communicating with constituents and taking care of constituent problems and also in building coalitions, both within and across parties. They also spend much more time than men studying proposed legislation. On the other hand, there is no discernible difference between the sexes on activities normally associated with legislative individualism—the sorts of undertakings Mayhew (1974) called advertising, position taking, and credit claiming. Women and men do not differ in the amounts of effort spent introducing new legislation, pork-barreling, or campaigning and fund-raising. In sum, women appear to be better team players within the legislature than are men.

Again, in keeping with previous research, we confirm that women legislators are substantially more liberal than men. Here, the multivariate analysis is particularly useful in showing that this difference is neither an artifact of the particular states from which women are elected, nor of their parties, nor even of the demographic characteristics of their particular legislative districts. The ideological differences are robust when all of these factors are controlled. Our results also show that the gender difference is particularly pronounced within the Democratic Party.

Finally, having illustrated quite clearly the nature and extent of gender differences among state legislators, we return to the question of whether these differences bode well or ill for women's electoral prospects in the late 1990s. The increase in professionalization among women candidates over the past 20 years proved instrumental to the gains women made in state legislative representation in the environment of the 1970s and 1980s. But the current backlash against precisely this kind of state legislator, which is best embodied in the popular movement for state legislative term limits of the early 1990s, may indicate a deteriorating electoral environment for women's candidacies. Specifically, we find that the very sorts of groups that are most likely to support women candidates have been less central to the support coalitions of the new state legislators, those first elected in the 1990s. Conversely, groups most likely to support male candidates have been increasingly important supporters of new legislators.

What this suggests is that the combination of changes in the nature of women state legislators on the one hand, and changes in the mid-1990s electoral environment on the other, may be working at cross-purposes. Women adapted remarkably well to the increasingly professionalized state legislative environment of the past 20 years and began to reap electoral rewards. Should the strikingly conservative and antiprofessional environment of the mid-1990s continue, women candidates will once again need to adapt so that progress may continue.

Notes

1. In order to contain the cost, we selected 77 percent of the members of lower chambers. The number of legislators sampled in each chamber was proportionate to the state population, with a minimum of 70 or the maximum size of the chamber if that was less than 70. (In addition, we sampled all presiding officers and majority and minority leaders.)

2. The response rate was 47 percent. Logistic regression analysis indicated that there were significant differences across a set of individual and contextual variables in the probability of responding. The coefficients from the regression were used to

estimate the probability that individuals with given characteristics responded to the survey. These probabilities were then multiplied by the initial selection probabilities to form an overall probability of selection/response. Respondents were then weighted by a factor proportionate to the inverse of the overall probability. The factor was chosen so that the number of respondents in the weighted data set was the same as that in the unweighted data set.

3. Using a three-category dependent variable ("Yes," "Don't know," "No"), the regression coefficient for gender was .09 when entered in a bivariate regression. It jumped to .12 when a dozen control variables were added.

4. For campaign headquarters and campaign managers, we examined a multivariate logit using the same control variables as used for careerism. In both instances, the coefficient for gender remained significant and sizable, though slightly reduced, after introducing the controls.

5. Our conclusions are drawn from responses to five-point scales for each activity ranging from "a great deal" to "hardly any" time spent. Table 6.3 shows only the difference in the percentage of respondents who report spending "a great deal" of time on a given activity, and so does not reflect the full range of gender differences. However, regression analysis confirms that the pattern of differences suggested in the table is robust when the full range of the scale is considered.

6. Using district-level data from Lilley, DeFranco, and Diefenderfer (1994), we included average income and the percentage in each district who were college educated, in manufacturing industries, in service industries, working for the government, farmers, age 55 and over, received Social Security, black, Hispanic, and Asian. A similar procedure at the congressional level (and with somewhat different variables due to availability) was shown to distinguish well between liberal and conservative districts (Powell, 1991).

7

The Geography of Gender Power
Women in State Legislatures

BARBARA NORRANDER AND CLYDE WILCOX

Although the number of women in state legislatures nationwide has increased slowly but steadily over the past three decades, there remain sharp differences among state legislatures in the percentage of women who serve there. In 1995 women constituted only 4.3 percent of the state legislature of Alabama, but nearly 40 percent of the legislature in Washington. The absolute number of women in legislatures ranged from 6 in Alabama to 127 in the large legislature of New Hampshire. In twelve states, women constituted fewer than 15 percent of state legislators, a threshold that Kanter (1977) described as signifying the critical mass needed for women to begin to assert their unique voice in decision making, whereas in three states women comprise more than 30 percent of legislators.

This uneven distribution of women across state legislatures is nothing new. In 1964, women comprised fewer than 1 percent of legislators in six states, while in Connecticut, New Hampshire, and Vermont they were near or above the 15 percent mark. Werner (1968) reported that the latter three states, each of which had very large state legislatures, contained almost half of all women serving in state legislatures nationwide. At that point, she hypothesizes, these large legislatures (which ranged in 1964 from 276 to 424 members) resembled town meetings, and they were more likely to include women because of the proximity of grass-roots contact in these small districts and of the lessened cost of campaigning.

In 1994, neither Connecticut nor New Hampshire stood out among the states with the most women in state legislatures. Although there is considerable continuity among the states with the largest numbers of women in state legislatures, the rates of progress have also been uneven across the states. Between 1964 and 1994, for example, the percentage of women in New Hampshire's legislature grew from 15 percent to nearly 25 percent, but in

Washington it went from less than 7 percent to 40 percent.[1] Utah went from slightly less than 6 percent to only 14 percent.

A number of social scientists have sought to explain the uneven distribution of women in state legislatures, and the uneven rates of progress in different states (Werner, 1968; Rule, 1993). The 1992 election brought many new women into state legislatures nationwide, after a decade of steady increases (Thomas, 1994b, also 1994a). Moreover, the uneven progress of women across states suggests that the sources of women's legislative strength today may be quite different from those of the past.

In this chapter we examine the patterns of women in state legislatures throughout the past 30 years, and explore the patterns of progress across the states. We then examine explanations for women's legislative strength, and test these explanations for 1995 using data we have compiled from a variety of sources. We conclude with some thoughts about the future of women in state legislatures.

The Geography of Women's Representation in Legislatures

We begin with a straightforward examination of the geography of women's representation in state legislatures. Table 7.1 shows the percentage of women in each state's legislature in 1964, 1974, 1984, 1994, and 1995.[2] Figures 7.1 and 7.2 show these data geographically in two years exactly thirty years apart: 1964 and 1994. Table 7.2 shows the average number of women in state legislatures by region in 1964, 1974, 1984, and 1995.

Several things are evident from these data. Throughout this period, women were most numerous in legislatures in the Northeast and the West and least numerous in the South and the mid-Atlantic region. Second, the data in Table 7.2 show that growth has been more rapid in recent years in the West and Midwest, and that as of 1995 the West had drawn even with the Northeast as the region with the highest proportion of women legislators. Third, the progress within regions has been uneven. Note, for example, the different growth rates in Maine and New Hampshire in the Northeast, and of Kansas and Nebraska in the Central Plains. Finally, although the first four data points show that most states increased the number of women in their legislatures in each decade, comparing data from 1994 and 1995 suggests that in any given election women might advance in some states while losing ground in others. In 1994 Republican gains in state legislatures led to a loss of women in states where women had been primarily confined to the Democratic Party and gains in states where women are well represented among Republican candidates.

Figure 7.1 shows the trends in a few selected states between 1964 and 1994, and compares this with the national trend during this period. Alabama, California, and Kansas all began with few women in state legislatures, but Alabama remains a male bastion in 1994 whereas California was slightly above the national average and Kansas was among the leading states. In

TABLE 7.1

Women in State Legislatures, 1964–1995

	1964	1974	1984	1994	1995	Change
Alabama	1	1	4	6	4	3
Alaska	3	12	10	22	23	20
Arizona	8	14	18	33	30	22
Arkansas	4	2	5	11	13	9
California	1	3	12	24	21	20
Colorado	7	8	25	35	31	24
Connecticut	15	10	21	26	27	12
Delaware	4	11	16	16	21	17
Florida	3	4	16	18	19	16
Georgia	0	1	8	17	18	18
Hawaii	4	5	20	25	20	16
Idaho	1	7	14	30	28	27
Illinois	2	5	11	23	23	21
Indiana	2	6	12	19	22	20
Iowa	3	7	9	15	18	15
Kansas	1	2	13	29	28	27
Kentucky	4	4	7	6	8	4
Louisiana	1	2	3	9	10	9
Maine	6	9	22	32	26	20
Maryland	6	6	19	25	29	23
Massachusetts	3	3	9	23	24	21
Michigan	2	4	9	21	22	20
Minnesota	1	3	13	27	25	24
Mississippi	2	3	2	12	12	10
Missouri	1	6	10	20	20	19
Montana	2	6	6	20	24	22
Nebraska	2	2	14	18	25	23
Nevada	6	8	8	16	35	29
New Hampshire	15	20	27	24	30	15
New Jersey	4	8	8	9	13	9
New Mexico	1	2	6	26	21	20
New York	1	3	10	11	18	17
North Carolina	3	5	15	25	17	14
North Dakota	2	8	10	13	15	13
Ohio	5	6	9	20	24	19
Oklahoma	1	1	7	12	11	10
Oregon	10	12	21	17	29	19
Pennsylvania	5	3	4	14	12	7
Rhode Island	3	3	12	25	24	21
South Carolina	1	3	7	13	12	11
South Dakota	2	6	13	20	18	16
Tennessee	2	3	8	12	14	12
Texas	2	3	6	17	18	16

continued

TABLE 7.1
Continued

	1964	1974	1984	1994	1995	Change
Utah	6	6	7	14	14	8
Vermont	18	11	18	33	30	12
Virginia	2	4	9	11	11	9
Washington	7	9	18	40	40	33
West Virginia	4	7	10	17	15	11
Wisconsin	2	5	20	27	24	22
Wyoming	4	5	20	24	21	17

Sources: 1964 from Werner (1968), 1974 and 1984 from Rule and Zimmerman (1995), 1994 from Van Dunk and Holbrook (1994).

contrast, Oregon and Connecticut were among the leaders in 1964, and both experienced slow growth in the next three decades. Clearly these states have experienced different patterns of progress in electing women to legislative office.

Explaining State Differences in Number of Women in State Legislatures

How might we account for the differences in representation of women in state legislatures? Several sets of explanations have been offered. First, it is clear that the number of women legislators depends on the number of women willing to run for that office. Research has shown that women are not disadvantaged among voters when they seek elective office (Darcy, Welch, and Clark, 1994; Darcy and Schramm, 1977; Ekstrand and Eckert, 1981; Burrell, 1994), so if women in one state are more likely to run for state legislative office than women in another state, it seems likely that more women in that state will be elected.

The supply of women candidates depends on several factors. First, there must be a pool of potential women candidates ready to seek office when

TABLE 7.2
Regional Patterns in Women's Representation in Legislatures, Average per Region

	1964	1974	1984	1995	Change
Northeast	9.7	9.3	18.1	26.8	17.1
Mid-Atlantic	3.4	6.3	9.5	16.1	12.7
Midwest	2.1	5.0	11.9	22.0	19.9
South	2.3	3.3	8.4	14.0	11.7
West	4.5	7.5	14.2	25.8	21.3
National average	20.7	12.0	5.7	3.8	16.9

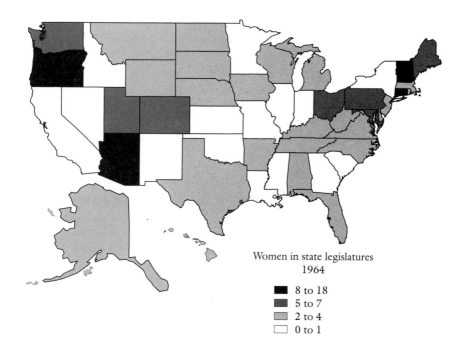

Women in state legislatures
1964

■ 8 to 18
■ 5 to 7
▨ 2 to 4
□ 0 to 1

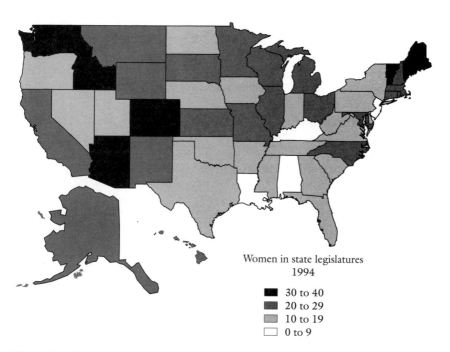

Women in state legislatures
1994

■ 30 to 40
■ 20 to 29
▨ 10 to 19
□ 0 to 9

Figure 7.1. Women in state legislatures, 1964 and 1994.

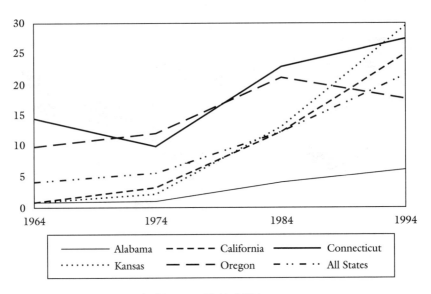

Figure 7.2. Women in state legislatures, 1964–1994.

electoral conditions are favorable (Darcy and Schramm, 1977; Welch, 1978; but see also Rule, 1981). In state legislative races, this eligibility pool includes many individuals who have held local office. The pool also includes those who have been active in community affairs, have name recognition within the community, have ties to important established political groups, or have other resources that help win elected office. Because legislative office in many states is a part-time job, some seek elected office to further their professional careers in law or real estate. Potential women candidates are likely to be in the labor force, and to work in professional occupations.

Of course, members of the potential candidate pool must decide to run for office before they can win election. Candidates may be recruited by party committees, and they might also be persuaded to run by interest groups such as the National Women's Political Caucus (see Chapter 2 of this volume), the National Organization for Women (NOW) for feminists, and Concerned Women for America (CWA) for religious conservatives. Thus, it may be that women will be more likely to run and subsequently win election in states with well-organized interest groups that recruit female candidates and in states where party officials actively recruit candidates and endorse them in primary elections (Darcy and Schramm, 1977; Volgy, Schwarz, and Gottlieb, 1986; Flammang, 1985). Yet members of the candidate pool do not automatically agree to seek election when asked; instead they weigh a number of important factors, including some important characteristics of our political system.

Running for office costs money, and women in America generally have less money than men. Moreover, women are less likely than men to give large donations to candidates, suggesting perhaps that women might initially view the costs of campaigning as a barrier to entry into elected politics.[3] Although research shows that women raise as much money as men once incumbency and other factors are conrolled, many women in the potential candidate pool might not know this. Thus women may be more likely to run in states that provide public funding, or that limit the size of contributions and therefore the costs of campaigns.

Other aspects of the system may influence women's decisions to run. Women may be relatively more likely to seek office in states where districts are small, thereby allowing more effective personal campaigning (Nechemias, 1985, 1987; Rule, 1981; Hill, 1981). They may be more likely to seek office in states where the commuting time to the state capital is small (Nechemias, 1987; but see also Darcy, Welch, and Clark, 1994).

Moreover, women may be more likely to decide to run if they come from states with political cultures that support women in politics. Although political culture is a complex and often controversial concept, Elazar (1984) classified states into three categories: those with moralistic cultures in which politics is considered public business, traditional cultures where politics is generally controlled by an established and male elite, and individualistic cultures where individual politicians advance their own careers by helping different groups achieve their political goals (Rule, 1993). Women have been more likely to seek elected office in moralistic states than in those with traditional or individualistic cultures (Hill, 1981; Nechemias, 1985, 1987).

Women may also be more likely to run in states or regions in which voters show less bias against women candidates, or where gender roles are less traditional. States with well-educated, urbanized electorates are likely to show the least voter bias and therefore to invite more candidacies by women (Nechemias, 1987; but see Rule, 1981). It is also likely that states with liberal, Democratic electorates will have more women in their state legislatures, although recent efforts by Republicans to recruit women candidates, including those from the Christian Right movement, may lessen that relationship.

Third, there may be aspects of the job of being a state legislator that make it more or less attractive to women. These job characteristics might work in two ways. On the one hand, the more attractive the position of state legislator, the more candidates who will seek the position and hence the more crowded the field. On the other hand, as Carey, Niemi, and Powell show in this volume, women who run for state legislative office are now as likely as men to have further political ambition (see also Constantini, 1990), so they should be as attracted by these characteristics as are men. The pay scale for the office, the power of the legislature relative to the governor, and the number of staff available may affect candidacy decisions and thereby the number of women in the legislature (Squire, 1992; Nechemias, 1985; Rule, 1981; Hill, 1981).

There are also systemic factors that affect the number of women in legislatures. Although most states apportion their legislative seats through single-member districts, some have districts with multiple members. These multimember districts appear to elect more women, in part because parties and voters appear to seek to balance the slates of legislators in such districts (Darcy, Welch, and Clark, 1994). In addition, because men are more likely to be incumbents and incumbents are difficult to defeat in elections, women will probably be more numerous in the legislatures of states that experience high turnover. When incumbents retire from the legislature, their seats are open for new candidates to win, and this creates opportunities for women (Andersen and Thorson, 1984).

Data and Methods

To test whether these factors affect the proportion of women in state legislatures, we assembled a data set that contains measures from a variety of sources. As measures of the pool of potential women candidates we include data for each state on women in the electorate, women who own their own firms, and women who hold executive and professional jobs. Later we use a summary measure that combines these four items.

To measure recruitment efforts, we consider whether the party endorses in the primary election. We also include a measure of the number of NOW chapters per state, and membership in CWA in each state.

We examine a variety of state campaign finance laws, including whether the state provides public funds for state legislative candidates and whether there are limits on the amount of contributions by corporations, unions, PACs, parties, individuals, and family members. To account for other factors that might influence candidacy decisions by women, we include measures of the average size of the legislative district and the average distance to the state capitol.

As measures of political culture, we include Elazar's (1984) typology, which highlights the traditionalistic, moralistic, and individualistic cultures. An interval-level measure of political culture by Sharkansky (1969) is also included. We have measures of the socioeconomic status and urbanism of the electorate in each state, as well as its ideology and partisanship. Finally, we investigate the impact of the religious composition of the state population. It is likely that in places where there are high proportions of conservative Protestant denominations there will be fewer women in the legislatures.

To determine if attractiveness of legislative office affects proportionality, we have a measure of the salary and staff for state legislators, and of the governor's strength relative to the legislature. Finally, we have measures of systemic factors such as multimember districts and turnover of legislative seats.

Results

Our analysis proceeds in three stages. First, we examine the relationships between each measure listed in the preceding section and the proportion of women in the legislature. Next, we look at how each measure affects the percentage of women in the legislature once other indicators are taken into account. Finally, we look at differences in the percentage of women legislators across time.

Table 7.3 shows the correlations between each indicator and the percentage of women in legislatures in 1995. The first column shows the overall correlation nationwide; the second the correlation among northeastern, midwestern, and western states, where women are relatively more numerous in legislatures; and the third column the correlation among southern and mid-Atlantic states, where women are less numerous. The final column shows the correlation between this regional split and the indicator itself.

The data in Table 7.3 show that women are significantly more likely to sit in legislatures in states where there is a large pool of potential women candidates. Each of the indicators we selected and the overall scale we constructed from them are strongly correlated with the number of women in state legislatures nationwide. This pattern is repeated in the southern and mid-Atlantic states, though not in other regions.[4] The strong correlations in the final column indicate that the pool of candidates is significantly larger in the Northeast, Midwest, and West than in the South, and is, therefore, a good explanation of regional differences.

The data also suggest that our measures of party activity in elections do not predict the proportion of women in state legislatures. Although party organizations can encourage women to run and even (in some states) endorse them in the primary, differences in party rules and strength do not appear to be related to this recruitment activity. Presumably these rules must exist in conjunction with sympathetic attitudes among party elites before women are actively recruited by party organizations.

The data do show, however, that interest group strength is a good bivariate predictor of women's legislative representation. Nationally, the number of NOW chapters per state is a solid predictor of women in state legislatures. Although CWA membership does not predict nationally or in any of the regions shown in Table 7.3, it is a strong and significant predictor in the South alone, where the CWA is generally strong.

The campaign finance laws do not predict candidacies nationwide, although limits on PAC, individual, candidate, and family contributions are significantly correlated with *decreased* women's candidacies in the Northeast, Midwest, and West. It may be that women see such limits as forcing them to spend more time fund-raising, or it may be that such limits prevent feminist PACs from easily raising money to support candidacies. Distance from the state capital and state size are not related to candidacy decisions.

State political culture is a significant predictor of women in legislatures nationally, and in the South and Mid-Atlantic. As previous research indicates, women are more likely to hold seats in states with moralistic political cultures and less likely to sit in legislatures in states with traditionalistic cultures. In the South and Mid-Atlantic, women are more likely to hold office in individualistic states, possibly because southern states are either traditionalistic or individualistic. Our alternative measure of political culture, the Sharkansky scale, is also a significant predictor of women's representation.

TABLE 7.3

Correlates of Women Legislators in 1995

	All States	Non-South Mid-Atlantic	South Mid-Atlantic	Regional Difference
Pool of women for candidacies				
Women pool scale	.61*	.17	.68*	−.51*
Working women	.46*	−.09	.44***	−.56*
Women own firms	.52*	.15	.73*	−.39*
Women professionals	.34**	.05	.48**	−.27***
Women executives	.57*	.30***	.66*	−.36*
Recruitment				
Party recruitment scale	.25***	−.14	.43***	−.25***
State party strength	−.11	−.11	−.19	.0
Local party strength	.23	−.03	+.36	−.16
Legislative caucus campaign fund	.22	.04	.22	−.20
Party endorses in primary	.08	−.26	.33	−.19
NOW chapters	.31**	.20	.29	−.24***
CWA membership	.15	−.09	.35	−.26***
Campaign finance				
Corporation limits	.09	.08	.04	−.07
Union limits	−.12	−.11	−.27	−.00
PAC limits	−.23	−.43**	−.27	−.06
Party limits	.09	.14	−.17	−.12
Individual limits	−.19	−.31***	−.34	−.07
Candidate's own money	−.18	−.42**	−.38	−.16
Family's own money	−.10	−.37**	.07	−.07
Public financing	−.02	−.20	−.22	−.19
Other factors				
Number of seats by population	.23	.01	.02	−.33**
Distance to state capital	.07	−.02	.07	−.11
State geographic size	.10	−.04	.02	−.18
Political culture				
Political culture (Sharkansky)	−.60*	−.16	−.20	.76*
Moralistic states	.42*	.01	.18	−.60*
Traditionalistic states	−.59*	.03	−.52**	.63*
Individualistic states	.09	−.01	.48**	.07
Characteristics of electorate				
SES scale	.37*	.28	.53**	−.13
Income	.37*	.27	.51**	−.15
College graduates	.46*	.24	.57**	−.29**
Urbanism	.10	.17	.40***	.12
Conservative ideology	−.65*	−.26	−.62*	.58*
Republican party identification	.24***	.16	.05	−.23
Catholic	.25***	−.06	.17	−.35**
Fundamentalist/Pentecostal	−.29**	.20	−.38	.26***
Evangelical	.13	−.04	−.04	.20
Mormon	.01	−.25	−.04	−.20

Desirability of office				
Legislative professionalism scale	.00	.02	.1	.07
Salary	−.00	−.03	.24	.09
Staff	−.10	.02	.10	.21
Length of session	.11	.05	.05	−.11
Governor's strength	−.05	−.34***	.36	.06
Systemic factors				
Turnover in seats	.36**	.17	.03	−.41*
Multimember districts	.31**	.32***	.38	−.09
Over time				
With 1984	.68*	.46*	.79*	
With 1974	.55*	.41**	.47**	
With 1964	.49*	.48*	.41***	
N	50	31	19	50

* = .01
** = .05
*** = .10

Characteristics of the electorate are also meaningful predictors of women in legislatures. Income and education are significant nationally and in the South and Mid-Atlantic, whereas urbanism is significant only in one region. Ideology is significant nationally and in the South and Mid-Atlantic, with liberal citizens more likely to lead to women in legislatures. Partisanship predicts proportionality nationally, although the relationship is not large. Interestingly, women are more likely to win election in states with more Republican electorates. Finally, states with substantial numbers of fundamentalist and Pentecostal Christians elect significantly fewer women, while states with large numbers of Catholics elect more women.

The attractiveness of the office does not seem to influence women's representation in legislatures. Women are not more or less likely to be found in professionalized legislatures, which offer higher salaries and more staff and remain in session for lengthy periods. In the Northeast, Midwest, and West, however, women are somewhat less likely to occupy seats in states where the governor has significant power.

Finally, systemic factors do influence the number of women in state legislatures. As previous research has indicated, women are more common in states that have multimember districts and in those that have higher levels of turnover.

Multivariate Results

Although many factors are associated with increased numbers of women in state legislatures, our multivariate analysis shown in Table 7.4 illustrates that the best predictors of women's representation in 1995 are those which have been significant in past studies. General state ideology is the single strongest predictor, and presumably a more focused measure of support for gender equality would have been even more powerful. Sharkansky's measure of state political culture is also significant, with states with moralistic cultures more likely to elect women.

The number of women in the candidate pool predicts women in state legislatures, even after controls for other cultural variables. Two structural measures predict increased numbers of women legislators: multimember districts and turnover in legislative office. The more turnover in a legislature, the more likely that newcomer groups will have an opportunity for access. The results shown in Table 7.4 illustrate the impact of turnover.

The most surprising result is that increasing numbers of fundamentalists and Pentecostals in state electorates appears to lead to *more* women in state legislatures. This result is extremely robust, and is the result of holding constant ideology and culture of the state, and of the candidate pool. Without these controls, the relationship is strongly negative, which tells us something important about recent recruitment efforts by Republicans, especially in the South. In conservative states, Republicans recruit women who do not fit our definition of the candidate pool (professional or executive occupation, business owners, college educated) but who are part of a conservative religious network based in churches rather than in standard political networks. Once we have held constant political culture and the "regular" candidate pool, these conservative churches provide an additional pool of candidates who have a political base in these religious institutions, and who have developed skills and networks through their religious work.[5]

Summing up the results so far, it appears that the best predictors of women's presence in state legislatures are ideology of the state, political culture, the proportion of women in the candidate pool, multimember districts,

TABLE 7.4
Multivariate Sources of Women in State Legislatures

	Beta	*t*
Ideology	−.48*	−3.63
Fundamentalists/Pentecostals	.28**	2.49
Political culture (Sharkansky)	−.61***	−1.74
Candidate pool	.27**	2.30
Multimember districts	.17***	1.76
Turnover	.18***	1.80
N		
R²		

* = .01
** = .05
*** = .10

level of turnover, and, interestingly, the proportions of conservative Protestant religious denominations.

Explaining Changes in Women in State Legislatures

Figure 7.1 and Table 7.1 both show that states differ widely in the history of their election of women to state legislatures. Although Alabama and California were tied with only 1 percent women in 1964, by 1995 their paths had greatly diverged. Similarly, although Kansas and Connecticut were tied in 1995 with 27 percent women, their progress began at very different levels.

How might we explain which states have made rapid progress and which have not? To answer this question, we first identified different clusters of states, based on their histories of electing women.[6] The best solution produced four sets of states. They are detailed in Table 7.5. The first cluster consists of those states that have consistently elected the fewest women to their legislatures. The second includes those states that have consistently ranked at around the national average of women in state legislatures. The final two clusters are more interesting: those that once had a sizable lead over all other states, and those which once trailed but which have experienced the most rapid growth in electing women. In 1964, the Early Leaders had more than three times as many women in their state legislatures as the Recent Progress states, but by 1996 this lead had fallen to 3 percent. States classified as Recent Progress made substantial gains, primarily between 1984 and 1994.

How might we explain the rapid progress of the states that have gained during the past decade? How do these states differ from the traditional leaders in electing women? With only 14 states in the two categories, statistical analysis can be at best suggestive. First, the states that have made more recent

TABLE 7.5
Progress of States in Electing Women

	1964	1974	1984	1995	1996
Consistently Low	2.57	3.86	6.45	11.69	12.53
Average	2.14	4.52	12.43	21.19	21.11
Early Leaders	10.62	11.63	21.25	32.31	30.26
Recent Progress	3.60	6.83	12.17	25.63	27.77

Consistently Low: Alabama, Arkansas, Kentucky, Louisiana, Mississippi, New Jersey, North Dakota, Pennsylvania, South Carolina, Tennessee, Texas, Utah, Virginia, West Virginia (15 states).

Average: California, Deleware, Florida, Georgia, Hawaii, Illinois, Indiana, Iowa, Massachusetts, Michigan, Minnesota, Missouri, Montana, Nebraska, New Mexico, New York, North Carolina, Rhode Island, South Dakota, Wisconsin, Wyoming (21 states).

Early Leaders: Arizona, Colorado, Connecticut, Maine, New Hampshire, Oregon, Vermont, Washington (8 states).

Recent Progress: Arkansas, Idaho, Kansas, Maryland, Nevada, Ohio (6 states).

progress differ from those that have traditionally ranked first in that they have only moderately liberal citizens, whereas those states that have traditionally had the most women legislators have solidly liberal voters. Second, although Early Leader states have generally had moralistic political cultures, those with more recent gains have come from individualistic political cultures. Third, the Early Leaders have generally been states with substantial Catholic populations, whereas the Recent Progress states are not. Fourth, Early Leader states are marked by significantly higher levels of education in the electorate. Finally, the states that initially made great progress are marked by strong interest group activity (by NOW and CWA), whereas states with more recent gains are not.

These data suggest that women initially made gains in states that provided the most hospitable climates—liberal and well-educated voters, moralistic politics, Catholic religious strength, organized feminist and antifeminist groups that recruited women candidates, multimember districts, and high legislative turnover.

More recently, women have begun to make rapid progress in the set of states that might be thought of as constituting the "second tier" of hospitality to women candidates. These states have voters who are not quite as well educated or as liberal as the Early Leader states, but who are better educated and more liberal than in states with fewer women legislators. So far they lack the organized interest group activity that can help to recruit women candidates.

If this interpretation is correct, then women may be poised to make rapid progress in other states as well, for there are a number of states in the Average set which have generally moderate to liberal voters, nontraditional political cultures, and sizable candidate pools.

Conclusions

The three decades covered by this study have produced gains for women in all states, but this progress has been decidedly uneven. In 1995, the range in women's representation was quite large, with states in the Deep South and the mid-Atlantic region trailing the rest of the country by a wide margin.

The best predictors of the percentage of women in state legislatures are various measures of political culture including state ideology, culture, and religion. The trend over time indicates that the once sizable lead among northeastern states with very large legislatures has evaporated, and midwestern and western states have almost caught up. In the past decade, however, those states in the second tier of women-friendly cultures have made the greatest gains. Moreover, there are a number of states with relatively similar political cultures and sizable candidate pools that appear poised to make gains in the next decade.

There are also significant barriers to women's progress. Foremost are conservative electorates and traditional political cultures. When these conditions exist, rules that enable party officials to intervene in the nomination process work to the detriment of women candidates.

Some systemic factors facilitate women's election—especially multimember districts and high levels of turnover. Other types of structural factors appear to be less relevant, although they may have had an effect at one time. States with professionalized legislatures do not elect more or fewer women, public financing and campaign finance limits do not help women and may hurt them in some regions, and very large legislatures are no longer a good predictor of high proportions of women in the legislature. Indeed, one of the most striking trends in these data is the gradually eroding lead of New Hampshire, Connecticut, and Vermont, which at one time accounted for a substantial percentage of all women legislators.

Notes

1. The 1994 Republican victories in Washington reduced the number of women in that state's legislature to slightly less than 40 percent.
2. We combine the upper and lower houses in all states except Nebraska, which has a unicameral legislature.
3. In fact, women who run for office generally do not suffer from a disadvantage in fund-raising. But first-time women candidates may doubt this fact, and fear to run because of costs.
4. It should be noted that these regional correlations apply only to variation within the region. That is, the low correlations in the Northeast, Midwest, and West indicate that the available pool is not much of a factor in those regions, although it does help explain why women are more common in legislatures there than in the South.
5. It is important to note that although Table 7.4 shows the best-fitting model, there are other specifications that would include other statistically significant predictors. We experimented with a variety of models, and other variables were significant in each of them. Indeed, nearly every variable that is significantly correlated with women in the legislatures in Table 7.3 could end up as a significant predictor in a reasonable regression model.
6. Specifically, we clustered the states based on the percentage of women in their legislatures in 1964, 1974, 1984, and 1995.

8

Women at the National Level
An Update on Roll Call Voting Behavior

JANET CLARK[1]

One of the questions concerning the small numbers of women in Congress is whether or not their numbers make a difference in regard to the types of policy passed. As women increase their proportion of seats, will legislation become more attuned to women's problems in society? Since the discovery of the "gender gap" in attitudes among the general population, it has been assumed that women's issues would be better represented if there were more women in Congress. One way to measure whether the increased representation of women in Congress over the past decade or so has, in fact, led to more congressional support for their special concerns is to compare the voting behavior of women legislators with that of the men. Such studies of Congress have been carried out by several individuals in every decade since the 1960s.[2]

This chapter will update the earlier findings by analyzing voting behavior in the 103rd (1993–94) Congress and first year of the 104th (1995–96) Congress. Based on theories of representation and previous findings regarding voting of women legislators, two possibilities are likely. First, women in the 103rd Congress may be more liberal than men, and this difference may be even greater than in previous studies because of the large number of liberal Democratic women newly elected in 1992, the "year of the woman." However, the gender gap in voting may lessen in the 104th Congress, because the 1994 election resulted in the defeat of some liberal Democratic women and the election of a number of conservative, often antifeminist women.

If female legislators do vote differently than men, and especially if they are more attentive to issues of special interest to women, then it becomes even more important to elect more women to Congress. Dissatisfaction with the low representation of women in Congress hinges on certain normative assumptions of democracy regarding participation and representation of all segments of society. According to Pitkin, advocates of "descriptive representation" argue that legislative bodies should be a microcosm of the society, with all social groups represented proportionally. They assume that legislators represent constituents whose social characteristics they share. Exclusion or underrepresentation of any social group may cause distortion of policy outcomes (Pitkin 1967). If women in general hold policy preferences which are different from men's, then the fact that women hold only 10 percent of the seats in Congress is cause for concern.

Women's Representation in Congress: The Evolving Context

An evaluation of women's representation in Congress should consider three questions. First, do women have distinctive political views and interests? If they do not, the question of how well they are represented as a group could become moot because they would not really represent a "political" group. Second, if women do constitute a distinctive political group, how well are they represented in government (e.g., Congress, cabinet and subcabinet positions, etc.)? Finally, if women do attain significant representation, do women decision makers act distinctively? After all, if women have specific interests as a group, these interests can be promoted by women in Congress only if women representatives act differently than men.

Women and men do have different attitudes on many political issues. Early studies found men's and women's attitudes to be relatively similar except for issues related to morality and to the use of violence or force in law enforcement or international affairs. More recently, however, there has been a divergence of attitudes among the two sexes on additional social issues including the role of women, minority rights, social welfare, and protection of the environment. These differences have promoted a growing partisan and ideological split between men and women, ranging from 6 to 10 per cent (Clark and Clark, 1996:79). Although feminism may have contributed to the growth of these differences by increasing gender consciousness, it does not explain all of the gender gap. Differences in attitudes exist among both men and women independently of their levels of support for feminism (Cook and Wilcox, 1991:1121).

Studies of women legislators in American states indicate that they have distinctive attitudes and behavior as well, especially when the proportion of women legislators increases beyond token levels (Saint-Germain, 1989; Thomas, 1994a; Thomas and Welch, 1991). In particular, women legislators have different priorities than their male counterparts. They are more likely to place legislation regarding children and families at the top of their list. They also place more emphasis on human services, the environment, and social issues. If more women were in legislative bodies, it is expected that legislatures would be more likely to address child care, health, and retirement issues (Welch and Thomas, 1991:14). Ultimately, when women's representation reaches parity with men's, it is possible that they not only will change the product of legislatures but also may transform the way in which legislatures do business. And relationships within legislative bodies might more nearly conform to women's conception of power (Thomas, 1994a:151–52). According to feminist theorists, women define power as empowerment, the "power to," whereas men define it as dominion, "power over" (Deutchman, 1991:3). That means that women are more likely to use power inclusively to achieve individual and collective goals, whereas men are more likely to work individually and in a hierarchical fashion.

Thus, women have some specific political interests, and considerable evidence, especially from state legislatures, has now accumulated to show that women representatives actively seek to promote this agenda. When we look at the national level of government, though, the question of women's representation becomes more problematic because women's representation in Congress has remained in the range of tokenism for almost the entire period since women were given the right to vote and hold office. In the late 1960s, for example, there were only 10 women in the House of Representatives, or just under 2.5 percent of the total House membership. As Table 8.1 shows, this gradually increased to about 5 percent during the 1980s and jumped to 11 percent after the 1992 elections.

Despite the extremely low numbers of women before the early 1990s, it is nevertheless easy to discern the existence of a gender gap in congressional voting patterns. The index of support for conservative issues compiled by the American Conservative Union (ACU), a standardized measure often used in congressional voting studies, is used here to describe and compare the

TABLE 8.1
Gender Gap in House of Representatives on ACU Scores

Year	Women in the House		Difference between women's and men's scores on ACU index
	N	Percent	
1969–70	10	2.3	
1971–73	13	3.0	
1973–74	16	3.7	−28
1975–76	19	4.4	−20
1977–78	18	4.1	−17
1979–80	16	3.7	−16
1981–82	21	4.8	−14
1983–84	22	5.1	−13
1985–86	23	5.3	−7
1987–88	23	5.3	−5
1989–90	29	6.6	−13
1991–92	29	6.6	−14
1993–94	48	11.0	−15
1995–96	47	10.8	−24*

Sources: McGlen and O'Connor, 1995:77; Vega and Firestone, 1995:216; Welch, 1985:129.
*Not ACU score, but a similar support index for a sample of voting on 18 selected bills.

ideological voting of members of Congress. This index includes a wide range of issues and ranks individual members of Congress from 0 to 100 depending on the percentage of time they support ACU positions, with high scores indicating more conservative voting. The "gender gaps" reported in Table 8.1 represent the women's average ACU score minus the men's for a given year. For 1993–94, for example, the average woman in Congress voted with the ACU 31 percent of the time, while the average man did so 46 percent of the time. Thus, the gender gap was:

$$31 - 46 = -15$$

The relationship between the growth of women's representation in Congress and the extent of the gender gap went through two stages. Earlier studies show that the increase in the numbers of women in Congress was not accompanied by a consistent increase in the size of the gender gap. Rather, the gender gap in congressional voting declined steadily over the 1970s and 1980s and only began to increase again at the start of the 1990s (Vega and Firestone, 1995; Welch, 1985). The gender gap was highest in 1973–74 when the difference between women's and men's ACU scores was -28. The difference ultimately declined to -5 in 1987–88 and then increased again to -13 in 1989–92 and -15 in 1993–94.

Why the voting behavior of men and women in Congress began to converge and then diverged again is open to speculation. Possibly the women elected in the early 1970s, the early days of the contemporary feminist movement, were likely to be more aggressive and more liberal in their orientations, because only those with strongly held ideological views took the extraordinary step of running for Congress. The success of the movement then provided increased access to public office for women so that women candidates were less distinctive, and more moderate and conservative women were also willing to run for office. Moreover, Welch speculates that the increased opportunity for women might have placed increased pressure on women in office to conform to male standards in Congress (Welch, 1985:128).

However, by the 1990s the impact of the gender gap in the general public and in political representatives may have again translated into more distinctiveness in congresswomen's voting. The feminization of poverty and the decline in economic opportunities felt by the general population may be reflected in congressional voting. Interestingly, the renewed jump in the gender gap occurred after the 1988 elections, four years before the "year of the woman" 1992 elections, which had almost no impact on the width of the gender gap.

The Gender Gap after the Year of the Woman and the Republican Revolution

This study first looks at voting patterns in the House of Representatives in 1994 by comparing men's and women's ratings by the American Conservative

Union. Then it examines voting patterns in 1995, following the takeover of Republican leadership for the first time in many decades. It describes the impact of gender on eighteen bills selected from House votes published in the *Congressional Quarterly*. Two criteria for selection were used: bills that were particularly relevant to the Republican program and bills of special interest to women.[3] Both measures of voting are related not only to gender but also to party and other salient characteristics.[4]

Table 8.2 provides a more detailed picture of the summary figure in Table 8.1 that men scored 15 points higher (46 to 31) on the ACU index than women in 1994, producing a gender gap equal to that of the late 1970s. As would be expected, Republicans were far more conservative than Democrats, with an ACU score over four times as high (85 to 19). However, the fact that there were far more Democratic than Republican women did not account for the overall gender gap in the full House since the gender gap within each party approximately equaled that for the entire House. Thus, while Republican women, on average, voted with the ACU almost 10 times more frequently than their Democratic women colleagues (68 percent to 7 percent), both were almost equally more liberal than their male colleagues in the same party: Democratic women by 13 points and Republican women by 17 points. Thus, by the 103rd Congress gender had clearly emerged as a significant factor in House voting (Dodson et al., 1995), consistent with our general image of the consequences of the 1992 year of the woman.

Since ACU scores were not available for new representatives elected in 1994, a support score was developed for the 18 votes used here based on the position of the Republican leadership.[5] Table 8.3 presents the analysis of this support score, showing that voting patterns are consistent with the

TABLE 8.2
1994 ACU Scores for 1995 House Holdovers, by Party and Sex

	Average ACU Score	N^*
Entire House	45	321
Women	31	23
Men	46	298
Gender gap	−15	
Democrats	19	191
Women	7	14
Men	20	177
Gender gap	−13	
Republicans	84	129
Women	68	9
Men	85	120
Gender gap	−17	

*Newly elected members have no ACU scores.

assumption that the 1994 Republican "revolution" brought more conservatism and partisanship to the House, thereby undercutting gender-based voting somewhat. Nevertheless, gender retained its significant influence on voting.

Similarly to the report of 1994 ACU scores in Table 8.2, Table 8.3 breaks down the 1995 average Republican support scores by party and sex. Overall, the gender gap of −24 for the entire House was significantly higher than for the 1994 ACU index. But given the different method of sampling votes, this may not represent a real change. In another facet of Table 3, however, the gender gap within each party appears quite significant. For the Democrats, the gender gap on the 1995 Republican support score was exactly the same as for the 1994 ACU score (−13), but among Republicans it was halved, dropping from −17 to −8. Thus, consistent with our general image of the 1994 Republican revolution, the newly elected GOP women were far more conservative than those elected previously, and therefore women became far less distinctive within the Republican Party than they had been earlier.

Normally, one would expect women to be more likely to vote together on some issues than on others. Thus, separate analyses were conducted for each of the 18 votes. As expected, gender was important in some areas but not in others. In regard to votes on budgetary issues, party was almost exclusively the determinant on the four general budget items included in the sample of votes. Perhaps surprisingly, Medicare revision and foreign aid also fit this pattern. Voting on the defense budget was similar as well, but with a slight tendency for women to vote against increasing the defense budget. For 1995 at least, the budget became an almost purely straight-line partisan battle.

The breakdown of voting on a representative budget issue by party and gender in Table 8.4 confirms this pattern. Table 8.4 is a multivariate table

TABLE 8.3
1995 Republican Support Scores, by Party and Sex

	Average Republican Support Score	*N*
Entire House	61	435
Women	39	47
Men	63	388
Gender gap	−24	
Democrats	24	205
Women	13	30
Men	26	175
Gender gap	−13	
Republicans	93	230
Women	86	17
Men	94	213
Gender gap	−8	

for the vote on the Concurrent Budget Resolution, with three components: the breakdown of the vote for the full House by sex; the vote by sex for the Democrats; and the vote by sex for the Republicans. For the full House, men appear to be much more supportive (57 percent voting Yes) than women (36 percent voting Yes). However, breaking down the women and men representatives into parties shows this association to be spurious: the real relationship is that party determined how a representative voted, and the apparent tendency of women to be much less supportive than men is caused by the fact that there were far more Democratic than Republican congresswomen. All Democratic women and most Democratic men voted No. All Republican women and all but one Republican man voted Yes.

Abortion is perhaps the most central women's issue in contemporary politics. Thus, it might be expected to evoke a somewhat less party-line response than the budget issues just described. This indeed turns out to be the case for the four votes on abortion that were included in this study. For each of these votes party had the largest impact on vote, but gender had an important secondary influence as well. Table 8.5 presents the breakdown for the vote on permitting abortion at defense facilities by party and sex. Party was clearly the dominant influence here. As on the budget issues, gender had an extremely strong relationship with the vote for the entire House: 81 percent of the women but only 42 percent of the men voted Yes. On this issue, unlike the budget votes, however, controlling for party has hardly any effect on this association. For the Republicans, 53 percent of the women but only 15 percent of the men voted Yes, whereas among the Democrats, 97 percent of the women and 76 percent of the men voted Yes. Thus, women were substantially more supportive of permitting abortions than were men, even after party was controlled.

The final set of votes concerns government regulation to promote public protection, an area where, due to the gender gap in the general public, women

TABLE 8.4
Vote on Concurrent Budget Resolution, by Sex and Party

	Male	Female
Entire House	N = 386	N = 47
No	43%	64%
Yes	57%	36%
Democrats	N = 173	N = 30
No	94%	100%
Yes	6%	0
Republicans	N = 213	N = 17
No	.5%	0
Yes	99.5%	100%

TABLE 8.5
Vote on Allowing Abortions at Defense Facilities, by Sex and Party

	Male	Female
Entire House	$N = 379$	$N = 47$
No	58%	19%
Yes	42%	81%
Democrats	$N = 169$	$N = 30$
No	24%	3%
Yes	76%	97%
Republicans	$N = 210$	$N = 17$
No	85%	47%
Yes	15%	53%

officeholders might be expected to have a distinctive liberal position. One subset of four bills was related to changing various government regulations. Overall, party was the predominant influence, but again gender had a significant secondary impact. Although gender was not as strong an influence in regard to regulation as for abortion, it did have a significant independent influence on three of the four regulatory issues: women were more likely than men to oppose revising the Clean Water Act, declaring a regulatory moratorium, and providing greater protection for private property rights.

Table 8.6 presents the vote on the Clean Water Act as an example. Public opinions polls have shown that American women are more concerned about protecting the environment than are men. It was expected that gender would have an impact on the vote to revise the Clean Water Act. While its independent impact was not quite as strong as for the abortion issue, it was still pronounced. Table 8.6 shows that women were only half as likely to support revision as men, 30 percent versus 59 percent. The relationship was almost as strong among the Republicans, for whom women were twice as likely as men (29 percent vs. 14 percent) to defect from the party position and vote against revision. Among the Democrats the relationship was even stronger than for the entire House: men were six times more likely than women (25 percent vs. 4 percent) to vote for the bill. Hence, the pattern in public opinion is mirrored among members of Congress.

The other three protection issues concerned crime. Women in the House were slightly more liberal than men on two of the crime issues. Moreover, gender was also related to the vote on Criminal Alien Deportation, the one issue with little partisan impact, but with a different pattern than the ones discussed so far in which women voted more liberally than men. This bill passed overwhelmingly, 382 to 19. Not surprisingly, race had an impact on the vote. Because of fears that it could be applied with a racial bias, African Americans supported it by only a small margin. However, African-

TABLE 8.6
Vote on Revising Clean Water Act, by Sex and Party

	Male	Female
Entire House	N = 381	N = 44
No	41%	70%
Yes	59%	30%
Democrats	N = 170	N = 27
No	75%	96%
Yes	25%	4%
Republicans	N = 211	N = 17
No	14%	29%
Yes	86%	71%

American women unanimously supported the bill, whereas African-American men opposed it by a narrow margin. Thus, African-American women appeared to vote in an atypically conservative manner on this bill, possibly out of concern for the high levels of crime in minority neighborhoods.

The decline in gender's impact on House voting in 1995 raises a question regarding the new class of women elected in 1995: Do they make a policy difference, and, if so, what kind? Given the increase in the impact of partisanship, one would expect cross-cutting effects by party. The new Republican women were expected to be conservative, partisan, and pro-life, and therefore to decrease the distinctiveness of women's voting. On the other hand, the new Democratic women were expected to be liberal, feminist, and activist on social issues, and therefore to contribute to the distinctiveness of women's voting. Thus, longer tenure in the House should be associated with less conservative voting for Republican women but with more conservative voting for Democratic women.

Tables 8.7 and 8.8 test this hypothesis by listing, respectively, the Republican and Democratic women of the 1995 House along with their 1994 ACU scores, 1995 Republican support scores, the vote for permitting abortions at defense facilities, and the vote for revising the Clean Water Act. Members are listed by years of tenure, and the Democrats are also sorted by race. As expected, the newly elected Republican women were distinctive, especially on the abortion vote. Among the seven new women, six voted against permitting abortions at military bases, with Sue Kelly of New York as the only exception. In stark contrast, eight of the ten holdover Republican women voted to support these abortions.

Table 8.8 shows that seniority had little correlation with the ACU and Republican support scores among Democratic women. Moreover, all but one of these congresswomen voted for permitting abortions at military bases, and all but one voted against revising the Clean Water Act. Therefore, the

TABLE 8.7
Voting Records of Republican Congresswomen

	Years of Tenure	ACU Score	Republican Support Score	Abortion at Defense Facilities	Revise Clean Water Act
Seastrand, Calif.	1	—	100.00	No	Yes
Chenoweth, Idaho	1	—	100.00	No	Yes
Kelly, N.Y.	1	—	83.33	Yes	Yes
Myrick, N.C.	1	—	100.00	No	Yes
Waldholtz, Utah	1	—	100.00	No	Yes
Smith, Wash.	1	—	100.00	No	Yes
Cubin, Wy.	1	—	94.12	No	Yes
Fowler, Fla.	3	90	88.89	Yes	Yes
Pryce, Ohio	3	67	88.89	Yes	Yes
Dunn, Wash.	3	86	88.89	Yes	Yes
Molinari, N.Y.	5	71	88.89	Yes	Yes
Ros-Lehtinen, Fla.	6	65	94.44	No	No
Morella, Md.	9	29	27.78	Yes	No
Myers, Kans.	11	57	77.78	Yes	No
Johnson, Conn.	13	52	64.71	Yes	No
Vucanovich, Nev.	13	100	100.00	No	Yes
Roukema, N.J.	15	50	61.11	Yes	No

hypothesis that the newly elected Democratic women would be more liberal than those with longer tenure is not supported by their votes in 1994 or 1995.

What do all these findings add up to? Clearly women members of Congress have long been more liberal than men in Congress, regardless of party, and their votes are distinctive from men's on a variety of issues. Even after the Republican revolution of 1994, women members, both Republicans and Democrats, supported the majority party positions less frequently than their male counterparts, although the differences were not as great as they had been in the past. As highlighted throughout this book, the party and ideology of women elected to office matter in terms of the extent to which women members have a distinctive policy impact. Having said this, however, women in office make a difference across party and ideological divides.

Women's Representation in Congress

The question of whether or not the numerical representation of women in Congress affects the types of policies passed remains. This study confirms many of the findings of earlier analyses that women and men in Congress do vote differently than men, and that the impact of party is stronger than the impact of gender. As Debra Dodson notes in Chapter 9, much depends on the type of women who are elected. When more Democratic women were

TABLE 8.8
Voting Records of Democratic Congresswomen

	Years of Tenure	ACU Score	Republican Support Score	Abortion at Defense Facilities	Revise Clean Water Act
Lofgren, Calif.	1	—	6.67	Yes	No
Rivers, Mich.	1	—	5.56	Yes	No
McCarthy, Mo.	1	—	5.56	Yes	No
Lincoln, Alaska	3	10	44.44	Yes	No
Woolsey, Calif.	3	0	.00	Yes	—
Eshoo, Calif.	3	0	5.56	Yes	No
Roybal-Allard, Calif.	3	0	5.56	Yes	No
Thurman, Fla.	3	19	29.41	Yes	No
Harman, Calif.	3	19	41.18	Yes	No
Danner, Mo.	3	29	44.44	Yes	Yes
Velazquez, N.Y.	3	0	5.56	Yes	No
Maloney, N.Y.	3	0	5.56	Yes	No
Furse, Ore.	3	5	5.88	Yes	No
Mink, Hawaii	5	0	11.11	Yes	No
Lowey, N.Y.	7	10	5.56	Yes	No
Pelosi, Calif.	8	0	5.56	Yes	No
Slaughter, N.Y.	9	0	11.11	Yes	No
Kennelly, Conn.	13	10	16.67	Yes	No
Kaptur, Ohio	13	20	33.33	No	No
DeLaura, Conn.	15	5	11.11	Yes	No
Schroeder, Col.	23	5	5.56	Yes	No
African American					
Lee, Tex.	1	—	11.11	Yes	No
Brown, Fla.	3	24	5.88	Yes	No
Meek, Fla.	3	10	11.76	Yes	No
McKinney, Ga.	3	0	6.25	Yes	No
Clayton, N.C.	3	0	5.56	Yes	No
Johnson, Tex.	3	19	11.11	Yes	No
Waters, Calif.	5	10	6.25	Yes	—
Collins, Mich.	5	0	.00	Yes	No
Collins, Ill.	22	6	18.75	Yes	—

elected, as in 1992, the significance of gender was enhanced, but when more conservative Republican women were elected, as in 1994, the gender gap in congressional voting was reduced. Having said that, there are issues of special interest to women where gender has an important independent influence. Since the priorities of women legislators are different from those of men, when the numbers of women in Congress grow beyond token levels the types of issues considered may change and the gender gap in voting may again increase.

Notes

1. The author wishes to thank Melanie Hill, Michelle Jordan, Tara Panter, and LaRhonda Brewer for their assistance in collecting the data and Professors Cal Clark and Jerry Perkins for their advice in preparing the analysis. They are not, however, responsible for any errors in interpretation.
2. Although many different approaches have been used, most researchers have found that the women of both political parties tended to be more liberal than their male counterparts. However, the difference was small and tended to be less important than party, constituency, and district type. For example, see Gehlen, 1977; Leader, 1977; Welch, 1985; Poole and Zeigler 1985; Vega and Firestone, 1995.
3. The author relied on recommendations of Women's Policy, Inc., for the selection of the women's issue votes.
4. Information regarding ACU scores, candidate characteristics, and district characteristics was taken from *The Almanac of American Politics 1996* (Barone and Ujifusa, 1995).
5. This index was the proportion of the 18 votes included in the analysis on which the representative voted with the Republican leadership. Non-votes were considered to be missing data.

9

Representing Women's Interests in the U.S. House of Representatives

Debra L. Dodson

The all-male Senate Judiciary Committee's performance in the Hill-Thomas hearings raised questions about the ability of a predominantly male Congress to represent women. Those 1991 hearings angered women across the nation and inspired them to open their checkbooks as never before to support women (particularly Democratic women) candidates during the 1992 campaign. Increased resources of women's PACs, unprecedented enthusiasm of women voters for women candidates in key races, greater tendencies of women candidates to "run as women," and the election of record numbers of women to the U.S. Congress in the 1992 elections seemed destined to create a new political era (Cook, Thomas, and Wilcox, 1994; see also Baruch and McCormick, 1993). With 54 women serving in the newly elected 103rd Congress, compared with only 31 in the 102nd, it seemed likely that more members of Congress would "act for" women because more of them would be women whose life experiences provided somewhat different lenses through which to view problems, policies, and legislative alternatives.

A critical question, however, was whether these record numbers of women who wanted to make a difference could do so in an institution like the U.S. Congress—a predominantly male institution whose members had come under fire for "just not getting it." The 103rd Congress seemed an ideal laboratory for exploring what would happen when the desire to make a difference on a whole range of policy issues collided with institutional norms, structures, processes, and realities. After all, even though record numbers of women were serving, they were still a small minority of members (initially 6 percent, then ultimately 7 percent in the Senate and 10.8 percent in the U.S. House) and they would be relative newcomers with less seniority, power, and knowledge that comes through experience.

The generous support of the Charles H. Revson Foundation enabled the Center for the American Woman and Politics (CAWP) to take full advantage of this laboratory, conducting interviews about women's roles and their impact on selected policies during the 103rd Congress (January 1993–January 1995). This chapter compares and contrasts the ways women made a difference in abortion rights policies (Dodson, 1995a), women's health policies (Schreiber, 1995), and health care reform (Dodson, 1995b) in the U.S. House of Representatives.

Collecting the Data

CAWP followed women members of the 103rd Congress from January 1993 through December 1994. CAWP conducted more than 250 in-depth, unstructured interviews with women members of Congress, congressional staff (working for members or committees), and lobbyists closely involved in at least one of seven policy areas (women's health, abortion, health care reform, the crime bill, NAFTA, internal congressional reform, and campaign finance reform).

During the summer of 1995, CAWP contacted all women representatives and senators, to discuss experiences in the 103rd Congress and involvement in shaping legislation pertaining to the policy issues on which the study focused. As of February 1996, CAWP had conducted post-103rd interviews with 43 of the 55 women who had served in the 103rd Congres.

Interviews with staff and lobbyists closely involved in the selected legislative areas provided behind-the-scenes insights into the actions of women members and comparative assessments of the actions of women and men. The vast majority of interviews were conducted between August 1994 and August 1995 with relevant, knowledgeable staffers and lobbyists, including Republicans and Democrats, feminists and nonfeminists, liberals and conservatives, and allies and opponents of the women members on specific issues. Most of the interviews were conducted in person, although a few were conducted by phone. This chapter draws on interviews with those who worked on abortion policy (50 staffers, 13 lobbyists, and 1 other), health care reform (64 staffers, 17 lobbyists, and 4 others), and women's health (49 staffers and 15 lobbyists).

The Basis for Difference

Not surprisingly, most women members of Congress saw women as having some common concerns, and the vast majority of women members interviewed—Republicans and Democrats alike—acknowledged feeling a responsibility to represent those special concerns of women, in addition to representing the concerns of their districts. Differences in the events and experiences that touch women's and men's lives contributed to gender differences in what they recognized as problems and what they defined as important.

Many respondents traced women's common concerns to the sexual division of labor, with women members quite often speaking of women's role as caregivers. For example, when asked what women have in common, Representative Lynn Woolsey (D-Calif.) replied, "The need to take care of . . . our parents, our children, each other, our husbands if we have them. We're the caretakers. It isn't that men don't care about these things. . . . It's just that it's more important to us."

Other types of personal experiences contributed to a recognition of both common concerns and the relevance of politics to those concerns. Representatives Marilyn Lloyd (D-Tenn.) and Barbara Vucanovich (R-Nev.), both breast cancer survivors, and Representative Rosa DeLauro (D-Conn.), an ovarian cancer survivor, brought unique personal experiences to the public debate about women's health issues. These close calls in their own lives raised their awareness of and commitment to women's health as a political issue. While there were some differences among them, Representative DeLauro explained her views this way,

> I had an interest in women's health issues . . . because I'm a survivor of ovarian cancer. I was stunned when I came here to find out that . . . research on women's health concerns was almost nonexistent, that women were not part of the clinical trials at the NIH [National Institutes of Health], there was no Office of Women's Research at the NIH. So the whole focus on women's health was important to me.

Yet the impact of the personal went beyond women's health issues and caregiving, with numerous women members directly or indirectly alluding to sex discrimination. As District of Columbia delegate Eleanor Holmes Norton, a civil rights attorney, explained,

> Much of my view of women comes out of the life I've lived and the commitments I've made long before even thinking about running for Congress. Growing up in a segregated city and going to segregated schools raised my consciousness very early about [racial] discrimination. . . . The transfer of that from blacks to women was almost automatic. . . . By the time I got to Congress, my view on women and my feeling of responsibility for pressing forward their demands was very well formed. . . . This was just another place, another forum, to act on them.

Having for whatever reason recognized shared concerns among women, the vast majority of women members felt a responsibility to bring those matters to the table. As Representative Deborah Pryce (R-Ohio) explained, "Women have to speak up for things that affect women, because the men don't—not out of malice but because it's just not of interest to them." Nor is it in their realm of experience, as Representative Nancy Johnson (D-Conn.) told us:

> We automatically think, "How will this affect the environment? How will this affect people at the work site?" But we really don't think, "How will this affect women who work at home? Women in the workplace with home responsibilities? Women who are single parents?" I know a lot more about the shape of women's

lives and the pattern of women's lives, so I need to look and see how public policy will affect those patterns and who it will help or hurt.

Although some of the women had come to Congress to focus on women's issues, others initially had been reluctant to do so. However, what these women encountered when they arrived left at least some of them feeling they had no choice but to speak for women. As Representative Marge Roukema (R-N.J.), a leader in the Family and Medical Leave effort, explained,

> When I first came to Congress . . . I really didn't want to be stereotyped as the woman legislator. I wanted to deal with . . . things like banking and finance. But I learned very quickly that if the women like me in Congress were not going to attend to some of these family concerns—whether it was jobs or children or . . . pension equity or whatever—then they weren't going to be attended to. So I quickly shed those biases.

A few of the women who felt a responsibility to act on behalf of women— even a few elected as recently as the 1990s—recalled their struggle with the legitimacy of acting on such concerns. Representative Patsy Mink (D-Hawaii) ultimately became one of the Congress's most consistent and tireless advocates for women, but she struggled with this concern as well, as she recalled,

> When I first came to Congress in 1965, I had a notion that my basic responsibility was to my constituents and my state. And gradually . . . I . . . realized that I had a far greater role to play. . . . It extended far beyond just caring for the constituents' needs. I had to speak for all the women in America. It was *not* something that I came to Congress understanding, but certainly it hit me very quickly after I arrived.

The acknowledgment by most women members of Congress that women's and men's lives give them different perspectives, combined with the sense of responsibility they felt to represent these different perspectives, provided a foundation for women to have a distinctive, collective, gender-related impact on public policy.

The question remained, however, of whether and how this potential for difference could be realized within Congress in any of these policy areas. At first glance, one might conclude that little was different because of women's presence. Women's health would seem to be a likely area where women might make a difference; however, in those few instances during the 103rd when up or down recorded floor votes were taken on women's health provisions, women and men were about equally supportive. Similarly, gender's relevance for health care reform was unclear, since women and men divided along partisan lines over the best plan, with little evidence of intraparty gender difference in cosponsorship of the major bills (Dodson, 1995b). Only on abortion rights did women cast consistently more feminist floor votes than their male colleagues (see Dodson, 1995a), but ironically, it is an area where some have concluded that women are prevented by institutional factors from having any substantial influence on the shape of those policies prior to the floor vote (Norton, 1995). Yet, as the discussion in this chapter will show, women managed to make a difference in all three policy areas, albeit in different ways along the path from introduction to passage and in ways that can often be missed by reliance on traditional quantitative measures (like roll call votes or cosponsorship) used in legislative studies.

Evidence of Difference: Defining the Agenda

In each of the three policy areas—women's health, abortion rights, and health care reform—the women members of the Congressional Caucus for Women's Issues (CCWI) seemed to reach some degree of consensus on a (formal or informal) agenda. With 41 of the 47 female U.S. House members plus the D.C. delegate being members of the CCWI, the bipartisan agreements forged within the Caucus reasonably can be considered the agenda of women members. The staff resources and structure of the Caucus went a long way toward fostering a collective voice among the women; without the Caucus women might well have supported similar policies, but coming together to work for those policies would have been far more difficult. As this section shows, however, the ease with which women could unite around a shared agenda varied across policy areas, as did the likelihood that the women members' agenda would be embraced by the entire chamber.

Women's Health

Women continued to do in the 103rd Congress what they had begun in previous Congresses: they defined women's health as a political problem, and they crafted and advanced a bipartisan legislative agenda to address it. One longtime Capitol Hill lobbyist explained, "If the women had not been there, there would be no women's health agenda. There never would have been. I think they are wholly and completely responsible. . . . I will go even a step further and say that the Caucus [Congressional Caucus for Women's Issues] is almost really the one that was responsible."

The Caucus initially introduced its bipartisan agenda for women's health, the Women's Health Equity Act (WHEA), in the 101st Congress. It was an 18-item omnibus bill to address gender inequalities in the treatment of women's health issues, with a particular focus on taxpayer-funded medical research. Women members continued to define the women's health agenda through WHEA, subsequently updating, revising, expanding, and reintroducing versions in both the 102nd and 103rd Congresses. By the 103rd, WHEA had increased to 32 provisions, 23 of which were sponsored solely by women (Congressional Caucus for Women's Issues, 1993). As in the past, sponsors of these measures included women from both parties.

These omnibus WHEA bills provided a variety of women's health provisions that could either stand alone or be attached to other pieces of legislation.

WHEA was not only the women's health agenda for women members, but also the agenda for the entire Congress. Virtually every women's health provision that passed or came close to passing in the 103rd Congress had its roots in the Caucus's WHEA bills. The influence of the Caucus was apparent in some measures sponsored by men. For example, when asked about women's influence on women's health provisions included in the NIH Revitalization Act, the Minority Health Improvement Act, and the Preventative Health Amendments—all sponsored by Representative Henry Waxman (D-Calif.)— one staffer explained:

> The input from the women members of Congress, specifically from the Women's Caucus, was absolutely the fundamental principal in getting these provisions in these bills. In every case . . . the initiative came from the Women's Caucus. . . . They [women members of the Caucus] were always willing to negotiate on these points, but I would say that they were the springboard for all of the [women's health] provisions that were incorporated into these bills.

Three factors were central to the women's success in reaching agreement on a women's health agenda and in turn influencing the Congressional agenda. First, by focusing more heavily on the allocation of federal dollars for health research, WHEA managed to avoid partisan conflict within the Caucus and within the Congress as a whole. Second, the rise of a grass-roots political movement to fight breast cancer increased constituent pressure on members both to support women's health measures and to take the problem seriously. Third, momentum created by these two factors was magnified by the absence of an organized political opposition to women's health.

Abortion Rights

If women's health is a case study in how women members forged a shared agenda that influenced the congressional agenda, abortion rights is a case study in how women can have at least some impact on the agenda when confronted by ideological and institutional obstacles. The pro-choice effort had been largely led in previous congresses by the predominantly male leadership of the Pro-choice Task Force. However, record gains for women in the 1992 elections brought into the 103rd Congress an infusion of members who cared passionately about reproductive rights. As a result, the CCWI adopted a pro-choice stand for the first time in its history, signaling women members' intention to shape congressional policy on abortion rights. The changes were summed up by one House staffer in the following way:

> Before [the 103rd Congress] the head of the abortion rights group was [Representative] Les AuCoin[(D-Ore.)], which I think kind of irritated a lot of women members. Not that he was ineffective, or that he didn't have good people working for him. . . . [But] Mr. AuCoin left, and someone else took that leadership spot, and it happens to be women. . . . I think the women have taken over more.

Nevertheless, this power shift was not effortless, and it was not as complete as one might assume given the success women had in shaping the women's health agenda.

Women members first had to agree among themselves on priorities, for a well-organized opposition to abortion rights meant that any pro-choice victory would be hard fought and require much in the way of political capital. When they began the session, the top priority was the Freedom of Choice Act (FOCA). But the increased presence of African-American women in the Congress caused the CCWI to reexamine its priorities and push funding to the top of its agenda instead. As one staffer explained:

> The area where you very strongly felt the increased diversity is in . . . what the focus on abortion was going to be. At the beginning of the 103rd Congress, the incumbent [veteran] congresswomen . . . were talking primarily about the Freedom of Choice Act and what the strategy should be around that, and [saying] we'll have it passed by the House in the summer. And primarily the African-American congresswomen said, "Wait a minute. That's not our priority. Our priority is funding and removing the restrictions on poor women's funding under Medicaid. It really means nothing for women to have this right to choose if they can't afford to pay for it and there isn't any funding."

The conflict among women over FOCA reflected to some degree the differences in the needs and concerns of their constituents. As one lobbyist noted,

> You have to remember that . . . people have different constituencies. For example, [Representative] Barbara Kennelly's [D-Conn.] district is not the same as [Representative] Maxine Waters's [D-Calif.] district. I mean Maxine Waters represents Compton, which is a very poor, almost 100 percent black district, and Barbara Kennelly's is probably the opposite. So I'm reluctant to say that the same amount of divisiveness that exists within the pro-choice movement exists between the Women's Caucus, because I'm not sitting in on those meetings, but . . .

Ultimately, the working consensus of the CCWI became that funding should be given priority over FOCA, and once that decision was made, the Caucus never took up FOCA again. There were no guarantees that women's priorities would sway their male colleagues. For one thing, women members were still a small proportion of the membership. Second, women had been ignored by longtime FOCA sponsor Representative Don Edwards (D-Calif.) despite the fact they had been a solid core of support for FOCA in Congress. Edwards, chair of the House Civil and Constitutional Rights Subcommittee, failed to consult them prior to introducing a version of FOCA some Caucus members found objectionable. A staffer explained:

> You've probably heard people talk about the first meeting of the Women's Caucus in 1993, when everything sort of hit the fan. That's when Pat Schroeder said, "They're introducing a bill [FOCA] that is weak on parental notice and

funding." . . . It got people agitated, and that's when they said, "Let's form a task force." . . . You know, it seems unbelievable to me . . . that FOCA would have been introduced without the senior woman on the committee, Pat Schroeder, the senior woman in the House, having looked at the bill. It just seems surprising to me.

The Caucus failed to get the changes in FOCA that would have addressed concerns about funding for poor women or minors' access to abortion. Nevertheless, in an indirect—albeit negative—way their agenda did affect FOCA's fate. Even with unity among pro-choice supporters FOCA would have had a difficult time passing, because the antiabortion forces both inside and outside Congress were well organized. However, the erosion of enthusiasm for FOCA among the women and the redirection of women's efforts elsewhere (e.g., lifting the Hyde ban, Freedom of Clinic Access [FACE], health care reform) deprived Representative Edwards of some of the energy he needed to launch a full battle. As a result, FOCA never made it through the rules committee and to the floor for a vote.

Health Care Reform

Women faced enormous obstacles in forging a shared bipartisan agenda on health care reform. Health care reform was, after all, being driven by the White House, an enormous array of economic interests wanted a voice in reforming this industry which accounts for one-seventh of the U.S. economy, the sharply partisan environment discouraged compromise, and women members themselves were divided over the best health care plan. Nevertheless, women members, working through the Congressional Caucus for Women's Issues, did to reach a tacit agreement on a relatively narrow agenda.

In theory, women's shared agenda was expressed in the Caucus's "Statement of Women's Health Principles" and articulated by Democratic and Republican representatives of the Caucus in testimony before House committees and subcommittees. Starting with the statement "Health care coverage should be available to all, regardless of income, employment status, preexisting conditions, or eligibility for other forms of public assistance," the principles were aimed at ensuring that any health care reform plan adopted would adequately address women's needs.

In practice, however, women members united across party lines on a much narrower, more informal agenda, comprised almost exclusively of specific concerns that Caucus members had worked on in the past. Staffers and lobbyists echoed the conclusions of this staff member who summed up women's impact on the health care reform agenda as follows:

Women in general . . . had a major impact [on health care reform] in . . . making sure that women's health wasn't relegated to the kind of back-bench status that it had received in previous years . . . and in just raising awareness about women's health issues, too, in terms of preventive services. I'm not just talking about access

to abortion, but I'm talking about mammograms and pap smears . . . raising the
level of understanding of how important and how critical those things were.

To this end, Caucus members of both parties met with first lady Hillary
Rodham Clinton early in the first session to discuss their concerns about
women's health coverage under health care reform. Majorities of CCWI
members signed on to letters to the White House both urging improvements
in coverage of cancer-detecting mammograms, pap smears, and pelvic exams
and reiterating their demand that abortion be included in the basic benefits
package. Women members of the Caucus held press conferences to keep these
concerns before the public, and they lobbied party leaders to convince them
that failure to address their agenda in health care reform would cost them a
large bloc of votes. Their focus on this narrow range of specifics rather than a
broader range of concerns addressed in the eight principles helped them avoid
partisan pitfalls that could have shattered their solid united front. By focusing
their energies on a niche that united them, they were large enough to create a
political din the House leadership (which was counting every vote) could not
ignore. Whether any Republican women would have voted for the Clinton
health plan because of these provisions (or others) is doubtful, but women's
efforts to maintain a high-profile, united front kept women's health concerns
and abortion rights on the political agenda far longer than many might have
expected.

Evidence of Difference: Incorporating the Women's Agenda into Legislation

Raising awareness of problems, developing agendas with solutions to those
problems, and getting male colleagues to buy into those agendas are important first steps—but they are only first steps. The next step is to incorporate
that agenda into legislation. Just how successful women were in doing this
varied depending on their positioning within the institution—who served on
relevant committees, the chairs of those relevant committees and subcommittees, the seniority of those supporting the agenda—and the level of opposition
to their agenda. Waiting until the bill gets to the House floor might be for
naught, since the rule governing debate may limit amendments and lobbying
the full chamber rather than simply a committee or subcommittee may take
a great deal more effort.

Women's Health

Committee assignments were important in determining whether the agendas
that women coalesced around would be reflected in legislation. This was
true even in the case of women's health—an issue no member wanted to
be seen as opposing. (As one women's health advocate put it, "When those
guys come out of committee, they don't want to be seen as voting against
breast cancer [research]—that doesn't look good. There's a certain amount of

bipartisanship based on the sort of 'mom and apple pie' issues that women's health now represents.") Although the momentum behind women's health remained strong and stable across the 102nd and 103rd Congresses, one major change between the two Congresses (in addition to the shift from a Bush to a Clinton administration) was that women members were added to the Appropriations' Labor, Health and Human Services subcommittee (Labor/HHS) during the 103rd Congress. No longer would women have to lobby the panel as outsiders, as one Democratic staffer explained:

> We got . . . women [on] a committee that had not had women on it since 1974. But when you added . . . [four] women onto an entity that had not had women on it before, . . . it . . . accelerated and increased an influence [support for women's health] that was already felt because of the involvement of people outside of the subcommittee itself with the issues that we handle. But it was a very significant change.

In the absence of women members, there almost certainly would have been some appropriations for women's health. However, it is significant that in an era of cutbacks, the addition of women to the Labor, Health and Human Services (Labor/HHS) subcommittee was accompanied by some substantial increases in women's health funding during the 103rd Congress: the National Cancer Institute's appropriation for breast cancer research increased 75 percent; Breast and Cervical Cancer Mortality Prevention Act appropriations increased by approximately a third; and the NIH Women's Health Initiative appropriations increased substantially (Congressional Caucus for Women's Issues, 1994c). In addition, language in the Labor/HHS committee report targeted monies for breast, cervical, and ovarian cancers; osteoporosis; lupus; and problems disproportionately affecting aging women. Getting this language into the report was significant because it meant that agencies could be held accountable in the next appropriations cycle for activities on these medical concerns.

Not surprisingly, the general consensus in interviews was that having women on that subcommittee played a critical role in increases for women's health programs. As one lobbyist recalled:

> Women on the Appropriations Committee . . . really went to bat for us. . . . It's very easy to get members of Congress to say they're *for* more money for breast cancer research, or they of course want to see the breast cancer epidemic ended. And of course they believe it's an important issue. But it's not so easy to find members of Congress who are willing to actually pick up the banner and go into battle on the issue. Nita Lowey did that. And Nancy Pelosi did it. Rosa DeLauro. The women members who were on the Appropriations Committee really went into battle on this issue.

With money limited, Representative Pelosi (D-Calif.) summed up the impact of women on that subcommittee in the 103rd: "It helps a great deal to have women at the table when the pie is being carved up. . . . Our presence there made a tremendous difference in the breast cancer money." More specifically, one Democratic staffer offered an example of how women's presence at the table made a difference:

> Having women in that [sub]committee had a very important impact. Mr. Porter [ranking minority member of the committee] . . . made the point over and over again about how he didn't like . . . the "targeted funding" for breast cancer and AIDS research. . . . Every time he was able to raise his concerns [in the subcommittee], we had three women to say, "Wait a minute. There's a reason we're doing this. It's because they've been neglected for so long."

Moreover, the three Democratic women in particular made the most of this opportunity by developing a team strategy to advance the women's health agenda.

The women acted as a bloc that represented the Caucus, not merely their own personal interests. Indeed, several women members who did not serve on Appropriations mentioned the important role that the women on Appropriations had played in funding their own priority programs— Representative Connie Morella (R-Md.) mentioned AIDS, Representative Patsy Mink (D-Hawaii) mentioned ovarian cancer, and then-Representative Olympia Snowe (R-Maine) mentioned osteoporosis. Having women on the subcommittee meant that the Caucus could turn responsibility over to them. As one staffer explained, "They [women on the subcommittee] would watch out for women's issues, and they would make women's health issues a priority. . . . It was a different relationship than us lobbying the entire Labor/HHS committee."

Abortion Rights

If it was important to have women on a committee to advocate for universally popular programs like finding a cure for breast cancer, their presence was even more critical on Labor/HHS Appropriations when it came to the ever-controversial issue of Medicaid funding of abortion. It is probably true that abortion rights legislation of some type would have been on the agenda regardless of whether women served on key committees; but without women on the Labor/HHS Appropriations subcommittee, the Caucus's priority of overturning the Hyde ban on Medicaid funding of abortions probably would not have been pursued as vigorously. The success Representatives Rosa DeLauro (D-Conn.), Nancy Pelosi (D-Calif.), and Nita Lowey (D-N.Y.) had in lifting the Hyde Amendment from the Labor/HHS Appropriations bill in subcommittee was a reflection of their commitment to choice and their willingness to challenge business as usual. As one staffer recounted:

> When I say the women were critical to this [removing the Hyde Amendment in the subcommittee], it has to do with the composition of the subcommittee,

fundamentally, which changed by their presence. . . . We probably had a majority for years on rape and incest. But as a courtesy to Mr. Natcher [the subcommittee chair], in fact, people did not raise that as a subcommittee issue. It was always dealt with in full committee or on the floor. . . . So you had a change in the composition, and the votes were just different in subcommittee. And women were part of that.

Nevertheless, having women in key committee positions committed to pursuing the CCWI's priorities could not ensure victory—it could only ensure that the issue was placed on the agenda. In a 31–18 vote, the full committee reversed the subcommittee action and restored the Hyde Amendment. Some blamed women for the loss, citing poor strategy on their part; others chalked up the win for Hyde to the ideological composition of the committee. The reasons for their loss in committee (and later their crushing defeat on the floor) remain a matter of debate. However, the commitment of a minority of members, particularly in the face of an organized opposition, could not ensure victory.

Health Care Reform

The politics of health care reform and abortion rights were alike in two respects: (1) both would have been on the agenda of the 103rd Congress regardless of whether women served; and (2) having women who supported the CCWI's agenda on relevant committees increased the likelihood that their shared agenda would be included in bills, for the Caucus members were limited in what they could accomplish as outsiders.

The Ways and Means Committee is a case in point. After much highly publicized criticism by women members about the inadequate women's health provisions in the Clinton health plan (e.g., biennial, rather than annual, mammography coverage for women 50 and older), the chair's markup (or amendments) in Ways and Means altered coverage to bring it closer to current medical standards. It provided biennial mammography coverage for women in their forties and annual coverage for women 50–64. However, in a cost-saving move, coverage then reverted to biennial coverage for women 65 and older. Both female members of the panel, Representatives Nancy Johnson (R-Conn.) and Barbara Kennelly (D-Conn.), offered amendments to strengthen mammography coverage and these were the only such amendments that came to a vote. But it was Kennelly who succeeded in improving the bill for women.

Representative Kennelly found the $40 million needed to cover the cost of annual mammograms for seniors, offered the amendment, and got it passed on a voice vote in the committee. Whether a male member of the committee would have offered the same amendment in the absence of women is unclear (although it is noteworthy that Representative Nancy Johnson offered the only other mammography provision that was brought to a vote in that committee). What is clear is that having an advocate for women's health needs on the committee was important, as this Republican staffer noted:

She [Mrs. Kennelly] was able to offer that amendment at the Ways and Means Committee [stage] and find the revenue to pay for it. An amendment like that would almost certainly have never passed on the floor. . . . For all practical purposes, the tax portions of it are locked off . . . any bill that comes out of the Ways and Means Committee. They are not subject to amendment [on the floor].

Women also made a substantial difference in the version of the Clinton health care reform bill drafted by the Education and Labor Committee, but they did so in a manner not initially apparent. Representative Pat Williams (D-Mont.), chair of Education and Labor's Labor-Management subcommittee, introduced a draft bill to his subcommittee that substantially improved the women's health and reproductive health coverage initially offered in the president's bill, to include biennial mammograms for women 40–49; annual mammograms for women 50 and older; annual pap smears; breast and cervical screening and family planning visits with no copayment; and full coverage for contraceptive drugs and devices for women with incomes 200 percent of poverty level (Congressional Caucus for Women's Issues, 1994c).

He strengthened those provisions in response to concerns women members of the subcommittee raised about the inadequacies of women's health coverage in the Clinton bill. It is important to understand that the markup process in the Labor-Management Subcommittee, for all practical purposes, began before the actual markup, in the committee's Democratic Caucus. The Democratic women on the subcommittee, led by Representative Patsy Mink (D-Hawaii), formed an informal task force on women's health, approached the subcommittee chair about their concerns, and convinced Williams to incorporate their recommendations into his markup. According to Representative Mink,

When we first met in our Education and Labor caucus, it [women's health coverage] was not an issue of any paramount concern, so I volunteered to write that portion [of the health care reform markup]. . . . But once we did [it] . . . everybody wanted to take ownership of it. There they were out there like they authored it, you know. I didn't care, I mean the point is to get it across and to get it included.

The Democratic women members involved in this effort lauded Pat Williams for his receptivity to their concerns. Had someone else chaired the subcommittee, these concerns might have been ignored. However, they firmly believed that strong women's health provisions were included because women served on the committee. As Representative Lynn Woolsey (D-Calif.) explained:

[Women's health coverage] was not on his [Representative Pat Williams's] radar screen. Once he "got it" . . . every time he talked about his plan, it was the first or second thing he brought forward. It was a real accomplishment, . . . but it had to come from us [the women members]. . . . [After all,] why haven't they had breast cancer research all these years? It's not that men don't want it. They are not even thinking about it.

Neither Republican woman serving on the committee—(Marge Roukema [R-N.J.], who was the ranking member of the subcommittee, or Susan Molinari [R-N.Y.], who served on the full committee—was involved in this collaborative effort. These two women nevertheless left their mark on reproductive rights coverage, for they were the only two Republicans who voted in the full committee against a motion that would have given the states the right to regulate abortion services. They were the swing votes that closed the door to what some saw as widespread abortion prohibitions at the state level. Had they followed the pattern of their male colleagues, the motion would have carried with a one-vote margin. But perhaps more important, a victory for the anti–abortion rights side on this would have made it easier for the Democratic leadership, worried about the votes of pro-life Democrats, to jettison abortion coverage when they melded provisions from Ways and Means' and Education and Labor's drafts into a Leadership bill that they thought could pass.

Evidence of Impact: Policy Victories That Might Have Been Defeats without Women

Women members of the 103rd Congress increased attention to women's health, developed an agenda that addressed women's health concerns, and (either directly or indirectly, working through male colleagues) incorporated portions of that agenda into legislation. To the extent that *anyone* made *any* difference in the ill-fated health care reform effort, women's support of a narrow range of concerns was responsible for the improvement of women's health provisions and the maintenance of some form of abortion coverage in committee drafts and the leadership compromise bill that was based on them. If the bill had made it to final passage, there is certainly reason to believe that women would have prevailed on at least some of these matters.

But it is on abortion rights (outside of health care reform) where the questions arise about women members' impact in the U.S. House. While lobbyists and staffers generally agreed that women brought new energy to the pro-choice effort (Dodson, 1995a), it was male, not female, members who had the highest-profile roles in the two major pro-choice victories—passage of FACE and removal of the ban on abortion coverage under the Federal Employees Health Benefit Program (FEHBP). Moreover, the male sponsors of FACE and FOCA—the two major pieces of reproductive rights–authorizing legislation—appear to have formulated their bills without seeking input from women members. While the battle for Medicaid funding may well have been fought—or as hard fought—because of women, they ultimately lost that battle badly. If we approach the question of women's impact on reproductive rights policy from a different perspective, however—asking whether FACE or the FEHBP abortion coverage would have gone down to defeat or died without

the efforts of women, rather than looking at who held credit-claiming roles—
then women's impact on abortion rights becomes more apparent.

Federal Employees Health Benefit Program

In 1994, for the first time since fiscal year 1984, the ban on abortion coverage
under the Federal Employees Health Benefit Program was lifted. Had everything gone according to plan, women in the House would have had little
role in this pro-choice victory. Treasury-Postal Subcommittee Chair Steny
Hoyer steered that provision through his Treasury-Postal Appropriations
Subcommittee (on which no women sat), through the full Appropriations
Committee, to the floor, and through the conference committee on what
was intended to be a low-profile path to victory. However, in the final step
toward passage, the vote on the conference report, it was quick action by
women members that may have saved the bill and kept abortion coverage
under health care reform a real possibility.

On the day scheduled for the vote on the conference report, Hoyer,
unaware of the eleventh-hour pro-life ambush planned for his Treasury-Postal
bill, assured women members that there was no danger of a pro-life challenge.
Fighting for the Hyde Amendment in the Labor/HHS Subcommittee bill had
been the pro-life caucus's highest priority, and as a result they had offered no
strong opposition to the Treasury Postal provision in committee, on the floor,
or in conference. Abortion was hardly even mentioned in the floor debate.
The real threat to passage seemed to be the growing partisan tensions between
House Republicans and the Clinton administration over staffing issues.

Later that day, however, women members learned of a late-starting effort
by the Pro-Life Caucus to defeat the conference report. A Democratic House
staffer recalled:

> [A pro-choice staffer for a pro-life member] . . . told people, "Something is going
> on tonight with Treasury Postal, because my boss keeps getting these calls."
> Presumably they're whip calls, right? So [Caucus staff and some staff for individual
> members] faxed something to all the women members saying, "Get to the floor—
> there's an ambush on this." . . . Women went to the floor and just stood on the
> floor. . . . (It [abortion coverage for federal employees] hadn't come up in the
> debate at all really, and it was a late-night vote, so people weren't aware.) . . .
> They [women members] went to the floor and just acted like normal whips and
> just did the thumb up, vote yes, to people who came in. [One woman member]
> grabbed at least one Democrat, pro-life, and stood with him while he voted the
> right way, and did not tell him what was going on. And mind you, this was after
> being assured by the chairman of the subcommittee there was no problem with
> this bill. This bill almost went down.

Armed with this information, the Congressional Caucus for Women's Issues
also alerted Hoyer and worked with him to call the vote earlier than originally
planned. With the bill passing by a single vote, 207–206, it seems quite likely

that women members of the U.S. House did have an impact on the fate of this bill.

Freedom of Clinic Access (FACE)

With Charles Schumer drafting FACE (rather than Pat Schroeder who previously voiced an interest in doing so), introducing it (after inviting Representative Connie Morella [R-Md.] to be a chief cosponsor), and chairing the subcommittee through which it passed, one could certainly ask just how much impact women had on FACE. Combined with the views of some staffers and lobbyists who argued that the escalating violence outside abortion clinics made it inevitable that FACE would pass regardless of women's actions, the question of whether women made a difference seems all the more justified. However, others saw women's roles as critical to the success of FACE. Representative Jolene Unsoeld (D-Wash.), who led the whip effort on the bill recounted:

> I do not believe it [FACE] would have happened regardless [of whether women were there or not]. . . . It took a strong effort, particularly from the women, to keep people focused on the need for this. . . . Part of that is timing. . . . Immediately after one of the shootings, that [passage] might have happened; but . . . all you have to do is put a little doubt in people's minds. . . . Trying to equate it with discrimination, religious discrimination . . . got a lot of people uneasy.

Women made a difference because Schumer had competing priorities—vying for his attention. Women House members, collectively and as individuals, kept FACE moving when its well-intentioned chief sponsor may have been tempted to let things slide. First, women members (primarily members of the CCWI) put pressure on Judiciary Chair Jack Brooks (D-Tex.) and Crime Subcommittee Chair Charles Schumer (R-N.Y.) to pass the bill and not let it languish as other, seemingly more pressing issues (like the Crime Bill) came to the fore. A Republican House staffer recalled:

> All the women were going to Jack Brooks constantly and to Chuck Schumer (and over to the Senate side as well) . . . saying, "You must pass this. You must do it quickly. We cannot afford to wait recess after recess." It kept getting put off. . . . "We've got to get this done. This is a high priority. Please pass it. Pass it, pass it, pass it." You know, there was just this dogged persistence again on this issue. . . . I think it was the women together as a force that really made the difference.

Second, women in key committee positions went above and beyond the call of duty to move FACE. The most obvious example was Representative Pat Schroeder (D-Colo.), the only woman serving on Judiciary during the 103rd. Although Schumer's decision to introduce FACE short-circuited Schroeder's plan to do so, Schroeder jumped in to carry Schumer's bill at critical times.

As one staffer commented, "It was my impression that FACE would not have happened without Pat Schroeder. From everything I have seen, that was her bill." Schroeder's efforts were seen as particularly critical in making sure that FACE made it through the conference committee. As the only woman on Judiciary, and hence the only female House member likely to sit on the FACE conference committee, Schroeder was uniquely situated among women members to make sure that the bill did not die. Commenting on this situation, one pro-choice advocate observed:

> It was Schroeder organizing some good, behind-the-scenes pressure to keep this moving forward, get it conferenced, get it back, get the conference report voted on, and exert the pressure. Not that Schumer was not interested in the legislation; it's just where it fell in his priorities. And I think Schroeder was very good, and very successful in pushing it forward and making sure that it didn't fall between the cracks.

Pat Schroeder may have been the only woman on Judiciary, but she was not the only woman who was able to use her committee position to keep FACE moving. Representative Louise Slaughter (D-N.Y.), the only woman on the Rules Committee, played an important role in getting FACE through the Rules Committee and to the floor in a form that would be supported by the bill's sponsors.

> It was important to have Louise there [on Rules]. . . . We one night spent hours working with Louise. . . . We were trying to get the bill to the floor to be conferenced . . . before the end of the session. . . . The Republicans had prevented it from going through the technical procedures that you have to go through before you can conference a bill. We were trying to figure out a way to get it to the floor before the end of the session. Louise Slaughter worked with us to try to figure out how to make that happen.

As Representative Louise Slaughter (D-N.Y.) recalled, "The majority of the Rules members were pro-life. . . . We [pro-choice Democrats] were always short. This came up time after time after time. There were times when I'd literally say to a couple of the members, please don't come. Let's just don't vote on this today. And we were able then to muster enough votes that we could get it down to the floor."

Finally, women used informal roles to catch things that were falling through the cracks and to carry FACE to the finish line. Representative Connie Morella (R-Md.), the Republican Schumer (D-N.Y.) invited to join him as chief sponsor of the bill, took on with a vengeance what could have been a largely ceremonial role. She did what her Democratic colleagues could not do, as one Republican staffer explained:

> The Judiciary Committee had a real hard time . . . dealing with the many issues that were before them all at once. And Morella's office was really the main office

doing all the lobbying on the Republican side. There really wasn't anyone else that could handle it at that point in time. They were holding the boat up on that side. And that's not to say that there weren't other Republicans being helpful—there were some. But they really had the main weight on our side of those that would support the bill, getting those people together, making sure they were fully cognizant of any possible amendment that would be introduced, and how . . . they should vote and why, and giving them the arguments ahead of time, and making sure they knew the second something was going to hit the fan.

Conclusion

In each of the three policy areas, women members of the 103rd Congress made a difference. The scope of that difference and how it manifested itself varied across the policy areas; but with methodological tools sufficiently flexible, their distinctive gender-related impact could be observed. Some policy areas are easier for women to reach bipartisan agreement on than others; concerns of race, class, and ideology seemed less relevant to women members' interactions on women's health, for example, than on abortion or health care reform. Women were better able to get the Caucus's consensus incorporated into legislation on health issues than in other areas, and this difference was partially due to committee assignments, the extent to which the membership of committees or the House would support them, and the degree of organized opposition to their efforts. As a small minority of members (and a minority that is lower in seniority, status, and committee power than men), women needed sympathetic male colleagues who would support their agenda and help them work to advance it. And, as almost any newly emerging group finds, the decision to attempt to take control of an area where many political battles have been fought previously places the group in the position of treading on territory already staked out by others, as happened with reproductive rights and FOCA in particular.

Many of the patterns observed in the 103rd are useful for understanding women's impact in the significantly more conservative 104th Congress, as well as in other Congresses. Even though the 104th Congress saw the entry of six very conservative Republican women members, if women are making a difference it will manifest itself in the same ways it did in the 103rd Congress—in a gender gap in roll call voting as well as in expansion of the agenda to include issues important to women, incorporation of these concerns into legislation, expansion of the debate to include perspectives reflecting women's life experiences, and a willingness of women to push legislation they value but that others are sponsoring.

At the same time, the change in partisan control elevated more women to leadership positions and key positions such as full committee chairs than had been held under Democratic control. However, it also made it more difficult for women to pursue an aggressive agenda of policies supported by the women's movement. For one thing, the decision by the newly emergent Republican leadership to defund the Congressional Caucus for Women's

Issues (along with, of course, other legislative service organizations) made it more difficult for women to come together to advance a collective agenda and to build bipartisan support for that agenda.

But perhaps more significantly, the shift of control to the Republican Party put the reins of leadership in the hands of men (for the most part) who during the 103rd Congress had opposed the majority of Republican women members on legislation like the Crime Bill, reauthorization of the NIH, the Assault Weapons Ban, FACE, the Brady Bill, and some legislation dealing with gays and lesbians in the military, and who were significantly more conservative on abortion funding and the Family and Medical Leave Act (Dodson et al., 1995). With those men controlling the floor agenda and committee action as well as doling out rewards and punishments, there is good reason to believe that the hurdles will be higher for those who want to "act for" women in the spirit of the women's movement.

And although the Republican women have been voting with their party more in the 104th than they did in the 103rd, women continue to diverge from their male colleagues on some issues (see Clark in this volume), taking more feminist and more liberal stands in roll call votes, and there is certainly evidence that they raise at least some different concerns from those of their male colleagues. Senator Nancy Kassebaum (R-Kans.), Senator Edward Kennedy (D-Mass.), and Representative Marge Roukema (R-N.J.), the sponsors of a bipartisan health care reform plan, have been among the most active in the effort to keep health care reform on the agenda (Women's Policy, Inc., 1996a:3). Representative Barbara Kennelly (D-Conn.) offered an amendment to the welfare reform bill in Ways and Means that would have eliminated the penalty for failure to establish paternity. Republican Representative Nancy Johnson (R-Conn.) crossed party lines to support that amendment, which ultimately failed. However, Representative Jennifer Dunn's (R-Wash.) amendment, which allowed recipients to collect any lost benefits once paternity was established, passed (Katz and Rubin, 1995). Democrats and GOP moderates, especially women, were critical to provisions in the welfare reform bill that sought to strengthen child support enforcement through establishment of new state and federal registries, new collection systems, and new hire registries for parents who refuse to comply (Katz and Rubin, 1995). Barbara Kennelly failed in her attempt to get a provision that would withhold drivers' licenses from noncustodial parents who fall behind in child support payments, but Marge Roukema's similar amendment offered on the House floor passed (Women's Policy, Inc., 1996b:29). Representative Nancy Johnson voted for the welfare bill rule, but only after reassurances from Senator Nancy Kassebaum that she would take care of child care matters in the Senate (Katz, 1995). Democratic women offered most of the amendments in the Judiciary Committee that would have allowed exceptions for women's health to be included in the bill banning the D and X abortion procedure. Representative Jan Meyers (R-Kans.) took the lead in fighting Representative Chris Smith's (R-N.J.) amendment which would have prohibited funding to any organization that provides abortion-related services overseas and withheld funding for the United Nations Fund for Population Assistance (UNFPA) until it discontinued assistance to the People's Republic of China (Women's Policy, Inc., 1995). Democratic and Republican women members fought efforts in the House to reduce funding for Violence Against Women Act (VAWA) (Women's Policy, Inc., 1996b:32). Clearly, in the 104th Congress, with its value on party unity, the methodological approaches used to assess the difference women make must be diverse enough to capture all of the varied ways in which women have had an impact.

Finally, two cautionary notes. First, when women members of Congress talk enthusiastically about women's shared concerns and the responsibility they feel to represent those concerns, they may convey an image of unity and consensus that fails to reflect the diversity among women. Acknowledging this diversity was a concern across all three policy areas. Women differ in the solutions they see to the problems that women face, they differ in the kinds of women they represent, and they differ in the extent to which these concerns are salient. As clichéd as it has become, women are not monolithic, and the 104th Congress brings that cliché to life. Second, men have played important roles in supporting women's agendas. Until women are chairs of powerful and key committees, hold half the leadership positions, and have the expertise that comes through years of experience, they will have to continue to build the strong ties to male colleagues that enable them to accomplish goals they could not otherwise accomplish.

10

African-American Women in State Elective Office in the South

Marsha J. Darling

This chapter assesses the emergence of African-American women in elective public office in the South in the decades since the civil rights and voting rights movements, and since the judicial and legislative interventions that signaled a new era in enforcement of the Fourteenth, Fifteenth, and Nineteenth Amendments to the Constitution. This assessment places the lives and careers of a sample of black women elected to public office over the past several decades in a historical, political, and cultural context reflecting the increasing political participation of black American women.

The theoretical foundation of this chapter is based on an understanding of the lives, careers, beliefs, values, and actions of African-American women in light of a cultural backdrop that includes the consequence of multiple discriminations—or the intersection of race, sex, and class—referred to here-after as "intersectionality." I also evaluate key issues in the legacy of historical and cultural self-help histories of southern black communities, which have strongly influenced the political behavior of African-American women.

This chapter provides historical analysis and data on the modern era and reports on current research which surveys a sample of African-American state legislators in the states of the former Confederacy. The survey project was developed to explore the nature of African-American female participation in public officeholding in the South.

Research Design

African-American women state legislators now occupy a previously unimag-inable place in American politics. Although a minuscule number of African-American women have been elected to high-ranking state and national public office in the earlier decades of this century, significant representation has occurred only since the passage of the Voting Rights Act (VRA). Never before was an active African-American self-help and race uplift movement able to effect the emergence of so crucial a level of male and female political leadership that shares and negotiates power in what, just a few decades ago, was a white-only domain.

This research contributes insights from recent oral history interviews with a group of African-American women who were elected to public office as state legislators in eight of the former Confederate states of the South during the turbulent two decades that followed passage of the Voting Rights Act of 1965. These states are Virginia, North Carolina, South Carolina, Georgia, Alabama, Louisiana, Mississippi, and Texas. Evaluating the rise of African-American women to state-level public officeholding during the period 1965–1985 permits an evaluation of the impact of the Voting Rights Act on the political aspirations of African-American women interested in running for public office in the South.

The in-depth interview was administered to nearly every former and current African-American female state legislator whose term in office began prior to 1985. In all, 15 African-American women were interviewed. Each two- to three-hour interview explored a wide range of issues and information, including family background, whether institutionalized self-help organizations operated in their midst as they grew up, the extent to which the civil rights and voting rights movements affected their political beliefs and behaviors, how they entered politics, and what the challenges have been to pursuing politics as a profession.

Theoretical Challenges

One of many challenges of this project has been to grapple with theoretical constructs that go beyond the narrow focus on gender that asks only if women behave differently from men and not the ways in which women are different from each other. It has become too acceptable to speak of a female identity as though the experience of female sex could be represented by one discourse, namely the identification of gender as a universal social construct. This discourse misses an explicit concurrent critique that evaluates the social construction of skin color *and* sex, or race *and* gender.

It is not enough to say that black women have existed in a society that values white skin and male sex. The vast majority of black women operate within at least two worlds: a black world, wherein, for most of the decades in this century, social status was based on one's degree of commitment to race uplift within the black community and, secondly, on one's status in the white world. Thus, we must analyze the politics of black women through the lens of the intersection of discrimination on both race and gender.

Practically, this kind of analysis is compelling because it requires us to ask what the real-world consequences are of the impact of race, gender, class, and sexuality and the ways oppositional and linear beliefs, paradigms, and actions create and sustain marginality and operate to establish multiple discriminations. Consequently, African-American women are often seen in dualistic terms either as appendages of African-American men or as women behaving according to a male model. Black women's activism on behalf of self-determination began as soon as resistance against enslavement began, and so the experiences of intersectionality and multiple discriminations have been defining for African-American belief and behavior all along.

Historical Assessment

There has been no one or two threshold movements that have "liberated" black women. Black women have a long tradition of involvement in organization and institution building, volunteerism, and a tradition of protest, resistance, and informal struggle against marginalization and exclusion. Unlike white-skinned women, who have railed against sexual subordination while exercising the benefits of skin color and, often, class privilege, African-American women and other women of color have experienced subordination based on their skin color, sex, and socioeconomic class (Darling, 1992). Hence, much of the impetus for challenging racism and sexism stems from the differential operation of many forms of privilege as it relates to the status of black and white women. The intersectionality that defines America's social landscape is responsible for the experiential differences in the social status of white-skinned women and women of color.

The demise of slavery and the amendments that followed brought the Constitution around to recognizing human rights for black women. Decades later, the suffrage movement often sold black women out as many white women sought to accommodate their own racial views and to ensure that southern states, which had disfranchised black male voters, would not allow black women to vote. It is not just that as women, black women were locked out of participation in formal politics, but rather as members of the black community, Black women were excluded and marginalized even when white women were allowed into the political arena.

Black women have had to struggle to gain human rights before attaining civil rights and the access to the political process that creates and defines voting and political rights. This point has implications for when and how African-American women have been able to challenge effectively the sexual subordination they confront outside as well as within black communities. Since the particular form of black women's oppression has been racial and sexual, the politicalization of the personal was unavoidable.

The legacy of the meanings of that intersection has been passed along from one generation of black females to another by the work of the black women's club movement and by the work of social action gospel women activists, especially in the Baptist denominations of black churches in the South, and activist sororities. In writing about the black women's movement in the black Baptist Church between 1880 and 1920, Evelyn Brooks Higginbotham notes:

> Black women likened their role to that of the biblical queen Esther, who had acted as an intermediary between the king and her people. They envisioned themselves as intermediaries between white America and their own people. Expressing the biblical analogy, Mrs. H. Davis compared Ida B. Wells to queen Esther and praised her crusade against lynching on the front page of the *National Baptist World*: "We have found in our own race a queen Esther, a woman of high talent, that has sounded the bugle for a defenseless race." (Higginbotham, 1993)

This is not a small point because it suggests that resistance and struggle against oppression indeed qualify as political acts, whether the nature of the action is covert or overt. Further, those who are involved as change agents are perceived of as intermediaries and as political people.

The tradition in this century of self-help, born of the struggle for freedom that set an indelible mark on the nineteenth century, occupied much of black women's organizing work in the decades preceding the civil rights movement. Black women had to empower themselves to challenge many constructed forms of privilege and morality to create something emancipating and self-affirming. The tenacity, moral purposefulness, and inclusive vision of an African-American female leadership has bred a strongly held belief in many black women that their virtue increases as does their calling to undertake public service in order to make a positive difference.

African-American women have been in the rank and file and the leadership of recent efforts and movements. Indeed, the training school for black leadership historically, the black church, would not have functioned as an effective philanthropic, fund-raising, and social action gospel institution without the work of African-American women (Davis, 1982; Pierce, Avery, and Carey, 1977).

Significant numbers of African-American women were particularly active and visible in direct action protest activities, namely civil rights and voting rights activism. In fighting for civil rights and voting rights, black women were fighting for their own rights as well, although black women often submerged their concerns about sexual subordination to the issue of racism (Chafe, 1977). Black women were among the most respected of civil and voting rights workers. Many put their lives on the line so that others could have access to public accommodations free of the humiliation of overt Jim Crow. Many knew firsthand how little separated them from anguish and even death in their insistence on working to advance voting rights. Black women's sense that attainment of political office was possible for them came out of the activism and organizing that preceded it (Baxter and Lansing, 1983; Githens and Prestage, 1977).

Many African-American women have perceived their subordination and oppression as warranting a personal commitment to challenge and transform black institutions and American society. There is no way in which black women act to challenge that social landscape that is not immediately political. After decades of self-help activism in communities, organizations, and institutions in African-American communities, black women have moved to involve themselves in public elective office because it is possible and because such service is a further extension of efforts to promote the extension of the two fiercely held agendas of self-help and race uplift.

As the research findings presented here reflect, African-American women who consider themselves progressive have little difficulty advancing a necessarily political and cultural agenda for the development of African-American communities with the challenge and imperative to represent an ethnically and culturally diverse constituency. One of the legacies of African-American social justice work in the United States has been the growth of a commitment to democratic processes, both within and without the black community.

Current Research

African-American women's involvement in elective public office in precisely those states in the South that have borne one of the country's ugliest legacies of racially derived marginalization and subordination is inseparable from the struggles and remedies necessary to open access to elective public office to black American citizens. In an essay published in 1977, Jewel L. Prestage noted a link between political activism and political officeholding for the 35 African-American women state legislators that she surveyed (Prestage, 1977; Bryce and Warrick, 1977).

Table 10.1 illustrates the dramatic rise in the numbers of African-American women elected to public office in the last three decades. The vast majority of African-American women and men were not able to vote or hold public office until well after the passage of the Nineteenth Amendment to the Constitution (Bass and DeVries, 1976; Key, 1949; Matthews and Prothro, 1966). Table 10.2 presents clear evidence of the adverse impact of Jim Crow disfranchisement.

Encouraged by the federal enforcement of provisions of the Voting Rights Act of 1965, which went a long way toward redressing some major concerns and disfranchising violations noted by the U.S. Commission on Civil Rights, the Justice Department's oversight of election mechanisms in many southern states, successful litigation that identified the subtle efforts of voting subterfuge to undermine the VRA, and efforts by legal advocacy organizations to establish the adverse impact of white vote-dilution efforts, many more African-Americans in the South registered and voted than ever before. The right to exercise the franchise has come for the first time ever in this century after far-reaching changes at the grass-roots, federal, judicial, and legislative levels (Lawson, 1976, 1991; Davidson and Grofman, 1994).

The disparity between the numbers of African-Americans in the voting-age population and the numbers of African-American women and men who were allowed to register to vote in southern states is depicted. Within six months of the Act's passage, upward of 75,000 voters had been registered by federal examiners, and voter registration among voting-age African-Americans increased to 62 percent in 1968 from 43 percent in 1964.

TABLE 10.1
Black Women Elected Officials Nationwide, by Year, 1969–1994

Year	Female Black Elected Officials	Absolute Increase	Percentage Increase
1969	131	—	—
1970	160	31	23.67
1971	225	65	40.6
1972	153	−72	−32.0
1973	345	192	125.5
1974	416	71	20.6
1975	530	114	27.4
1976	684	154	29.1
1977	782	98	14.3
1978	843	61	7.8
1979	882	39	4.6
1980	976	94	10.7
1981	1,021	45	4.6
1982	1,081	60	5.9
1983	1,223	142	13.1
1984	1,259	36	2.9
1985	1,359	100	7.9
1986	1,482	123	9.1
1987	1,564	82	5.5
1988	1,625	61	3.9
1989	1,814	189	11.6
1990	1,950	136	7.5
1991	2,053	103	5.3
1992	2,121	68	3.3
1993	2,332	211	9.9
1994	2,438	106	4.5

Source: Joint Center for Political and Economic Studies, Washington, D.C.

The significance of the Voting Rights Act for the election of African-American candidates to public office is captured in Table 10.3. There is a clear relationship between the removal of race-based barriers to black voter registration and participation (e.g., poll taxes, literacy tests, white-only primaries, property requirements, and physical intimidation and violence) and the increase in the number of African-American women and men elected to public office across the nation. In the year in which the Civil Rights Act of 1964 was passed, there was a total of 72 black state legislators in the South, compared with recent estimates of nearly 5,000.

The data are indicative of the unprecedented emergence of African-American women as elected officials, but they are also reflective of the far-reaching legal, social, and political changes that have swept the nation, and

TABLE 10.2
Black Voter Registration in Southern States, 1940–1988

Year	Blacks Registered	Black Voting-Age Population
1940	151,000	4,843,000
1946	595,000	4,869,000
1952	1,006,000	5,019,000
1956	1,238,000	4,955,000
1958	1,304,000	4,994,000
1960	1,463,000	5,090,000
1962	1,481,000	5,148,000
1964	2,165,000	5,173,000
1966	2,689,000	5,208,000
1968	3,112,000	5,299,000
1970	3,506,000	5,243,000
1972	3,448,000	6,178,000
1974	3,842,000	6,562,000
1976	4,149,000	6,931,000
1978	—	7,305,000
1980	4,254,000	7,718,000
1982	4,302,000	8,077,000
1984	5,596,000	8,368,000
1986	5,796,000	8,957,000
1988	5,842,000	9,171,000

Source: A portion of this information is provided by the Committee on the Status of Black Americans in *A Common Destiny: Blacks and American Society,* Jerald David Jaynes and Robin M. Williams, Jr., eds. (Washington, D.C.: National Academy Press, 1989).

particularly the South, in the past 40 years. Recent data collected by the Joint Center for Political and Economic Studies and the Center for the American Woman and Politics at Rutgers University reveal that 2,332 black female elected officials comprise 29.1 percent of all black elected officials across the country. Not surprisingly, as Table 10.4 illustrates, the South has the largest concentration of African-American women holding elective office, with 1,441, or 62.1 percent, of all black women elected to public office nationally.

Additionally, African-American women officeholders in the South constitute 4.8 percent of African-American officeholders across the region across all the above-mentioned categories. By comparison, there have been 5,683 African-American men elected to public office in the South (Bositis, 1992).

Although the number of African-American women elected to state office in the South is smaller than the numbers of African-American women elected to office at the county and municipal levels, and greater than the numbers of African-American women elected to mayoral offices within southern states, the number of African-American women state legislators is significant because attainment of election as state representative or senator often reflects earlier

TABLE 10.3
Black Elected Officials, by Region, 1941–1990

Year	Northeast	North Central	South	West	Total
1941	10	20	2	1	33
1947	21	35	6	4	66
1951	29	31	16	6	82
1965	63	104	87	26	280
1970	238	396	703	132	1,469
1975	503	869	1,913	218	3,503
1980	570	1,041	2,981	298	4,890
1985	694	1,150	3,801	371	6,016
1990	725	1,294	4,955	361	7,335

Source: A portion of this information is provided by the Committee on the Status of Black Americans in *A Common Destiny: Blacks and American Society,* Jerald David Jaynes and Robin M. Williams, Jr., eds. (Washington, D.C.: National Academy Press, 1989).

political success. The most recent numbers available show that there are 166 African-American women state legislators, 40 senators, and 126 representatives, representing 35 states. African-American women state legislators are 10.77 percent of all female state legislators. There are 161 African-American women Democrats, 3 Republicans, and 2 Independents. By comparison, there are 12 African-American elected officials serving at the federal level, including an African-American woman delegate to the House of Representatives from the District of Columbia (Center for the American Woman and Politics, 1996d).

These recent numbers represent impressive change from the period before the 1960s. Throughout the decades of political disfranchisement of most black men and the refusal, after 1920, of many southern districts to recognize and honor the voting rights of black women, seeking elective office was also linked with trying to achieve the visibility and recognition that were symbolically reserved to white males. Hence, while historically black women like Mary McLeod Bethune, Majesta Simpkins, Ida B. Wells-Barnett, Mary Church Terrell, and Sojourner Truth worked on behalf of greater human, civil, political, and educational rights for African-American people, the women they helped empower confronted the challenge of seeking elective and appointive offices (Prestage, 1980).

Table 10.5 presents the pattern of black women's involvement in educational, civic, and municipal public officeholding for 1969, 1973, 1975, and 1976 and illustrates the impact of the Voting Rights Act on the election of African-American women to local, state, and federal public office during the years following its passage. The gains from 1969 to 1976 are dramatic and impressive on most levels. Not surprisingly, however, women are much more numerous at the local level than on any other. The data also indicate that at the local level, most African-American women officeholders have

TABLE 10.4
Distribution of Black Women Officeholders by Office, 1993

	South	North	Midwest	West	Total
Federal	7	0	3	1	11
State	84	27	27	14	152
County	128	6	24	4	162
Mayoral	50	3	14	2	69
Municipal	757	76	192	24	1,049
Judicial/Law Enforcement	94	30	64	25	213
Education	321	143	148	54	666
Total	1,441	285	472	124	2,322

Source: Joint Center for Political and Economic Studies, Washington, D.C.

been concentrated in education and municipal government, reflecting black women's interest and training to assume leadership positions in areas that also mirror concerns for education, children, and families (Davis, 1982).

Interview Results

In the in-depth interviews with African-American women, I asked about constraints on participation in elective office in this century, what has made it possible for black women to seek and attain public office, the issues most pursued by them, and the ways black women officeholders make a difference. According to all of the women interviewed for this project, the greatest obstacles to securing elective office have been structural impediments, such as the inability to register and vote, and the inability to make one's vote count toward electing candidates of one's choice. Those interviewed also cited the curtailment of white gerrymandering, which fragmented black voters

TABLE 10.5
Distribution of Black Women Officeholders by Office

	1969	1973	1975	1976
Federal	1	4	4	4
State	16	29	35	38
Regional	—	—	—	10
County	7	17	31	39
Municipal	38	104	203	311
Judicial and Law Employment	16	2	34	39
Education	53	151	214	243
Total	131	307	521	684

Source: Joint Center for Political and Economic Studies, Washington, D.C.

into voting segments too small to affect the outcome of elections, and the curtailment of white vote-dilution strategies as essential to increasing the number of African-American elected officeholders. Because racially polarized voting dominates the South, voting districts wherein racial or language minorities elected candidates of their choice arose from the abolition of multimember districts and other minority vote-dilution strategies. In light of congressional insistence that effective minority voting representation be a part of the mandate of the Fifteenth Amendment and the Voting Rights Act, single-member districts with African-American voting majorities have been created. Through a number of significant judicial challenges and congressional amendments, the VRA has increased voting participaton and the number of successful candidacies for elective office (Davidson and Grofman, 1994). Each respondent interviewed for this project insisted that the most pressing constraints to minority representation have been held in check by vigilant enforcement of the Voting Rights Act and its amendments.

The ability of officeholders to stay in office has also depended, in part, on the composition and structure of the voting system in place in the district from which they were elected. In the decade immediately following the passage of the Voting Rights Act, the small number of African-American women elected to state office was linked not only with the extent of black voter registration and voting, but with the active process of white vote-dilution.

Beyond structural impediments to seeking and attaining office, confronting the task of mounting a campaign to seek elective office has been no small or easy task, according to those interviewed. Two issues surfaced as important impediments to elective office. First, African-American women candidates who entered elections and runoffs in the decade immediately following passage of the Voting Rights Act were challenged to engage in electoral politics at a point when some leaders of the civil rights and voting rights movement in the country were being assassinated. A number of prominent civil rights and voting rights movement leaders were killed, as were some local leaders. Many others, both male and female, were beaten, harassed, and politically intimidated. Hence, African-American women state legislators who were civil rights and voting rights activists and then became entrants into formal politics in the Deep South had to warily weigh the possibility and the risk of physical violence.

A second impediment to winning office has been money. Very little money from political PACs was ever available to blacks seeking office. The other alternative for raising sufficient funds to win office is personal and campaign loans. This was not an option for most blacks running for office. Historically, bank and even credit union lending to African-Americans has been anywhere from erratic to racist and sexist. The legacy of race-based disparate lending has been an especially corrosive constraint on fund-raising for political campaigns.

Because of such obstacles, many of those interviewed for this research noted that they had invested most of their life savings to attain office. This was, of course, possible only for those who had middle-class employment.

Whereas black civil rights lawyers and morticians were in a far better financial position to finance the costs of running a campaign, most of the African-American women in elective office at the state level since 1965 have been concentrated in fields and occupations that are not nearly as high paying as law, medicine, or mortuary.

Although most of the respondents in this study did not specify any sources of campaign funding other than personal, family and local community resources, a number of the African-American state legislators said that building visibility and counting on the assistance of volunteers from their communities (church, women's club, sorority, and professional clubs), and innovative ideas like fund-raising dinners, parties, rallies, and door-to-door hand-shaking and solicitation, proved crucial to getting the message out and increasing visibility and financial resources.

The interviews also suggest that once African-American women are elected, they seek to have an impact on issues that benefit their communities. Their goals are pursued through the selection of a political agenda and gaining access to committees that will further that agenda. Black women state legislators' issue agenda concerned having an impact on opportunities available to their constituents, especially those in poor rural areas. Specific issues included social benefits assistance to families, especially poor women and their children; women's reproductive rights issues of concern to African-American women, including forced sterilization; reform of the criminal justice system; and educational and job opportunities. Respondents reported that the way to best pursue legislative goals is through committee work. Hence, access to committees with jurisdiction over priority issues is key. Fortunately, committee access, they report, is good and African-American women state legislators are represented on a full range of committees including economic development, judiciary, local and urban government, education, aging, and elections/redistricting.

Those interviewed indicated, however, that although they feel successful in meeting their goals, constraints exist on their abilities to further them. Two of those constraints concern their status as African-American women vis-à-vis African-American men on one hand, and vis-à-vis white women, on the other. Some respondents reported that African-American male legislators often see the role of black female colleagues as supportors of black male political objectives and agendas. This is reflected in the fact that some state black caucuses are operated on the basis of male privilege.

Additionally, the divisive effect of white racism and paternalism among many white women legislators often seriously constrains coalition work across racial lines. A number of legislators reported that constraints exist concerning coalition building with white women and that they often derive from the continuing legacy of conflicting loyalties on the part of many white female legislators. Long accustomed to exercising white-skin privilege, some white female legislators refrain from working with African-American female legislators as equals in addressing and seeking solutions to problems. Some respondents

charged that conflicting loyalties often means that some white women legislators "sell out" African-American women if the issue is constructed in such
a way that assistance and resources can be racially determined.

For instance, state and federal assistance to needy children and women has
been a long-standing issue of importance to African-Americans. Many states
have a historical record of dispensing assistance in a disparate and racially
unequal manner, not just in the decades wherein Jim Crow laws and practices
legitimized the idea that whites were to receive the best and the most of
public resources, but also in the decades since the federal government has
intervened to promote civil rights for racial and language minorities. Thus, it
is often poor women of color and their children who are attacked as welfare
cheats and undeserving of aid. White female legislators can vote against
progressive efforts to hold constant public assistance benefits to poor women
and children because they believe that many more poor white women than
black women and their children will be allotted benefits without the stigma
of the racialization of worthiness.

Many African-American women officeholders believe that a constraint on
their ability to facilitate their legislative goals is the attention given to African-
American neoconservatives who compromise some of the interests and needs
of African-American communities as an indication of their willingness to give
priority to white political goals. Often, African-American neoconservatives
have been elected to office by black voters who do not know that some of the
candidates they have elected are establishing loyalties that exploit the voting
potential of black communities but compromise their often clearly stated
interests. The participation by some black neoconservatives in "blaming the
victim" for black inequality often thwarts the ability of progressive African-
American women legislators to form coalitions that seek effective political
change.

Conclusion

This chapter began by suggesting that the theoretical framework employed by
many social scientists in their evaluation of African-American female political
behavior is too narrowly constructed. In that framework, either African-
American women are seen as acting according to male norms, or African-
American gender is constructed in a manner that emphasizes gender identity
over racial identity. In reality, however, skin color and sex have always operated
together to affect the lives of African-American women.

By focusing on the intersection of race and sex, and by examining the
consequences of multiple discriminations, researchers can use a less simplistic
conceptual paradigm for evaluating African-American female behavior. The
argument in this chapter offers an explanation of the consequence of female
sex and brown skin, and provides historical evidence of an African-American
female–defined construction of their own behavior.

In addition, this chapter points to the value African-American women
have historically placed on the evolution of a two-pronged agenda for social

change in black communities and in American society. African-American women have placed emphasis on self-help / personal accountability and race uplift / collective responsibility. They have also been instrumental in undertaking social justice direct action protest geared toward acquiring human and civil rights. The process of African-American women's involvement in politics is inseparable from two series of events: a tradition of struggle as brown-skinned persons and as females, and the process of progressive persons promoting social and political change that have made African-American female involvement in formal politics possible. Thus, African-American women have also been involved in transforming the very institutions in American society charged with enforcement of the Constitution. African-American women can serve as state legislators because the political system in the United States has recently been made accountable to political participation by those previously excluded from or marginalized within the system.

Unprecedented numbers of African-American women have been elected to serve in public office, primarily since passage of the Voting Rights Act of 1965, and these African-American women officeholders have been concentrated in local-level offices. These numbers reflect the interests, training, and leadership strengths of African-American women elected to public office in the South since 1969, when they first began to break into the system. It may also reflect the barriers to running for and winning higher office.

Surmounting the obstacles to exercise of the franchise and officeholding, African-American women elected to public office identify a number of issues as crucial to their ability to win and hold public office, especially electoral structure, the fear of white violence, and the issues of mounting and paying for a campaign. Once in public office, African-American women have had to grapple with competing loyalties, partisan interests, and challenges to their coalition-building skills. While white racism and paternalism have presented many African-American women state legislators with strong challenges, state black caucuses have been important to building political effectiveness among black leaders. Yet, the operation of male privilege has hindered the working relationship between some African-American male and female leaders.

Making a difference in legislatures involves access to the full range of activities and venues. African-American women state legislators pursue goals which center on a social justice agenda, including social services, health and human services for the rural poor, reform of the criminal justice system, and aid to women and dependent children, and they do so from their positions on important legislative committees.

11

The Feminization of Leadership in State Legislatures

MARCIA LYNN WHICKER AND MALCOLM JEWELL

Research results offered in previous chapters in this volume suggest that if more women run for office, they will win. Factors that are likely to impel more women to run have also been discussed. Do these factors also enhance the likelihood of women becoming leaders in state legislatures? As women obtain leadership posts with state legislatures in greater numbers, do women and men lead in different ways? Why might women have leadership styles that differ from those of men? In this chapter, we discuss women's representation in legislative leadership and our research on leadership types and the ways in which women and men seek to lead. The implications for the conduct of legislative leadership as women gain greater access to these positions serves as the closing for the chapter.

Increased Numbers of Women Leaders in State Legislatures

Our study of legislative leadership was conducted during the spring and summer of 1991. We interviewed about 90 legislative leaders in 22 states, about one-third of them women, asking for information about leadership roles, styles, and techniques, as well as about their careers in the legislature (Jewell and Whicker 1994).

The proportion of legislators who are women increased from 4.5 percent in 1971 to 12.1 percent in 1981 and 20.6 percent in the 1993–96 period. Has there been comparable growth in the number of women legislative leaders and the proportion of all leaders who are women? We might expect the proportion of female leaders to lag behind the proportion of women in the legislature for the following reason. The number of women in the legislature may have to reach a certain threshold or critical mass before one or more women become leaders. And as long as the proportion of women legislators is growing steadily,

TABLE 11.1
Average Number and Proportions of Women in Leadership Positions in
1979–1996 Legislative Sessions, All States

Year	Number of Women Leaders	Total Number of Women Members	Women Members as Percent of Legislature	Women Leaders as Percent of Leaders	Women Leaders as Percent of Women Members
1993–96	194	1,529	20.6	19.2	12.7
1989–92	161	1,311	17.6	16.8	12.1
1985–88	106	1,137	15.2	12.2	9.2
1981–84	73	952	12.7	9.2	7.6
1979–80	55	770	10.3	7.2	7.1

Source: Center for the American Woman and Politics (CAWP), National Information Bank on Women in Public Office, Eagleton Institute of Politics, Rutgers University.

a substantial number of them will be first- or second-term members, who are unlikely to hold leadership positions.

Table 11.1 shows, over five time periods from 1979 to 1996, averages for the number of women members and women leaders in state legislatures, the proportion of legislators and of leaders who are women, and the proportion of female members who are leaders. During this period, the proportion of members who are women has doubled while the proportion of leaders who are women has increased by two and two-thirds. The gap between the two measures was about 3 percentage points in the first ten years and closer to 1 percentage point in the last eight years. The proportion of women who are leaders has grown by over three-fourths in this period.

It appears that in most states the proportion of women has passed whatever threshold is necessary to win leadership positions. In 1981 there were 24 states with no women in leadership; by 1995 only 11 states had no women leaders, and only 6 of these (mostly in the South) had none from 1989 through 1995 (see CAWP, 1995a).

Although the steady growth in the proportion of women legislators guarantees that a considerable number will be junior, there are enough women with some legislative seniority so that the proportion of leaders who are women is now close to the proportion of legislators who are women. In exactly half of the states, in at least one of the legislative sessions from 1989 through 1995, in at least one chamber a woman held one of the top positions: presiding officer or majority or minority leader. (The presiding officer in the senate is defined as the top elected senator; this would be the president pro tem if the lieutenant governor is senate president.)

It is well known that the proportion of women legislators differs considerably from state to state. Consistently near the top of the list are some of the less populated western and northeastern states. At the bottom are many of the southern and border states and a few highly urbanized states such as New Jersey and Pennsylvania. We would expect to find the highest proportion of female leaders in states with the largest percentage of women members, because there is a larger pool to draw from and perhaps more political support for choosing women as leaders. And we would expect to find very few women leaders in states with few women members.

Table 11.2 provides the same information as Table 11.1, on a state-by-state basis, for two time periods, 1989–91 and 1993–95. It also indicates if there was at least one leader in a top leadership position (presiding officer [P] or majority or minority leader [L]) during each time period. In each of the columns the numbers are the averages for the two legislative sessions; the numbers are rounded off except for the numbers of leaders, where the numbers are small. The states are listed in order of the percentage of members who were women in the 1989–95 periods.

There is a huge variation in the number of leaders (and particularly assistant leaders) for each state who are listed in official publications. There are at least 10 states with more than 25 persons in leadership (most of them in the house). Most states have at least eight to ten leaders. But in a few southern states, in one or both chambers, there is no majority or minority leader, and the total women in leadership may be only three or four. For this reason the total number of women leaders and the percentage of women members who are leaders are somewhat misleading. A better measure of women in leadership is women leaders as a percentage of all leaders, compared to women as a percentage of all legislators.

For the most part the proportion of leaders who are female is roughly the same as the proportion of female legislators. Three of the states having a much lower proportion of women leaders than of women members are surprising: California (in the lower chamber), New York, and Pennsylvania. Pennsylvania chooses more than twenty leaders, and it had one woman leader in only one of the four legislative sessions. California averaged 26 women members in the 1993–95 period, and only one of them served as a leader for a single term. Women leaders were almost as scarce in New York, particularly in 1989–91, despite there being almost 60 persons in leadership. Perhaps the structure of leadership is more rigid and more difficult to break into in these states. New Mexico and Montana, each averaging only one female leader, lagged way behind female membership. Nebraska had no women leaders during this period, but the unicameral nonpartisan legislature elects only two leaders.

There are eight southern and border states having few if any leaders. Oklahoma had one female leader in two of four sessions; South Carolina and Kentucky had a female leader only once; and Arkansas, Mississippi, Virginia, Louisiana, and Alabama had no women in leadership. Five of these states (South Carolina, Arkansas, Mississippi, Louisiana, and Alabama) had five or fewer persons in leadership because they did not have majority or minority leaders. The proportion of women in the legislatures of these eight states ranged from 6 percent to 12 percent, at the bottom of the list. The same

TABLE 11.2
Average Number and Proportions of Women in Leadership Positions in 1989–1991 and 1993–1995 Legislative Sessions, by State

State	Number of Women Leaders 89-91	Number of Women Leaders 93-95	Total Number of Women Members 89-91	Total Number of Women Members 93-95	Women Members as Percent of Legislature 89-91	Women Members as Percent of Legislature 93-95	Women Leaders as Percent of Leaders 89-91	Women Leaders as Percent of Leaders 93-95	Women Leaders as Percent of Women Members 89-91	Women Leaders as Percent of Women Members 93-95	Number of Women in Top Leadership Roles 89-91	Number of Women in Top Leadership Roles 93-95
Washington	12.5	14	44	58	30	39	33	40	28	24	P, L	P
Arizona	2.5	4.5	29	29	32	32	19	28	9	16	P	L
Colorado	4	4.5	30	33	30	33	24	27	13	14	L	L
New Hampshire	11	15	136	135	32	32	42	28	8	11	L	L
Vermont	2	3	56	58	31	32	20	30	4	5	L	L
Nevada	1.5	4.5	13	20	21	31	14	27	12	23		L
Idaho	3	5	34	31	27	29	21	36	9	16		L
Kansas	4.5	4	44	47	26	29	22	20	10	9		L
Maine	2.5	2.5	59	54	32	29	25	25	4	5	L	L
Oregon	5	8	20	26	22	28	24	30	25	31	P	P, L
Connecticut	12	13	42	49	23	26	25	24	29	27	L	L
Maryland	4.5	7	43	50	23	27	26	25	10	14	L	
Wisconsin	5	5.5	33	34	25	26	22	24	15	16		
Rhode Island	8	12.5	24	37	16	24	20	28	34	34		
Massachusetts	3	3	37	47	18	24	19	19	8	6		
Illinois	6	6	33	41	18	23	17	18	18	15		
Wyoming	2	4	23	21	24	23	15	29	9	19		
Minnesota	5	6	40	53	20	26	19	22	13	11	L	L
Ohio	2	2.5	18	30	14	23	11	14	11	8		P
Hawaii	9.5	8	20	17	26	22	30	27	49	47	L	P, L
California	2.5	0.5	20	26	17	22	15	3	13	2		L
Alaska	0.5	2.5	14	14	23	22	8	47	4	17		
Montana	1	1	29	33	19	22	8	8	3	3		P, L

Nebraska	0	0	9	11	18	22	0	0	0	0	
Michigan	15.5	11.5	22	32	15	21	20	23	70	36	
Indiana	4.5	7	24	31	16	21	15	23	19	23	
New Mexico	1	1	15	23	13	22	7	7	7	4	
Missouri	2	2.5	31	38	15	19	10	12	6	7	
South Dakota	3.5	2	23	20	22	19	19	10	15	10	P L
Florida	4	3	28	30	17	18	18	18	14	10	P L
Delaware	1	1	9	11	15	18	10	10	11	9	L L
North Carolina	1.5	2	25	30	15	17	12	15	6	7	L
Georgia	1.5	3	28	42	12	18	10	17	5	7	
New York	1.5	5.5	26	37	12	17	4	10	6	15	
Texas	0.5	0.5	21	31	12	17	17	17	2	2	
Iowa	5	5.5	24	25	16	16	22	23	21	22	
North Dakota	2	1	24	23	15	16	14	7	9	4	P P
West Virginia	1	1.5	26	21	19	16	9	14	4	7	L L
Utah	0.5	1.5	12	15	12	14	4	11	4	10	L
New Jersey	3.5	4	12	16	10	13	9	12	29	25	
Tennessee	2	2.5	14	17	11	13	13	14	14	15	
South Carolina	0	0.5	17	22	10	13	0	10	0	2	L
Arkansas	0	0	10	16	7	12	0	0	0	0	
Mississippi	0	0	11	20	6	11	0	0	0	0	
Pennsylvania	0	0.5	21	28	8	11	0	3	0	2	
Virginia	0	0	16	17	11	12	0	0	0	0	
Oklahoma	0.5	0.5	13	15	9	10	2	2	4	3	
Louisiana	0	0	4	13	2	9	0	0	0	0	
Kentucky	0.5	0	7	9	5	7	3	0	7	0	
Alabama	0	0	8	7	6	5	0	0	0	0	

Source: Same as for Table 11.1.

167

traditional political culture that makes it difficult for women to be elected to the legislature probably makes it difficult for them to win leadership posts.

In 1985, when women held almost 11 percent of leadership posts and almost 15 percent of legislative seats, there were 17 states without female legislative leaders. Nine of these had fewer than 10 percent women members; only five of the states with women leaders had fewer than 10 percent female members. This suggests that the threshold of female membership necessary to elect a woman to leadership may be about 10 percent. If the proportion is smaller, women may lack the political clout to break into leadership ranks.

If women are to gain significant power in the legislature, it is obviously more important to elect women to top leadership positions and not merely to positions as assistant leaders. We define top positions as the house speaker, the senate president or president pro tem (whichever is the top elected senator), and the majority and minority leaders. In the four legislatures from 1989 through 1995, 74 women held one of those positions, less than 7 percent of all the top leadership positions. The number rose from 13 in 1989 to 17 in 1991 to 26 in 1993, and then dropped to 18 in 1995. Of these 74 women, 58 percent were Republicans. Seventeen were presiding officers, 24 majority leaders, and 33 minority leaders; the proportions were the same for Democrats and Republicans. The minority party seems more willing to gamble on a woman as leader.

There were 48 different women who held the 74 positions. That means that during these four legislatures, the average leader had served in a top leadership position for one and a half terms. This understates the actual tenure of leaders in top positions. Nine of the women serving in 1989 had held a top position one or more times prior to 1989, and some of the 18 women serving in 1995 will obviously be elected to a comparable position in 1997.

The nine states with the largest number of women in top positions are ones we would expect, based on the data in Table 11.3. These states, each with four or five top female positions from 1989 through 1995, are Washington, Arizona, New Hampshire, Vermont, Maine, Connecticut, Hawaii, Alaska, and Delaware. Arizona was unique in this time period because in 1993 there was a female house speaker and a female senate president. Delaware was unique because all four terms were served by one woman, the minority leader (who has had six terms and first served in that office in 1985). Only half of the states had any women in major leadership positions during the 1989–95 period. Among the states without a top female leader were eight southern states and several border states, but also such states as Wisconsin, California, Illinois, Michigan, New York, and Pennsylvania.

It is interesting to track the careers of the women who have served as house speaker or senate presiding officer. Between 1989 and 1995, seven women served a total of eight terms as speaker and eight women served nine terms as senate presiding officer. One house speaker had served two previous terms as speaker prior to 1989, and one senate president pro tem had served three previous terms in that post. (In the 1983–87 period, two other women served one term as speaker and one served one term as senate president pro tem.) Of the seven women serving as speaker between 1989 and 1995, five had served as speaker pro tem, majority leader, or majority whip before becoming speaker, and one had been minority leader. One presiding officer in the senate had also been minority leader, but the others had not held a major leadership post.

The trend toward increased numbers of women in leadership roles in state legislatures is the first aspect of "the feminization of leadership." As the number of women women members has grown and as their share of the total number of legislators has increased, the number of women in leadership has grown too. While the percentage of women in leadership roles lags slightly behind the proportion of women in the legislature, the linkage between the two shares is positive and the trend is upward. Women, then, not only are gaining a larger share of legislative seats but also are assuming a growing share of leadership roles.

Prevalence of "Female" Leadership Types among State Legislative Leaders

Do women lead differently than men? During 1991, we interviewed in semistructured interviews over 90 legislative leaders (presiding officers, majority and minority leaders, and, in some states, several other appointed or elected party leaders) in 22 states. Although our sample was not random, there was considerable diversity in the states selected. We selected states where women had attained leadership positions, but we also selected to attain variation on variables dealing with other aspects of leadership potential discussed in *Legislative Leadership in the American States* (Jewell and Whicker, 1994). We remain indebted to the State Legislative Leadership Foundation for both the introductions that gave us access to leaders and the funding that made the project possible.

We wanted to examine differences between male and female leadership. And, based on anecdotal evidence that a shift from "male" to "female" leadership styles and goals was occurring, even among male leaders, we also wanted to find out if men were adopting more "female" leadership styles. For the purpose of reporting our results here, we were able to classify 42 male and 20 female leaders into different leadership types.

In order to classify the types of leaders, we had to first construct a leadership typology appropriate to legislative settings. A typology is a classification using categories that can be aligned along two or more dimensions. We developed a typology for state legislative leaders using two major dimensions: leadership styles (command, coordinating, and consensus leadership styles) and leadership goals (power, policy, and process goals). Both dimensions range from a narrow focus on the self and the personal to a broader focus on others and the system as a whole. The intersection of these two dimensions results in a nine-cell or nine-category leadership typology. Based on past research and cultural norms, we labeled some types as "male" and some as "female." We expected that cultural norms and socialization would make men more oriented toward a command style of leadership than women. Women would be more oriented toward a consensus style of leadership than men. We expected both genders to adopt a coordinating leadership style.

We also expected that men would be more oriented toward power goals than women, while women would be more oriented toward process goals than men. Both genders would be oriented toward policy goals, but different policy goals on occasion, associated with gender-linked agendas.

When we applied these gender-linked proclivities to our nine leadership types, male types were clustered in the upper left portion of our two-dimensional table (command/power, command/policy, coordinating/power, and coordinating/policy types) (Table 11.3). Female types were clustered in the lower right portion (consensus/process, consensus/policy, coordinating/process, and coordinating/policy types). The only leadership type that was expected to be both "male" and "female" in character was the coordinating/policy type. Two leadership types had conflicting male and female orientations and were not expected to be adopted frequently by either men or women (command/process and consensus/power types).

We hypothesize that when the need to control on both dimensions is similar, there will be high internal consistency between two dimensions, low cognitive dissonance, and a high probability of the leadership type being adopted. Using a genetic metaphor, we refer to this leadership type as "dominant." When the need to control on the two dimensions is dissimilar, we expect low internal consistency between the two dimensions, high cognitive dissonance, and a low probability of the leadership type being adopted. The leadership type will be "recessive," indicating that it could occur but infrequently. When the two needs to control are mixed and somewhat divergent, the resulting leadership types will be "hybrid," indicating a moderate probability of occur-

TABLE 11.3
Personal Leadership Type Classification Based on Leadership Style and Goals, and Expected Gender-Linkages

	Legislative Goal		
Leadership Style	Power	Policy	Process
Command	Command/power (male)	Command/policy (male)	Command/process
Coordinating	Coordinating/power (male)	Coordinating/policy (male & female)	Coordinating/process (female)
Consensus	Consensus/power	Consensus/policy (female)	Consensus/process (female)

ring. Note that dominance, hybridness, and recessiveness are not the same as gender-linked orientations among leadership types.

In this fashion, we identified three dominant leadership types: command/policy (male), coordinating/policy (both male and female), and consensus/process (female). Four types were hybrid: command/policy (male), coordinating/power (male), coordinating/process (female), and consensus/policy (female). Two types were recessive and not likely to be adopted by either gender: command/process and consensus/power. Descriptions of each of these types are provided in Table 11.4.

To what extent were these gender-linked expectations about leadership types observed and which types were more prevalent, "male" or "female" types? Anecdotal evidence had indicated that with the increasing professionalization of legislatures, members were becoming more resistant to autocratic leadership types. Several leaders in various states who had exhibited a more controlling type had been overthrown in recent years, including Irv Stohlberg in Connecticut and Liston Ramsey in North Carolina.

Our interviews confirmed that women were more likely to adopt "female" types than were men. Women leaders repeatedly told us that they were interested in cooperating, building consensus, and creating a harmonious workplace. Both men and women saw men as more willing on occasion to be strong and directive, and to "try to run the show." Also, women rarely expressed concern about power goals, whereas men sometimes did. So we did find gender differences, with men having a higher probability of adopting a "male" style than women, and women having a higher probability of adopting a "female" style than men. No women in our sample exhibited the most "male" type—command/power, whereas four men evidenced this type. Indeed, we found only one female leader who had a command leadership style, whereas twelve men did.

What was even more interesting was the extent to which we observed that most leaders, both male and female, gravitated toward "female" leadership types, a second aspect of the "feminization" of state legislative leadership (see Table 11.5). The most commonly occurring leadership type among men was a "female" type, the coordinating/process type. When we looked at clusters of leadership types, 95 percent of our women leaders adopted female styles, but so did 71 percent of the men leaders we interviewed. Plainly, men were adopting leadership styles that previously, on the basis of cultural norms and socialization, were associated with women. Only 25 percent of women we interviewed adopted a male type, but a majority of men were also unlikely to adopt a male type (45 percent). This shift toward more harmonious, less controlling leadership types that we found within state legislatures parallels the shift toward more participative and less autocratic leadership styles that has been found in corporations and other settings (Maccoby, 1976; Ouchi, 1981). As more men shift to leadership types that women have been more likely to adopt, we may need to relabel these from "female types" to "other-directed types."

TABLE 11.4

The Nine Legislative Leadership Types

Dominant Leadership Types

Command/Power Leadership (a male type)
> High need to control others; high need to control personal institutional role to assure career enhancement and ambitions; suppresses conflict; focuses on the inputs of the policy process; controlling, ambitious for external recognition, and perceived to be self-centered and career driven with no compensating focus on policy outputs; most likely to be overthrown by fellow legislators.

Coordinating/Policy Leadership (Both a male and female type)
> Moderate need to control others; moderate need to control personal institutional role to ensure that it is compatible with and enhances desired policy outcomes; negotiates conflict; focuses on the output of the policy process; builds coalitions to achieve policy goals; often enjoyed prior role as committee chair as much or more than general leadership.

Consensus/Process Leadership (A female type)
> Low need to control others; low need to control personal institutional role; will assume a variety of roles as long as each facilitates institutional functioning; accommodates conflict; focuses on the mechanics of the policy process; is supportive, conciliatory, eager to let everyone have a say, free with information, and concerned with feelings of fellow legislators and harmony.

Hybrid Leadership Types

Command/Policy Leadership (A male type)
> High need to control others; moderate need to control personal institutional role to enhance policy outcomes; suppresses conflict; focuses on outputs of the policy process; is strong, directive, ideological, partisan, visionary, and distrustful of those who do not vote right.

Coordinating/Power Leadership (A male type)
> Moderate need to control others; high need to control personal institutional role to enhance own ambitions; negotiates conflict; focuses on the inputs of the policy process; takes occasional ideological stands without being strongly ideological; focuses on the short run; has strong external ties.

Coordinating/Process Leadership (A female type)
> Moderate need to control others; low need to control personal institutional role; will embrace many leadership tasks; negotiates conflict; focuses on the mechanics of the policy process; allows some rank and file dissension but clamps down on perceived excesses; interested in smooth legislative functioning.

Consensus/Policy Leadership (A female type)
    Low need to control others; moderate need to control personal
    institutional role to assure compatibility with desired policy outcomes;
    accommodates conflict; focuses on the outputs of the policy process; is
    supportive, democratic, persuasive on the issues; is interested in teaching
    or showing the value of preferred positions but will not push for
    preferences at the expense of relationships with fellow legislators.

Recessive Leadership Types

Command/Process Leadership (Infrequent, neither male nor female type)
    High need to control others; low need to control own institutional role;
    suppresses conflict; focuses on the mechanics of the policy process; is
    strong, controlling, legislative career–oriented; concerned with
    modernization and institutional improvements.

Consensus/Power Leadership (Infrequent, neither male nor female type)
    Low need to control others; high need to control personal institutional
    role to facilitate career advancement; accommodates conflict; focuses on
    the inputs of the policy process; craves power but fears alienating others;
    often gets bored and may voluntarily quit when power needs are thwarted.

TABLE 11.5
Observed Clusters of Leadership Types, Total and by Gender

	Total	Men	Women
Hypothesized male types (Command/power, command/policy, coordinating/power, coordinating/policy)	24 (39%)	19 (45%)	5 (25%)
All hypothesized non-male types	38 (61%)	23 (55%)	15 (75%)
Hypothesized female types (Coordinating/policy, coordinating/process, consensus/policy, consensus/process)	49 (79%)	30 (71%)	19 (95%)
All hypothesized non-female types	13 (21%)	12 (48%)	1 (5%)
Hypothesized overlapping type (coordinating/policy)	12 (19%)	8 (19%)	4 (20%)

Conclusion

The increase in the numbers of women serving in state legislatures that occurred in statehouses during the 1980s has resulted in the "feminization" of state legislative leaders in two ways. First, the number of women leaders has increased as the number of women elected to office has grown, lagging only slightly behind membership increases, proportionately. Second, although expected gender differences still exist, with women more likely than men to adopt a "female" leadership type and men more likely than women to adopt a "male" leadership type, men have gravitated toward "female" leadership types. Men are more likely to adopt a "female" type that emphasizes consensus and system concerns than they are to adopt a "male" type that emphasizes control, command, and narrow personal ambitions. Nor did most of the leaders we interviewed necessarily think that this "feminization" of leadership resulted in weaker leaders, but rather that it is a necessary trend given underlying shifts in the nature of state legislatures. Given the long-term nature of many of the factors prompting this "feminization" of leadership in state legislatures, it is a trend that is likely to continue into the foreseeable future.

12

Getting Things Done
Women Committee Chairpersons in State Legislatures

CINDY SIMON ROSENTHAL

. . . power can be thought of in terms of three "gettings": getting
one's way, getting along with others, and getting things done.
J. Goodschilds, 1979, cited in *Lips*, 1981:37

When Kaye Steinmetz retired from the Missouri House of Representatives
in 1994, she was honored by the Columbia *Missourian* as the first woman
ever to be named "Statesman of the Year." While ironically titled, the award
was much deserved. During her 18-year career as a legislator, she led a 10-
year-long struggle to establish a family court system, spearheaded efforts to
improve the regulation of child care facilities, and sponsored legislation to
prevent and prosecute child abuse.[1]

In her career, Steinmetz dedicated herself almost single-mindedly to the
task of children's legislation. It was not an agenda pursued with an eye
toward future political opportunities, nor was it a path to power that others
had already pioneered. Representative Steinmetz first had to convince her
presiding officer of the need for a committee focused on issues affecting
families and children. She overcame that hurdle by quietly encouraging a
network of interest groups to lobby the speaker for a special committee. In
1983 she was appointed the first chair of the House Committee on Children,
Youth, and Families, a position she held until her retirement.

Once appointed a committee chair, Representative Steinmetz pursued
leadership strategies with the single goal of getting legislation passed. Her approach is typical of many women committee chairs, whose primary focus is on
getting things done. For many women chairing state legislative committees, a

175

no-nonsense emphasis on task offers one strategy for overcoming the reality of women's relative numerical underrepresentation.

Among the leadership experiences and styles of male and female committee chairs in the 50 state legislatures, task commitment is a characteristic that clearly distinguishes women and men committee chairs. On average, women are more likely than men to point to their dedication to task as a key reason for winning committee leadership positions and as a feature of their leadership style in running a committee.

The Two Sides of Leadership

Humanistic theories of leadership posit that the central function of a leader is to balance the freedom and motivations of individuals within an organization with the need to accomplish organizational goals (see, for example, McGregor, 1960; Blake and Mouton, 1985; Hersey and Blanchard, 1977; Argyris, 1964; Fiedler, 1967; Likert, 1961). While given various names, these two dimensions of leadership comprise a concern for nurturing and maintaining interpersonal relationships and a focus on completing tasks or goals.

Often, women and men are seen as differing in terms of these two dimensions of leadership style. Stereotypes about women's roles in the family, in the work force, and in society at large have tended to color the picture of female leaders as emphasizing personal relations and sensitivity to the feelings of individual followers. Such stereotypes continue to be perpetuated by media images of women as professional caregivers, self-effacing volunteers, or women who stand behind more prominent men (Jamieson, 1995:chaps. 7 and 8). By contrast, masculine images of leadership have tended to emphasize decisiveness and take-charge strategies that are often described with metaphors drawn from male-dominated team sports and the military.

While much scholarly attention has been given to women's ability and inclination toward maintaining interpersonal relationships, less appreciated is the importance of task in the style and experiences of female political leaders. Eagly and Johnson (1990:247) reviewed 370 studies and found that *both* interpersonal relationships and task accomplishment are emphasized by women to a greater extent than by men. That seems to be the case among legislative committee chairs as well (see Rosenthal, 1995b).

For women operating within institutions populated predominantly by men, there are sound reasons to emphasize task accomplishment. Goodschild argues that power-wielding (i.e., "getting one's way") may pose a psychological dilemma for leaders who also highly value getting along with others (Lips, 1981:37). She suggests that a focus on "getting the job done" allows the leader to resolve the conflict. Similarly, a focus on task allows women a means of avoiding the double binds of certain female stereotypes. Morrison, White, and Van Velson (1987:4) conclude that executive women combine toughness and femininity and stay within a "narrow band of acceptable behavior" in order to contradict stereotypes that might imply weakness. Many women in politics recall situations such as those prompting Kay Steinmetz to remark: "More than once, I had to prove I was tough while remaining a 'lady.'"

Finally, women often must overcome organizational and structural realities of being less powerful (Kanter, 1977). A woman who can demonstrate task competence in a leadership role has an opportunity to dispel societal predispositions that tend to portray women as less powerful. Success in achieving one's goals generates confidence and builds up the leader's credit among followers, even reluctant or doubtful ones. By gaining recognition of one's competence, "the leader can subsequently depart from the group norms and move the group in novel ways, yet still be accepted by the group." (Bass, 1990:98)

Studying State Legislative Chairs

Electoral success by significant numbers of women has brought more women into political leadership roles. Since 1969 the number of women successfully winning state legislative seats has increased five-fold. As the number of female legislators has increased, women have also gained a greater share of committee chairships. Between 1985 and 1993, the Center for the American Woman and Politics reported that women committee chairs increased in number from just under 10 percent to 16.4 percent of the 2,094 standing committee chairs. In 1994, women chaired standing or statutory committees in every state legislature except South Carolina. In 15 states, women held 20 percent or more of the available committee posts. In Arizona, women held half of the committee leadership jobs. In total, 353 women chaired standing or statutory committees in state legislatures in 1994 (CAWP, 1991, 1993; see Table 12.1).

Committee chairs thus represent a significant pool of elected women officeholders with institutional leadership responsibilities, and their numbers allow for comparison of leadership behavior in different settings. Rieselbach (1992:2) argues that "as discrete units of analysis, committees lend themselves to efforts to investigate the power and leadership phenomena." Committee work is, in effect, a "middle management" level of legislative leadership and is where policy is formulated. Furthermore, "committee power lies at the heart of the whole transactional system of reciprocity, brokerage and exchange" which characterizes legislative leadership more broadly (Burns, 1978: chap. 13).

The committee chair provides a rich setting in which to explore the interplay of task orientation and interpersonal considerations, because the job clearly calls for both. Task concerns of the chair include controlling the agenda, determining which bills will be heard and when, managing the allocation of time, and directing the flow of discussion by recognizing members who wish to speak. The chair is also the focal point of myriad personal relationships dealing with members on the committee, bill sponsors, other committee chairs, the leadership, interest groups, and agency personnel. Thus the committee venue provides an opportunity for a chair to gravitate toward task or interpersonal concerns or to hew toward a balanced approach.

TABLE 12.1

Women's Representation in State Legislatures, 1994

State	Percent Female Members	Percent Female Chairs	Percent Female Leaders
Alabama	5.0	9.8	0
Alaska	21.7	8.7	60.0
Arizona	35.6	50.0	41.2
Arkansas	9.6	3.7	0
California	23.3	14.3	4.8
Colorado	35.0	33.3	23.5
Connecticut	25.1	19.6	21.6
Delaware	14.5	17.0	10.0
Florida	17.5	6.1	27.8
Georgia	17.4	6.9	16.7
Hawaii	23.7	19.4	29.4
Idaho	30.5	41.7	35.7
Illinois	23.2	19.1	20.6
Indiana	19.3	11.1	22.6
Iowa	14.7	13.9	24.0
Kansas	29.1	29.1	20.0
Kentucky	4.3	3.0	0
Louisiana	7.6	3.1	0
Maine	31.7	46.0	20.0
Maryland	23.9	16.7	18.5
Massachusetts	23.0	13.0	13.3
Michigan	20.3	21.6	21.9
Minnesota	27.4	17.9	28.6
Mississippi	10.9	7.9	0
Missouri	18.8	19.8	19.0
Montana	20.0	15.6	8.3
Nebraska	20.4	11.1	0
Nevada	27.0	25.0	20.0
New Hampshire	33.5	32.0	30.0
New Jersey	12.5	7.5	14.7
New Mexico	19.6	11.5	0
New York	16.6	6.9	8.8
North Carolina	18.2	18.2	15.4
North Dakota	16.3	12.5	14.3
Ohio	21.2	16.1	11.1
Oklahoma	9.4	10.9	3.2
Oregon	27.8	33.3	30.3
Pennsylvania	9.9	4.3	0
Rhode Island	24.7	23.1	28.9
South Carolina	12.9	0	0
South Dakota	20.0	24.0	9.5
Tennessee	12.1	3.4	12.0
Texas	16.0	11.4	0

Utah	13.5	9.8	8.3
Vermont	33.9	11.4	30.0
Virginia	12.1	6.5	0
Washington	39.5	33.3	47.1
West Virginia	16.4	18.6	18.2
Wisconsin	27.3	30.8	20.8
Wyoming	24.4	2.5	33.3

Source: Center for American Women in Politics (1993).

This study takes advantage of the growing cadre of women committee chairs and marshals the considerable literature from organizational behavior and public management to understand legislative leadership behavior. Three complementary data sources are used: (1) a 1994 mailed national survey of male and female committee chairs, (2) focused peer group interviews with women committee chairs in 1994, and (3) interviews, field work, and direct observation of committee chairs in three state legislatures during legislative sessions in 1995. The questionnaire covers: (1) demographic and career characteristics; (2) self-assessment of leadership traits; (3) committee operations; and (4) attitudes about conflict, power, ambition, and peer relationships. The survey was sent to all 353 women and a random sample of approximately 500 men who chaired standing or statutory committees as of March 1994.[2] Completed surveys were received from 136 women, a response rate of 39.0 percent, and 156 men, a response rate of 28.3 percent. The focus groups involved 17 women from 12 states,[3] and field work involved more than 60 face-to-face interviews and observation of 41 committee hearings or meetings.

Who Chairs Legislative Committees?

In many ways, the profile of male and female committee chairs is not unlike the picture presented by scholars who studied women state legislators in the 1970s and 1980s (see especially Diamond, 1977; and Thomas, 1994a). Female committee chairs in the 1990s on average defer their political careers until midlife. Female committee chairs also are more likely to be older than their male colleagues, to wait until their children are older before entering politics, and to postpone electoral ambitions until after the prime years of domestic or marital responsibilities.

Educational and occupational differences also remain in the 1990s and may have widened. Women committee chairs lag behind their male colleagues in obtaining advanced degrees, are less likely to be employed outside of the home, and are more likely to have developed their leadership skills in community and volunteer settings. In 1994, 53 percent of the male committee chairs held college degrees beyond a baccalaureate, whereas only 43 percent of the women did. By a margin of almost three to one, male committee chairs in 1994 were more likely than female chairs to have acquired a law, medical, or graduate business degree. Table 12.2 provides comparison of demographic data, education, and occupational background of legislative committee chairs in 1994.

The table also reports the most significant preparatory leadership experience of legislative committee chairs. Female chairs in the mid-1990s are three times more likely to cite their volunteer or community service activities as formative leadership experiences than were men. Notably, however, both male and female committee chairs identified some kind of professional experience more frequently than any other type of preparatory leadership experience. Male committee chairs, however, were much more likely to cite only profes-

TABLE 12.2
Background Characteristics of Committee Chairs

	Women (Percent)	Men (Percent)
Born before 1948*	83.8	72.2*
Have kids under 18 at home***	20.0	42.5***
Respondent's education**		
H.S. graduate	2.2	2.6**
Some college	20.9	13.9
College degree	34.3	30.5
Masters degree	26.9	14.6
JD, MD, MBA	13.4	35.1
Doctorate	2.2	3.3
Main occupation prior to legislator***		
Professional/managerial	53.8	56.5
Clerical	8.3	.7
Farming/ranching	2.3	12.9
Skilled crafts/labor/transport	1.5	7.5
Not employed outside home	22.0	4.1
Sales/service	12.1	18.4
Prior experience judged most important		
Preparation for role as a committee chair***		
Professional[1]	32.4	42.3
Legislative service	10.3	17.1
Prior government/political office	19.3	13.0
Community service/volunteer work	28.4	8.9
Personal factors	5.5	4.1
Other[2]	4.1	14.6

*$p < .05$; **$p < .01$; ***$p < .001$, based on Pearson χ^2 statistic.
[1]Includes all job or work-related experiences including business occupations, teaching, union positions, and military service.
[2]Includes issue interests, school experiences, and special educational training such as parliamentary procedure.
Note: The responses on prior leadership preparation were coded from the following open-ended question: What experience, either professional, volunteer, or otherwise, has most prepared you for being a committee chair? Answers were coded to multiple categories when appropriate ($N=91$ men, 123 different responses; and 83 women, 145 separate responses).

sional experience, whereas women typically cited professional background in combination with other experiences.

The legislative careers of women, committee leaders differ in important ways from the men. Women are significantly more likely to consider themselves full-time legislators: 64.9 percent of the women, compared with 37.3 percent of the men. Women chairs on average have fewer total years of legislative service than their male colleagues and have one less year of service as a committee chair. The difference in committee experience, however, disappears when the total years of legislative service are controlled. Simply put, women have fewer years of experience as committee chairs because they have been in the legislature for a shorter period of time.

In fact, it appears that women have been on a fast track, moving into their committee posts more quickly than their male colleagues. Of substantive and statistical significance, women, on average, are appointed to lead a committee after fewer years of legislative service. This may represent a limited form of affirmative action within legislatures, a conscious effort by legislative leaders to achieve a more descriptively representative team of committee chairs, or an indication of the hard work women do. (See Chapter 6 for more information on women's perceptions of working harder than men.)

As leaders of legislative committees, women tend to be overrepresented on the traditional "care" committees of human services, health, education, and children's issues but have continued to expand their influence in virtually every area and to erode further the male dominance of business committees (Thomas, 1994a:66). In the 1993–94 biennium, women chaired 17.7 percent of the 215 legislative committees focusing on business, labor, insurance, utilities, transportation, or consumer affairs; at the same time, women chaired 34.9 percent of the human resources, health, aging, and youth committees.[4]

In sum, the profile of women committee chairs suggests that some of the differences between male and female rank-and-file officeholders long reported in the literature are also true of committee chairs.

Getting the Job of Committee Chair

Committee chairs are appointed based on a variety of criteria including their reputation, skill, expertise, work habits, and loyalty. In some state legislatures, seniority looms large. While there seems to be little difference in most reasons for their appointment, women place greater emphasis on skill and work commitment. Significantly more so than the male committee chairs, women tend to emphasize appointment factors that suggest they can get the job done. Women chairs also are more likely to cite gender as a factor in their appointment as committee chair. And once on the job, they are likely to perceive themselves as working harder than the average committee chair.

Evaluating the importance of 11 different appointment criteria, male and female committee chairs give almost identical ratings of the importance of loyalty to and ability to work with leadership, subject-matter expertise, personal reputation with other legislators and interest groups, and regional and racial balance. The male chairs ranked only one factor—seniority—more important in their appointments than did the women, but the difference was not significant. Only three factors distinguish male and female chairs, and two seem to be closely related to women's perception of the importance of task orientation (see Table 12.3).

On average, women rate their "ability to get things done" and "willingness to spend time" as significantly more important than do men as factors in their appointment. Indeed, almost 60 percent of the women rated their commitment of time as "extremely important," compared with only a third of the men. The third appointment factor distinguishing men and women committee chairs is sex of legislator. Three times as many women chairs as men identified gender as "important" to "extremely important." Among all of the factors weighed in the appointment of committee chairs, however, sex and race on average were considered the least important by committee chairs. Responses to open-ended questions and personal interviews suggest that sex may influence appointments in several ways—balancing a leadership team, matching up certain issues with a female chair, and accepting committee assignments that no one else wants.

When asked to compare themselves with other committee chairs, women and men did not differ at all in the frequency with which they felt: (1) taken seriously, (2) sought out for advice, or (3) more effective. On some comparisons, however, there are significant gender differences. Women are significantly more likely to describe themselves as working harder and lobbying harder than the average chair. More than 70 percent of the women said they worked harder than the average chair, compared with 56.9 percent of the men. Forty percent of the women reported lobbying harder for their

TABLE 12.3
Factors Considered Important in Appointment as Committee Chair

	Mean Rating		Percent Rating Factor Extremely Important	
	Women	Men	Women	Men
Willingness to spend time	4.4	3.9**	58.5	35.8**
Ability to get things done	4.3	4.0*	47.7	39.5*
Gender[1]	2.1	1.4**	31.4	10.9**

*$p < .01$; **$p < .001$. Significance levels for means are for t-tests for difference of means on independent samples by gender. Significant levels for the ratings of "extremely important" are based on the Pearson's chi-square statistic.

Note: The reasons that the committee chair perceived important in his or her appointment to head a committee were ranked on a five-point scale ranging from 1 for "not at all important" to 3 for "important" to 5 for "extremely important."

[1] Because so few committee chairs rated gender as an "extremely important" criteria, the percentages shown in the second column represent ratings from "important" to "extremely important."

issues than other chairs in their legislature; only 22.2 percent of the men said they lobbied harder than other chairs. Female committee chairs are also less likely to feel included in key decisions. The perception of harder work is particularly striking among those legislators who describe themselves as part-time rather than full-time lawmakers. Among those who consider themselves "citizen" solons, 78.7 percent of the women feel they work harder than other committee chairs, compared with 52.1 percent of the part-time male chairs.

This difference in perception may be more of a qualitative than a quantitative difference, however. There is no significant difference in the average number of hours per week that male and female chairs report spending on committee business. But women participating in the focus groups perceived themselves as working harder—perhaps more persistently and thoroughly or on tougher issues—than male committee chairs.

An Arizona house member commented:

> The first thing we all say about women, no matter the party, is that the women work harder. The women are more likely to read the bills than the men. The men, because they know it all anyway, don't even bother reading the bills. They are the least prepared on your committee generally, unless a lobbyist has gotten to them and given them some amendments to write. (focus group, July 28, 1994)

While careful not to suggest that her male colleagues do not fulfill their job responsibilities, an Ohio state senator added, "Some of the men take on the lighter committees, and we [the women] are more willing to take on committees that require more work" (focus group, July 27, 1994). An Oklahoma state senator captured the seeming ambiguity between perceptions of hard work and hours spent: "It's just our way of life. We organize. We take care of the details. We feel like we have to work twice as hard. I don't even know if the men know that we feel this way. We all worked just as hard to get here. We're all elected the same way. But I think we [women] do it to ourselves" (personal interview, December 15, 1994).

Leadership Traits: Task and Interpersonal Emphasis

When asked to describe their leadership style, female committee chairs tend to emphasize traits consistent with an emphasis toward interpersonal skills *and* task orientation. The survey asked legislative committee chairs to weigh "the extent to which you think the following traits characterize *your* style." In all, the respondents ranked 22 traits on a scale ranging from 1 for "not very characteristic" to 5 for "extremely characteristic."

The average scores for men and women reveal distinct differences that are statistically significant on 11 of the 22 items. Looking more closely at the 11 traits, 6 are particularly noteworthy in terms of the percentage of women and men who rate the traits as "extremely characteristic." Table 12.4 summarizes the key traits. Women, on average, are much more likely to describe themselves as more task-oriented, managerial, assertive, skilled at interpersonal dealings, frank and direct, and team-oriented. On these six traits, the percentage of women choosing the category "extremely characteristic" was one and a half to two times greater than for men. This cluster of six traits clearly combines the essential elements of a leadership style emphasizing both interpersonal relationships and task commitment.

On average, male committee chairs rated four traits as more characteristic than their female colleagues, but the differences reach statistical significance on only one trait and only a few respondents rated the traits as extremely characteristic. These results are also shown in Table 4. The more male traits included being competitive, willing to intimidate, opportunistic, and trusting. Men were significantly more likely than women to describe themselves as opportunistic. The traits of competitiveness, willingness to intimidate, and opportunism suggest a more power-oriented or authoritative style, but that style seems characteristic of only a subset of the male chairs.

The survey also included one indirect measure of the traits associated

TABLE 12.4
Gender Differences in Traits Considered Characteristic of One's Style as Committee Chair

	Mean Rating		Percent Rating Factor Extremely Important	
	Women	Men	Women	Men
Traits women chairs rated significantly more characteristic				
Assertive	4.0	3.7**	26.9	15.9*
Interpersonal skills	4.1	3.6***	37.3	19.9***
Team-oriented	4.2	3.9*	44.0	25.8**
Task-oriented	4.2	3.8***	38.8	23.8**
Managerial	3.7	3.4*	24.6	12.6**
Frank and direct	4.3	4.1*	53.0	38.4*
Traits male chairs rated more characteristic[1]				
Trusting	3.7	3.9	26.1	30.5
Competitive	3.3	3.5	22.4	21.9
Opportunistic	2.1	2.5**	2.2	4.6**
Willing to intimidate	1.8	2.0	1.5	4.6

*$p < .05$; **$p < .01$; ***$p < .001$. Significance levels for means are for t-tests for difference of means on independent samples by gender. Significant levels for the ratings of "extremely characteristic" are based on the Pearson's chi-square statistic.
Note: Committee chairs ranked each trait on a five-point scale ranging from 1 for "not very characteristic" to 3 for "characteristic" to 5 for "extremely characteristic."
[1]When all five response categories are examined, the male-female differences are only slightly more revealing. For example, combining response categories 4 and 5, 47.1 percent of the women compared with 55.7 percent of the men describe themselves as somewhat or extremely competitive, and 54.5 percent of the women compared with 70.2 percent of the men describe themselves as somewhat or extremely trusting. Similarly, 18.7 percent of the women compared with 29.1 percent of the men characterize their style at least to a degree as "willing to use intimidation"; 29.1 percent of the women compared with 49.9 percent of the men characterize their style as "opportunistic."

with committee leadership style—Fiedler's "least preferred coworker" (LPC) instrument (Fiedler, 1967). The instrument has proven to be a reliable means of assessing a person's underlying predisposition toward task behaviors (e.g., controlling, structuring, directing) versus interpersonal behaviors (e.g., supporting, empathizing, considerateness). The instrument is useful because it provides an indirect measure of task versus interpersonal attentiveness that avoids gendered stereotypes.[5] For example, women who are hard-driving and detached may nonetheless describe themselves as nurturing because of a desire to present themselves in a culturally acceptable light.

In completing the LPC instrument, a person is asked to think about the most difficult coworker with whom one has had to work. Then the respondent rates that coworker on 18 personality features (e.g., kindness, warmth, disposition, openness, etc.) using an eight-point scale. Negative assessments of a coworker yield a low score, and a positive evaluation of the person produces a high score. A high score on the LPC (73 or above) is interpreted as an orientation to personal relationships, a low score (63 or below) reflects task motivation and is interpreted as a high need to accomplish the task. Interpretations of a middle score (64–72) indicate a person who is flexible with regard to task and "socio-independent" or less concerned about opinions of others (Fiedler and Garcia, 1987:76–77).

Table 12.5 reports the results for the LPC instrument. On average, the women chairs are more task-oriented than their male colleagues.[6] And, using the three LPC categories, female chairs fall more frequently into the category of task-motivated (i.e., low LPC score) than into the other categories.

The LPC scores suggest a subtle but distinct difference in women's emphasis on task. But the self-assessment of traits and the focus groups and individual interviews reinforce a linkage between task orientation and interpersonal relations. The focus groups described task commitment in terms of persistence and patience but intertwined with an emphasis on group or collective effort. As Kaye Steinmetz showed, the way to get the job done is rarely by dint of individual effort but rather through concerted collaboration with others. A Colorado legislator noted: "The task orientation is a very different characteristic of women than men: setting a goal and seeing it

TABLE 12.5
Least Preferred Coworker Scores for Committee Chairs

	LPC Score for Chairs	
	Women	Men
Task-motivated (≤63)	55.3%	42.7%
Middle group (64–72)	16.3	17.5
Relationship-motivated (≥73)	28.5	39.9

through and making sure that everybody else is brought along" (focus group, July 28, 1994).

Task Commitment: Key to Success or Potential Barrier?

In the minds of some experts, a management style combining a high regard for task commitment and sensitivity to interpersonal relationships is ideal (Blake and Mouton, 1985) and constitutes a "female advantage" in the new postindustrial economy (Helgesen, 1990). Clearly, for many women chairing state legislative committees, a dedication to a policy agenda and a focus on the details of the job reap not only satisfaction but success. Just as Kaye Steinmetz accomplished significant policy goals, other female committee chairs are using their positions to rewrite state law and transform policy. There is, however, a potential downside that some legislators identify.

Consider the comments of Speaker Jo Ann Davidson of the Ohio House of Representatives who cited task commitment as a barrier that keeps women from seeking more powerful leadership positions:

> I simply think a lot of it [the lack of women in legislative leadership] has to do with women seeking leadership. If you have ever tried to recruit women to the legislature, you know what I mean. . . . There is a good illustration in the audience today. When I first tried to get her to run for the legislature she was mayor of her community and she had to finish that job. I think many of the women in the legislature came in with an agenda and they have to finish that. They really have not focused as much on seeking leadership positions. (Davidson, 1994)

Two Arizona women had a similar experience of being hesitant to pursue an elected leadership office until they finished work on issues within their committees. A third lawmaker from Arizona told of a conversation that she had with a younger male colleague:

> He said to me, "You ought to just run for Congress because you are never going to be in leadership here." I have chaired a committee since my second term, and I said to him, "You know, maybe I am not going to be in leadership, but I don't think that is the goal here. The goal is: Are you successful in getting your agenda completed? All the bills that I sponsor, that I care about, I get passed. That is what I am here to do." (focus group, July 28, 1994).

In conclusion, an emphasis on getting the job done seems to provide women committee chairs an avenue to obtain power and represents an alternative leadership style to ones based on the exercise of raw power or positional authority. Rather than pursuing power to command or direct others, women committee chairs appear to be more comfortable developing their influence through group efforts aimed at solving a problem or achieving a desired outcome. The emphasis on "getting the job done" may, however, prevent or at least temporarily sidetrack women from moving up the political ladder.

Notes

1. Information about Representative Steinmetz came from a personal interview, January 15, 1996, and focus group comments, July 27, 1994, New Orleans, Louisiana.

2. The response rate is based on the original sample minus questionnaires returned as undeliverable or because the individual was no longer a committee chair. Responses were received from every state except Tennessee. Female committee chairs in the study represent 42 states. Six of the eight states with no female respondents had three or fewer female committee chairs; the lack of responses in the other two states is largely attributable to timing of the survey and session schedules.

3. Convenience sampling was used to select the participants; nonetheless, the participants represented 12 different states, both parties (8 Republicans and 9 Democrats), and different legislative tenures (3 to 20 years). Each focus group lasted 90 minutes, was recorded and transcribed, and then coded by selected topics for analysis. Participants spoke with the understanding that they would not be quoted directly.

4. These calculations are derived using the subject-matter listings of committee chairs developed by the Council of State Governments (CSG, 1993). No attempt was made to check the accuracy of the categories. Among the respondents to the 1994 survey, women chairs are similarly concentrated on human services committees and are significantly more likely than men to head these committees. Also among the respondents, almost identical percentages of men and women chair budget and taxation, business, and government committees. This suggests that the types of committees represented in the survey sample are fairly comparable to the CSG listing.

5. For a brief review of the history of the score, its reliability and interpretation, and both corroborating and critical research, see Fiedler and Garcia, 1987.

6. For both male and female committee chairs, the LPC scores fall slightly below the norms established for the scale (Fiedler's norms: $\bar{X}$ = 68.75, s.d. 21.8; committee chairs: $\bar{X}$ = 66.92, s.d. 20.47 for men; $\bar{X}$ = 62.24, s.d. 19.29 for women). In other words, as a group, legislators are more task-oriented than other people.

13

In a Different Voice

Women and the Policy Process

LYN KATHLENE

"Are elected women really different from men in political office?" This is probably the most common question I am asked by students, colleagues, journalists, and friends. The question of "difference," however, is deceivingly simple. It masks the complexity that leads us to ponder what impact women will have as they make gains in numbers and in positions of power in our male-dominated legislatures. The first difficulty with answering the question of women's difference and impact is that no individual or group of "similar" individuals exists independent of the social, economic, and political environment in which they live. Women across the country are not a homogeneous group promoting "the women's agenda," nor are women "just like men," because our society socializes individuals based on their sex (Lips, 1995). There is tremendous diversity among women based on race, class, ethnicity, culture, region of the country, and other factors; yet, at the same time, there are important commonalities women share based on, for example, the female reproductive reality of pregnancy and birth, as well as gendered socialization that has "assigned" to females such roles as primary caretakers of young children and elderly family members.

The second difficulty in attempting to empirically measure or determine what impact elected women have in politics stems from the institutional and social constraints within which women work. All organizations are the creations of people. In this country, white middle- and upper-class males historically have held the political, economic, and social power, and therefore only a numerically small portion of the U.S. population had the "authority" to define and create our institutions. Consequently, the distribution of power within organizations (see, e.g., Ragins and Sundstrom, 1989; Sigel, 1996), the formal rules and informal norms that guide daily operations (see, e.g., Edelsky, 1981; Ferguson, 1984; Acker, 1992), and even the design of buildings, layout of interior spaces, and configuration of furniture (Spain, 1992; Weisman, 1992; Kathlene, 1995b) are all gendered.

Studying how women are changing the policy process (i.e., how issues become public policy problems, how problems are conceptualized, how solutions are crafted, and how legislation gets passed) requires incorporating into our research designs the gendered dimensions of both individuals and institutions. To illustrate the approach, this chapter synthesizes and combines some of my previous research to demonstrate that gendering, in its varied forms, is essentially about power, and that power is differentially distributed among individuals and groups in society (Duerst-Lahti and Kelly, 1995). In order to analyze the attitudes and behavior of legislators, I developed attitudinal constructs reflecting gendered orientations applicable to the process of making policy. These constructs guide the analysis in two ways. First, an examination of how state legislators talk about formulating policies, followed by their conceptualization of crime and prison policies, reveals how legislators' attitudinal orientations toward policy making are gendered and have an impact on both the process and the substance of public policy. Second, an analysis of legislators' verbal behavior in committee hearings, in the context of the institutional rules and norms of committee procedures, uncovers how the structure of the hearing—the hierarchical power differences among the participants as well as the physical setting of the room—is gendered and therefore systematically affects who controls the discussion in legislative hearings. The combined results of the three types of analysis—discourse analysis of interviews with legislators, content analysis of proposed legislation, and conversational analysis of committee hearing participants—paint a complex picture of how the social construction of gender is embedded in individual legislators' worldviews and undergirds our legislative institutions. Finally, the implications of these gendered patterns are discussed in terms of democratic procedures and the impact on women's policy issues.

Gender, the Individual, and Policy Orientations

Much of the research on women in politics has been spurred by the question, Will elected women bring a feminist agenda into politics? (this assumes that elected women will be feminist in attitude and action, and more feminist than men), or the less precise though arguably more provocative question, Do women speak "in a different voice"? This latter well-worn phrase owes its origin to psychologist Carol Gilligan, whose 1982 book is titled the same. Through an examination of how men and women reason about moral dilemmas, Gilligan found that men tend to be more concerned with people interfering with each other's rights, while women concern themselves with the possibility of omission, of not helping others when one could help them. The masculine approach is commonly referred to as an "ethic of justice," whereas the feminine approach is an "ethic of care." The roots of these gender differences are hypothesized to be sex-based socialization, and Gilligan focuses most heavily on childrearing practices (Chodorow, 1974), though many other scholars include differential sex-based life experiences (e.g., occupation and family responsibilities) as important determinants, too.

The influence of Gilligan's work cannot be overstated. While her research has been controversial (see, for example, Nails, O'Loughlin, and Walker, 1983; Hockmeyer, 1988), it has generated a wealth of theorizing and testing in the social sciences, including gender studies in political science. For example, recent empirical research in communication and psychology has found support for the "connectedness versus separateness" theories of gendered views of the social world (Turner, 1992; Gilligan et al., 1988; Gilligan, Lyons, and Hammer, 1990; Lang-Takac and Osterweil, 1992). My own interest in the policy-making process has been inspired by the possibilities that these theories and empirical findings imply for gender differences in the formulation of public policy generally, not limited to feminist or women's issues.

Consider what Gilligan's work implies about elected men and women as decision makers. Adapting her framework to the political process of formulating public policy, I have argued that men tend to be more *instrumental* in their behavior and attitudes. Their dominant and relatively independent position and function in society have socialized them to view people as autonomous individuals in a hierarchical, competitive world. People are essentially self-centered and self-serving; therefore, knowledge that is subjective is suspect and objective knowledge is revered. The view of people as self-centered and in competition with each other leads to a strong adherence to the protection of individual rights in order to guarantee individual freedoms. Hence, men are more likely to solve problems by applying an "ethic of justice."

Women, on the other hand, approach the world from a more *contextual* viewpoint. Their subordinate and relatively dependent position and function in society have socialized them to view individuals in connection with each other and with society. People's lives are interdependent, based on a continuous web of relationships. The world is not composed of distinct and separate spheres; thus women will not tend to view the world in terms of dichotomies. The public sphere is not separate from the private sphere. Subjective knowledge is not superior or necessarily distinct from objective knowledge. Because women see individuals in terms of their symbiotic relationships to each other, women are more likely to be concerned with addressing the interrelated needs of individuals. Women, therefore, are inclined to adopt an "ethic of care" orientation. Table 13.1 summarizes the values and approaches embedded in the attitudinal orientations (for a more detailed discussion of the constructs, see Kathlene, 1989).

It is important to remember that the attitudinal constructs describe "ideal types" in a theoretical world of only two options. Obviously, such a gross simplification violates the very assumptions of complex interactions and subtle but important gendered behaviors. A more realistic description of a person in a given situation would probably consist of some combination of attributes from the two constructs, whether by an individual's preference or through external pressure. Nevertheless, the question that arises is whether or not

TABLE 13.1
Main Attributes of the Attitudinal Orientations

Instrumentalism	Contextualism
View self as autonomous	View self in connection with community/others
Human interactions are separate and competitive	Human interactions are part of a continuous web of relationships
Distinguishes between objective and subjective knowledge; favors objective	Integrates objective and subjective knowledge; believes both have bias
Main focus is protecting individual's rights	Main focus is addressing needs
Sees the public and private spheres as distinct	Sees the interaction between the public and private spheres

people, based on their sex, tend to rely more on one approach than the other, especially in a *similar context.*

These attitudinal constructs have, in part, guided my analysis and interpretation of data collected from the 1989 Colorado statehouse during the regular legislative session. The Colorado legislature has long been among the states with the highest proportion of elected women. During 1989 Colorado ranked fifth among the 50 states in the number of women elected to state government, with 33 percent (22 out of 65) seated in the House and 20 percent (7 out of 35) in the Senate (CAWP, 1989). As is the case in most bicameral states, far more women were serving in the Colorado House than in the Senate, both in numbers and in percentage of the chamber. This project focuses exclusively on the House because of the greater number of women.

The following analyses rely on subsets of several distinct but related databases: interviews with 61 of the 65 state legislators; the content of all 360 proposed bills; and taped and transcribed committee hearing debates of 68 bills introduced in the House. The research design triangulates multiple simultaneous databases and multiple methodologies (Hakim, 1987) to capture a complex picture of legislators working within the constraints of social and institutional gendered conventions.

Using the attitudinal constructs and the assumptions derived from the constructs, I expected to find that women and men have differing conceptualizations of and behaviors toward formulating policy. Specific to the following analyses, the constructs suggest that given women's world of interrelationships,

1. Women will formulate policy differently from men because they will be more likely to see a problem as affecting many people and groups and will take into account a broader range of information sources when making policy.

2. Women will conceptualize some policy issues in different terms than will men. In explaining their position, the language they use may be misunderstood (because the men have an alternative conceptualization) or may be discounted as tangential to the relevant policy problem and solution. Women may encounter resistance that thwarts passage of their bills.

Both of the above propositions reveal that bringing women into the political arena is not as simple as changing issue priorities. Although women (maybe even particularly feminist women) will bring a heightened sensitivity and interest in women's issues, the differences between men and women are likely to be more profound than the issues area. Women may approach women's issues not just more often than men, but from an unconventional standpoint. If women define women's issues as policy relevant because they see the issue from a broader perspective that includes public action, it may not be the women's issue that is being rejected but rather the conceptualization of the public and private spheres. Of course, this can be true for many policy areas, not just women's issues. And overcoming this institutionalized conceptual bias requires more than increasing the number of women. If women see the world as webs of interrelationships composed of a myriad of legitimate needs rather than competing claims of differing levels of importance, women will be more inclined to include men's conceptualization of the problem (as another equally legitimate concern) than vice versa (because men have elevated certain claims while dismissing others). Hence, women's approaches may be undermined or transformed in the legislative process. In short, sex as understood in the gender framework produces a complicated picture of legislative decision making.

Gendered Approaches to Formulating Policy

Sources of Information Utilized

An important aspect of policy formulation is the initial research a legislator engages in before drafting a bill. Research involves the use of a variety of information sources that will influence and mold the proposed legislation. Sources can include people—constituents, fellow legislators, local politicians, staff personnel, professionals, citizens, and friends. Sources also can be items of data, such as previous research, reports, books, articles, laws in other states or countries, and so forth.

One indicator of a contextual versus instrumental approach to policy making is the number and variety of sources a legislator uses (1) to keep informed in general and (2) to formulate a particular bill. More resources represent a contextual orientation, which recognizes the complexity of the environment and the need to integrate many sources of information in order to incorporate as many of the affected and interested people as possible. An instrumental approach relies on fewer information sources, most likely the ones viewed as more politically legitimate, more "objective." For example, experts will be highly valued. The use of fewer select resources arises from the notion that problems stem from separate and competitive claims; hence, reliance on people deemed most directly "knowledgeable" in the area of interest. but not necessarily those most affected.

In two separate sets of interviews with Colorado state legislators (Kathlene, 1989), I found gender differences in the number and types of resources used to develop legislative bills. Table 13.2 reports descriptive statistics on resource range, mean, and mode (if any) of the number of responses, by sex, party identification, age, and freshman status in the legislature. The mean and mode are both statistical measures that indicate where the bulk of scores lie in a distribution. The mean is an arithmetic average calculated by dividing the sum of the number of resources mentioned by the number of legislators. The mode reports the most frequently reported number of resources. A small sample t-test of sample means is used to determine if there are statistically significant differences within the categories. The range and mode are helpful in understanding the t-test significance levels because both provide additional information about the distribution not readily apparent in the mean.

In both sets of interviews, only sex differences were statistically significant; party, generational age, and terms in the legislature were not significant predictors of the number of resources mentioned. Sex differences were even greater in an examination of "who," "which groups," and "what types" of informational sources are used. Table 13.3 lists six categories of resources legislators utilized when formulating bills.

Of the 55 different resources, only 13 (24 percent) were common words used by women and men. These distinct vocabularies indicate that women and men are relying on different resources when formulating policy, which suggests they may have different approaches to conceptualizing policy problems and researching solutions. For example, men claim that they became aware of policy problems more often through "experts" and political persons with specialized knowledge. In contrast, women became aware of problems more often through general information sources covering the full range of political geography, from their district to the world. Note that only women talked about receiving information from local and state political leaders. And even though both men and women spoke about their reliance on lobbyists, for women it was more an unfortunate fact of legislative life, whereas for men it was seen as a highly valued and essential resource. Moreover, an examination of resource usage by party affiliation revealed that men in both parties were more similar to each other than to their women co-partisans. Women, whether Democrats or Republicans, utilized a wider variety of resources outside the legislative institution than the males in their own party.

Policy Study: Alternative Views of Crime

Do these orientations about legislators' general approach to developing public policy apply to and affect their individual deliberations about specific policy problems and possible solutions? In a study examining how 47 legislators

TABLE 13.2
Number of Different Resources Reported by Colorado Legislators When Developing Public Policies, by Sex, Party, Age, and Freshman Status

Category	N	Range	Mean	Mode	t
Interview Study 1: 1985 Legislative Session, $n = 10$					
Female	5	4–8	5.8	6	2.53**
Male	5	2–6	3.4	3	
Democrat	3	2–8	5.3	—	.75
Republican	7	3–6	4.3	3	
<45 years old	5	3–8	4.8	3	.32
>45 years old	5	2–6	5.4	6	
Freshman	5	2–8	5.0	6	.59
Second + term	5	3–8	4.2	—	
Interview Study 2: 1989 Legislative Session, $n = 20$					
Female	8	4–10	6.9	7	1.85*
Male	12	2–8	5.4	4	
Democrat	8	2–10	6.4	7	.74
Republican	12	4–8	5.8	4	
<45 years old	7	2–8	5.7	6	−.50
>45 years old	13	4–10	6.2	7	
Freshman	4	5–7	6.3	7	.30
Second + term	16	2–10	5.9	4	

**p < .05.
*p < .10.

talked about the problem of crime (Kathlene, 1995a), I found that men tended to see criminals as autonomous individuals responsible for choosing a life of crime. Women, on the other hand, tended to see criminals as people acting within the context of societal opportunities, especially the lack of equal opportunities (i.e., access to healthy families, adequate education, economic prospects), and the lifelong processes that foster criminal behavior. These differences were significant even when I took party into account.

These gendered viewpoints on the origins of crime are directly related to the proposed policy solutions. Since men focus on the crime event, the policy questions they ponder are more narrowly defined, such as how to improve the administrative aspects of the criminal justice system or the prison system, how to keep criminals off the streets, and how to make criminals take responsibility for their behavior. Women's view of crime as a lifetime process led to broader policy questions such as how to prevent people from turning to a life of crime and how to make the criminal a functioning part of society after incarceration.

TABLE 13.3
Six Categories of Resource Nouns Mentioned by Legislators, 1989 Session

Used by Females and Males	Used by Females Only	Used by Males Only
General population		
constituent(s, cy, cies)	citizen(s)	advisors
people	community	client
	country	consultants
	district	experts
	parents	industry
	world	some(one, body)
Political (elected)		
DA (public defenders)	city council(men)	
	county commissioners	
	leaders	
	legislators	
	mayor(s)	
Political (not elected)		
groups(s)	private attorneys	police officers
lobbyist(s)	organizations	insurance
judges	social workers	commissioner
meeting(s)	legislative council	special interests
	staff	
Government/private organizations		
department	public officials	agencies
NSCL	social services	
state(s)		
Personal experience		
myself	husband	relatives
	personal experience	
Studies/Media		
articles	history	letters
news/papers(s)	issue-statements	policy
	magazines	problems
	research	radio
		situations
		statutes
		stuff
		television

The 30 crime and prison bills introduced in the 1989 Colorado session revealed these same gendered views. Men focused on legal proceedings (such as rules regarding new evidence in criminal court cases), expanding existing laws to include new crimes, and increasing penalties in existing criminal law.

These crime bills, with their legal focus (92 percent) and "get tough on crime" approach, parallel the men's discussion and policy recommendations in the interviews, which focused on the crime event. Women, too, sponsored legal changes (37 percent) such as stricter sentencing, but this was not their overwhelming method. In fact, only women dealt with crime through prevention and intervention strategies—approaches that mirror their discussion of the relationship between society and criminal behavior. What of success rates? Only 37 percent of women's crime bills became law, compared with 83 percent of the men's crime bills. In particular, all of women's intervention and prevention bills were postponed indefinitely. While it may be pure sexism that prevented women's bills from becoming law, a more likely explanation stems from the hypothesis that women's contextual orientation resulted in a broader conception of crime, one that was at odds with the instrumental institutionalized discourse. Hence, women's policy approaches are not understood or appreciated, but seen at best as tangential to the problem at hand.

Gender, the Political Process, and Policy Outcomes

Gendered views of policy problems manifested at the individual level are complicated by gendered institutional arrangements and gendered social dynamics. Gender is a fundamental category of organization in nearly all societies (though how gender is constructed differs across societies); thus it manifests itself in the behavior and expectations of (1) an individual, (2) individuals interacting with one another, (3) the rules and norms guiding organizations or institutions, and (4) societal arrangements and opportunities (Ragins and Sundstrom, 1989).

Discovering that elected women and men have, for example, different orientations toward developing legislation is but the first, and perhaps the least complicated, level of documenting and understanding the effects of gender on politics. Individuals in the legislative arena must be able to "act upon" their convictions; yet there is ample evidence to presume that elected men and women are not equally situated with respect to political power even when they are institutional equals (e.g., hold the same positions, such as chairing a committee, etc.). Moreover, women, whether they be 10, 20, or 60 percent of an organization, work within the larger confines of gendered institutions and socially prescribed roles. Simply increasing the number of women in the workplace may not bring about gender equality. In fact, Yoder (1991) demonstrates that as women obtain more than a token presence in highly masculinized occupations such as law, the work environment becomes *more*, not less, resistant to increasing numbers of women, a phenomenon Yoder labels the "intrusiveness" effect; this effect may have to do with men seeing competition from women as a heightened threat as the proportions of women in the organization rises.

Yoder's assessment has serious implications for women in politics. Few social and occupational domains are more masculinized than politics. Because individual power and influence over policy making occurs mainly in legislative committees and subcommittees, women may face barriers not previously considered.

Gendered Verbal Dynamics in Committee Hearings

In the legislative setting, individuals (and therefore groups) exert influence primarily through two methods: (1) appointments to powerful positions, and (2) assignments to and participation in committees. Theoretically, in a gender-neutral institution, all committee chairs have the power to set the agenda and guide committee discussions. If women have more of an interest in certain types of issues, as research on their legislative priorities and sponsorship of bills indicates (Thomas and Welch, 1991; Thomas, 1994; Saint-Germain, 1989), or if women have gendered conceptualizations of policy problems, as the examination of resources and views of crime indicates, then, in an equitable setting, female committee chairs would have opportunities to imprint their concerns while directing the hearings. Similarly, if committees are composed of some critical mass of women, then the effects of tokenism and marginalization should be lessened (Kanter, 1977), allowing women to join freely in the debate on bills. Additionally, research on leadership styles has found that women tend to lead more democratically, while men tend to be more autocratic (Eagly and Johnson, 1990). Women's style of leadership may bring unexpected changes to legislative policy making beyond gendered conceptualizations of policy problems to a change in the process of policy deliberation.

But gender affects more than just the individuals who occupy the legislature. The institution itself is gendered through the rules, norms, and expectations of how business should proceed. In our society, this gendering is also inextricably linked to power. Institutional structures such as legislatures embody and reward instrumental orientations and behavior while implicitly and explicitly devaluing, limiting, or marginalizing contextualism. If women are more likely to bring a contextual mode of thinking and acting into a masculinized arena, we cannot expect a transformation or even an easy integration of a feminized perspective into existing institutions. Indeed, understanding gender as a power construct that interacts at the individual, institutional, and societal levels suggests that women chairs—even when, or maybe especially when, they bring a more contextualized understanding of problems and lead the committee more democratically—may not receive the same respect or have the same influence over committee hearings as men. Similarly, Yoder's work suggests that the more feminized a committee becomes through increases in the proportion of women legislators at a hearing, the more overt resistance to women's presence will be displayed by men.

The purpose of legislative committee hearings is to discuss a proposed bill, allowing proponents and opponents to put forth their evidence and arguments. Examining the conversational dynamics of individuals participating in committee hearings is one important way to determine whether asymmetrical gender power dynamics exist in the process of formulating public policy. To determine "who holds the floor" in legislative committee hearings, 13.2 hours of committee discussion with 204 speakers acting in one of four positions (chair, committee member, sponsor, witness) were taped, transcribed, coded, and analyzed (Kathlene, 1994). Following is a summary of the results.

Committee Chairs   The position of a participant is important in terms of the institutional power conferred upon her or him. Committee chairs, by virtue of their task of running a hearing, are the most institutionally powerful participants at a hearing. In terms of verbal interaction, chairs have the ability to speak without waiting for acknowledgment. And their verbal contributions to the discussion can range from merely calling on other people to speak, in which case they act as a facilitator, to limiting other speakers by cutting them off, not calling on them, or dismissing or bolstering their remarks. Committee chairs can also bring to a hearing, more successfully than other participants, their own personal agenda, however tangentially related to the bill being heard. For example, a chairperson may have an underlying ideological position on the "proper role of government" that influences how she or he will conduct the meeting—the length of time allotted for hearing the bill as well as the tactics discussed above—which serves to either enhance or impede the passage of a bill out of their committee.

The analysis found that men and women chairs differed significantly in terms of their speaking behavior. Women chairing committees spoke less, took fewer turns, and made fewer interruptions than their male counterparts, suggesting that men and women have different leadership styles. Male chairs, beyond taking the floor away from speakers through interruptions, influenced and controlled committee hearing discussions through engaging in substantive comments more than did female chairs. Men, in one out of six turns, interjected personal opinions or guided the committee members and witnesses to a topic of their interest. Men used their position of power to control hearings in ways that we commonly associate with the notion of positional power and leadership. Conversely, women used their position of power to facilitate discussion among committee members, the sponsor, and witnesses—rarely interjecting their own opinion on the topic.

This gendered approach to leadership is illustrated in a hearing in which a "school choice" bill was being considered by the Education Committee, which was chaired by a woman. A controversial topic, the hearing lasted most of the afternoon. After several hours of testimony and debate in which the chair acted as a moderator only, she temporarily stopped the proceedings and asked the vice-chair to take over the remainder of the hearing. Handing the new chair her gavel, she explained she could no longer remain silent on the topic. By stepping down from her leadership position in the hearing, she now felt free to join in the debate. Formally and symbolically, she gave up the power to control the hearing because she could no longer act neutrally with regard to the topic. This gendered approach to chairing committees was demonstrated repeatedly in the conversational analysis of the twelve hearings where women acting as chairs refrained from making substantive remarks but men chairing committees freely entered the debate.

Do these gendered leadership styles differentially affect the gendered participation rates of committee members and witnesses? Clearly they do affect witnesses. For committee members the dynamics are complicated by interactions between the sex of the sponsor, the percentage of females present at the hearing, and the policy issue area.

Witnesses   In hearings chaired by a woman witnesses began speaking earlier, because the chair tended to move directly to witness testimony; whereas a man chairing the committee tended to delay witness testimony through his substantive questioning of sponsors, especially female sponsors, during the introduction of their bill. Male witnesses, under a female chair or when the hearing was on a family bill (a traditional "women's issue" area), demon-strated heightened verbal aggressiveness through their use of interruptions—most notably male witnesses interrupting female chairs. This is a breach of position power and suggests that male witnesses discriminate against women sometimes, presumably including those when women are in power and when women's traditional interests are being discussed.

Gender overrides position power, and the pattern persists in other dynam-ics. Regardless of who chaired the committee, female witnesses opposed to a bill had significantly less opportunity to participate in the hearing than male witnesses opposed to a bill. Female citizens (i.e., "non-experts") spoke less than male citizens, who were asked more questions by committee members. Although we might expect that citizens and witnesses opposed to bills would receive fewer opportunities to participate in the hearing, this was the case only for those who were female. Among the less "politically connected" witnesses, there appears to be a significant gender credibility gap. Male bureaucrats were engaged by committee members through questioning significantly more often than female bureaucrats. So even among the more politicized witnesses, there were gender differences.

Committee Members   Committee members are relatively free to engage in discussion at any point in time—unlike witnesses, who must wait for their initial turn and for subsequent requests for comments. Women committee members, on average, waited until more than two-thirds of the hearing was over before they uttered their first words, whereas men engaged halfway through the hearing. Men spoke longer and took more turns, and men made and encountered more interruptions than did women committee members.

The proportion of female legislators at the hearing and the sex of the chair and of the sponsor all affect the verbal participation of committee members. As women comprise greater proportions of the committee, men become significantly more vocal, supporting Yoder's "intrusiveness" theory. Similarly, male committee members engage earlier, and female committee members later, when the sponsor of the bill is a woman. An examination of the transcripts reveals that male committee members ask questions of a female sponsor immediately after her introduction and that more male committee members engage early in questioning witnesses who testify for a female-sponsored bill, regardless of the proportion of women at the hearing. Both behaviors tend not to be present when a man sponsors a bill. In other words, females, but not males, in positions of importance have their ideas scrutinized by rank-and-file men.

Neutralizing Gender Power

The conversational analysis of committee hearings suggests that women legislators, despite their numerical and positional gains, may be seriously disadvantaged in committee hearings. These findings are not surprising given our culture and the social construction of male power. Perhaps most disturbing are the results that substantiate Yoder's thesis of intrusiveness, which posits that men become more verbally aggressive and conversationally dominant as the proportion of women increases.

Does this leave us with no hope that women can participate equally with men in the near future? Perhaps yes, but again, other research in gender and nonverbal actions in group conversations indicate simple methods for neutralizing gender power. Seating arrangement, such as whether males and females are grouped together or interspersed, may be a powerful factor in verbal behavior (Swann, 1988). Given the importance of political friendships (Caldeira and Patterson, 1987) and women legislators' reports that they tend to find other women more friendly toward them (Blair and Stanley, 1991), perhaps women on committees would speak earlier and more often if they sat next to each other. In addition, other research has found that women are more aware of and responsive to nonverbal social and emotional cues (Buck et al., 1972; Eakins and Eakins, 1978; Wiley and Eskilson, 1985), suggesting that if the hearing table were shaped so that women could make visual contact with each other, their verbal activity might increase.

To address these speculations, a cluster analysis was performed that took into account the nonlinguistic features of a hearing. As the literature suggested, when women sat next to each other and/or could see each other (as in the case of a V-shaped table), women were more active participants in the committee hearings. Without this arrangement, women's voices were significantly muted (Kathlene, 1995b).

On the basis of the results of these two conversational analyses, women legislators are disadvantaged by asymmetrical gender power, which defies the group advantages that should accrue as the proportion of women increases in our legislatures. These power imbalances can be neutralized somewhat, however, by employing the following three strategies:

1. First and foremost, women committee members should sit next to at least one other woman.
2. A woman sponsor concerned about having a gender-balanced treatment of her bill should attempt to have a woman chair the hearing. The alternative,

having a woman-sponsored bill heard in a committee chaired by a man, received the most unbalanced gender treatment.

3. Women should seat themselves so they have eye contact with other women.

Discussion

Do women "speak in a different voice"? Yes, in important, albeit often subtle, ways women are bringing to the legislative process a gendered perspective on how to develop public policy. In their pursuit of learning about problems, women saw themselves serving, responding, and being connected to a wider range of people and groups than the men did. We might expect women to bring nontraditional sources into the political arena based simply on their different social experiences. Yet these different sources also can be understood as the result of differing attitudinal orientations that perceive a wider range of affected people and groups that need to be considered when formulating policy. That men relied on more traditionally political and expert sources is not simply a function of their more professional network but also of their propensity to evaluate and separate "important" from "unimportant" sources.

Obviously, the two notions of experience and attitudes are intertwined, but to understand these differing behaviors based solely on the networks of resources women and men have developed and not on their gendered attitudes about the social world leads to different conclusions. If the differences are the result of sex-based networks, we should not necessarily see women and men differing on the evaluation of and solutions to policy problems. Yet women and men did address criminal policy in very different terms. Women emphasized the societal link to crime, which lead them to speak about long-term preventive strategies as well as intervention measures. Men emphasized individual responsibility, which led them to propose stricter sentencing and increased prison space. These gender differences in the evaluation of criminal behavior are congruent with the differences found in legislative resources and information-gathering activities. In both cases, women approach the issue from a broader, interconnected perspective. The use of more resources and the propensity to activate contact with people can be understood in terms of women's role as the caretakers of relationships. It is precisely this relationship perspective, that leads women to see crime problems as part of a lifelong issue—problems stemming from early childhood experiences, poor education, and lack of opportunities in adulthood. Women tended to see the criminal as a person who is both a victim of circumstances and a perpetrator of a crime. Women's solutions, then, were multifaceted and long term.

Men tended to have a more bounded view, both of the sources of information that were valuable (in terms of the categories of sources they relied upon) and in their less active approach to gathering information. Useful sources were typically the traditional sources that were already part of the legislative environment. Thus, men did not need to participate in bringing together diverse groups because they acted within the bounds of the legislative status quo. Men's valuation of particular sources over other sources can be seen in both their reliance on and their action to acquire certain information. And, along the same lines, men expressed a more bounded definition of crime—they talked about criminals in terms of the crime itself rather than in terms of people in society. Their tendency to recommend and sponsor bills that responded directly to the crime event is more evidence that men tend to see the world as comprised of distinct actions that could be responded to in terms of the event itself. Thus, men did not tend to talk about or sponsor legislation that addressed crime from a long-term perspective; rather, they sponsored legislation that responded directly to the crime event.

Can women's "different voice" change the legislative process? The answer to this question is complex. The examination of verbal dynamics in committee hearings revealed the power dimensions of gender, which complicate women's direct impact on the process, especially women as committee members and witnesses. Nevertheless, women chairing committees demonstrated a gendered leadership style by their tendency to act as facilitators of committee hearings, rarely interjecting their own opinions. The importance of a more democratic leadership style cannot be overstated, for committee hearings in state legislatures are usually the first open public airing and discussion of a proposed policy. To "control" the dialogue at this point in the process is to increase the probability that policies will be poorly designed, and insensitive to the needs and realities of its target population and the public at large.

Autocratic leadership styles, which men are more likely to use, may have an important place later in the process after the public debate has been aired. But as this chapter has shown, men tend to control the policy debate early in the process. This has special significance for all public policy, but it is especially disconcerting for policy issues in which women have a special stake, for example, women's rights or women's issues. If male chairpersons have a propensity to interrupt speakers and choose the points to be discussed, women's issues will probably not receive a fair or informed hearing. If rank-and-file men are propelled to "take away" the floor from women when a female sponsors a bill or the issue heavily affects women, then women's imprint on the policy process will be undermined.

The existence of women's "different voice" stems from a complex socialization process that affects the process of formulating policy. The nuanced ways in which women think differently than men about societal problems speaks to the important impact gender can and does have on public policy. But a "different voice" is not easily integrated into existing gendered institutions. One solution is for us to become aware of how these individual and institutional gender processes work in order to devise workable strategies for circumventing some of the barriers to equitable participation. Women legislators as committee members and in leadership positions have already begun to create some of these opportunities and forums (whether by deliberate design or not), which are helping to equalize gender power differentials and to bring a "different voice" into the policy-making process.

14

Into the Twenty-First Century
Will Women Break the Political Glass Ceiling?

JEAN REITH SCHROEDEL AND NICOLA MAZUMDAR

We have been heah, Joe, foah two full days talkin' about "har*ass*
this" and "har*ass* that." Would you *puh-leeze* tell me when are we
gonna talk about her tits? Haw!
> Senator Howell Heflin of Alabama, as heard through an
> accidentally open mike at the Clarence Thomas Senate
> confirmation hearings, cited in *Southern*, 1994:330

This is the most well-reasoned, stable, trustworthy body I have
dealt with in 10 years of chamber management in three states.
> The male president of the Chamber of Commerce of
> Missoula County, commenting on Missoula County's all-
> female County Board of Commissioners, cited in *Manning*,
> 1988:44

As we move into the twenty-first century, the role of women in electoral
politics is in transition. The euphoria generated by the elections of 1992,
dubbed the "year of the woman" because the number of women in the House
of Representatives nearly doubled and the number in the Senate tripled, faded
as the nation's politics turned to the right in the 1994 elections.[1] Yet, as
analysis in this book shows, if one looks beyond the rhetoric and the hype,
the 1994 elections did not reverse the long-term trend of increasing numbers
of women officeholders in all levels of government. In fact, we argue that
women's prospects for achieving electoral success are greater now than at
any point in the country's history. Moreover, we believe that the impact of
women officeholders may be qualitatively different than in the past. However,

this relatively optimistic prediction is not written in stone. If women wish to achieve political clout commensurate with their numbers in the population, they will have to be willing to make increasing their numbers and their power a priority. As the early chapters of this book show, when women run, they win. It is important, then, to examine the prospects for increasing the pool of women candidates. Before doing so, we review the status of current research on women officeholders and their impact to illustrate the political stakes of equal representation.

Does Underrepresentation Matter?

As Sue Thomas argues in the Introduction to this volume, the underlying question is, Why should we elect more women into office? For example, should one care that the total number of women who have served in Congress to date is a scant 170, as compared with over 11,000 men (United States House Historian's Office, 1995). Some will see the imbalance in these figures as primarily raising questions of fairness and equity. Does fundamental fairness dictate gender parity in representation? Does it mean only that there must be equal opportunity to be elected to office? These questions are not as easy to answer as they may appear, particularly because it is so difficult to bracket out culturally ingrained preconceptions about women. Gender biases are often unconscious and pervasive. Furthermore, in the United States the idea of group rights has become increasingly inflammatory. And when the "group" is women there is an additional complication, which frequently takes the form of a debate over the "proper place" of a women—in essence a debate not over equity but over women's role in society.

Some debate whether effective representation requires that representatives demographically mirror the constituency they represent. The question here is, Do women need to be present to be represented? The short answer to this is, Yes, it does make a difference. One need only look at the circumstances behind the development of the Women's Health Initiative to know that the presence of women in Congress is the difference between life and death for thousands o f women in this country. As Debra Dodson discusses in this volume, the Women's Health Initiative is the large-scale National Institute of Health (NIH)–funded longitudinal study of three diseases of crucial importance to women—heart disease, breast cancer, and osteoporosis. The law was enacted only because women in Congress asked the General Accounting Office (GAO) in 1990 to issue a report on the gender composition of NIH-funded research. The GAO report revealed a systematic exclusion of women from research important to their health (Glazer, 1994:424). For example, although women are almost twice as likely to die from a heart attack than men (Glazer, 1994:411), NIH-funded research was conducted almost exclusively with male subjects. Yet recent studies show that women exhibit a range of complaints that don't fit the typical male profile, such as pain in the stomach or jaw (Glazer, 1994:411). Women's exclusion from research often meant that the male body was studied as if it were the normal human body, and findings from these studies were applied to the treatment of women with little regard to the effect of gender differences on the treatment and progress of these diseases. The recent momentum in women's health can be traced to this report and to aggressive follow-up by women legislators on its implications.

To examine the question of why we should elect more women requires an approach that integrates the complexities of the issue and enables us to reasonably project the effect of more women officeholders on both public policy and political processes. Our approach to answering this question begins with a brief examination of the nature of representation. Second, we summarize recent research which identifies the distinctive contributions made by women elected officials as well as areas where gender does *not* appear to make a difference. Is there a "gender gap" in issue orientations and policy outcomes? Are women officeholders ideologically different from their male counterparts? Do men and women have different political and governing styles? Third, we utilize insights from group and organizational theory to show how increased proportional representation affects the nature of group behavior. For instance, how do attitudes and behaviors change when a group moves from 5 percent to 15 percent and then to 40 percent of an organization? Does this change imply that there will be shifts in public policies and in the way elected officials conduct their business?

The Nature of Representation

"Representation" of one form or another is a defining feature of modern democracies. Two primary variants of representation are "agency representation" and "sociological representation." In agency representation, we choose an agent to act on our behalf, and we attempt to ensure accountability by making the agent stand for elections. We hope that will suffice. The agent may have little in common with his constituency but must somehow be able to divine what is in their best interests. The alternative approach, sociological representation, is to elect someone who shares our background, our culture, and our worldview. We trust that his or her similarity to us will give the representative a deep understanding of our needs, and therefore a more reliable representation of our interests.

Providing role models is one by-product of sociological representation. Representative Carrie Meek (D-Fla.), whose grandparents were slaves and parents were sharecroppers, and who was at one time a domestic worker, makes this point in the following story:

> You know when I get a thrill? When some of the little girls come to my office, the little interns. One little girl, I met her in the hall; she came to intern for someone else and she said, "I just want to take a picture with you. . . . I'm so proud to see a woman like you, a black woman." She's a little black girl and little tears came to her eyes. And she said, "Just let me have a picture." And to see that kind of—I guess the word I want is admiration, for me and for the fact that I'm a

woman . . . and that one day they'll be here, right? See, ten years ago, or fifteen years ago, she wouldn't have thought she could be here. But now she thinks she can be here, and that is a great part of what I see here, too—when the young come along and they see it can happen. (Margolies-Mezvinsky, 1994:142)

Although the ability to provide a role model is the most readily apparent aspect of Meek's story, this personal significance stands alongside the political significance of the increased legitimacy a system gains when groups of people can see that they are included in the system of power.

The virtue of sociological representation is that those in office will have a deeper understanding of how their decisions and policies will affect members of the groups to which they belong. One major difference between male and female officeholders is that men can never have the experience of bearing a child. Not only does this difference affect how male and female officeholders view issues, such as abortion and reproductive health, it also affects how individuals view a wide range of policies. Unlike any of her male colleagues, Representative Lynn Rivers (D-Mich.), knows what it is like to be a pregnant, unmarried high school student. In a similar vein, Representative Lynn Woolsey (D-Calif.) brings her experience of having been a welfare mother to negotiations about reforming Aid to Families with Dependent Children (AFDC).

Institutional Power

Not only is it essential that women be participants in policy debates, they must be part of a genuine discourse which can only ensue among equals, which means that women must be *in* power—not merely around the halls of power. Being elected to political office is only the first step in achieving political power. Women need to occupy key policy-making positions within political institutions. In legislatures the policy-making responsibilities are divided among the different substantive committees. Committees are responsible for drafting legislation and determining whether bills are reported out for consideration by the entire body. Those who are not on the committees have very little chance of affecting the content of the legislation. The most powerful actors are the committee and subcommittee chairs with jurisdiction over the policy.

Women have never been equal participants in policy debates, even on issues that affect primarily women. Despite the fact that reproductive policies have a far greater effect on women than on men, female legislators have been excluded almost entirely from playing a meaningful role in setting national policies in this area. Between 1969 and 1992 there were 10 committees and 19 subcommittees in the House of Representatives that considered reproductive policies. Only a handful of women have ever been members of these committees and no woman has ever served as the chair of a committee or subcommittee responsible for setting reproductive policies. Norton (1995) discovered that women's exclusion from these institutional positions of power resulted in their having very little influence on shaping reproductive policies.

Women are just beginning to accumulate sufficient amounts of political clout and seniority to achieve institutional positions of power at any level of government. For example, state representatives in Ohio recently elected their first woman to the position of Speaker of the House. By the early 1990s the proportion of women occupying key leadership positions within state legislatures was roughly equal to the percentages of women serving in those state legislatures. Not surprisingly, state legislatures where women comprised fewer than 10 percent of the membership had few women in leadership positions. On the other hand, eight out of the ten state legislatures with more than a quarter of the membership comprised of women had women in one of the top leadership positions in the upper or lower chamber (presiding officer, majority leader, or minority leader) (Jewell and Whicker, 1994:172).

In the 104th Congress (1995–1996) women serve on 16 of the 20 Senate committees and on all 20 of the House committees. However, as noted in the Introduction to this book, women are just beginning to build up the seniority necessary to begin occupying some of the key leadership positions within Congress. In the 104th Congress Nancy Kassebaum (R-Kans.) became the first woman to chair a major Senate committee, Labor and Human Resources. In the House of Representatives, Jan Meyers (R-Kans.) and Nancy Johnson (R-Conn.) became the first women to serve as chairs of standing committees in almost 20 years. In both the House and the Senate, women have been moving into key subcommittee positions. In the House, seven chairs and eight ranking minority members on subcommittees were women. The Senate had two female subcommittee chairs and another three women serving as ranking minority members.

Women Legislators: Issue Orientation and Ideology

In 1992, at the first official press conference held by the 24 new women elected to Congress, this bipartisan group stated their commitment to address four policy priorities: to fully fund Head Start for all eligible children, to pass family and medical leave legislation, to pass a Freedom of Choice Act, and to seriously address sexual harassment in the workplace (Margolies-Mezvinsky, 1994:33–34). To some extent these priorities reflected the events of the preceding years—administrative policies that gutted effective implementation of *Roe v. Wade* (1973) and a men's-locker-room approach by the Senate to the problem of sexual harassment during the Clarence Thomas confirmation hearings. To a larger extent, however, these priorities also reflected the congresswomen's deeply felt commitment to women's issues and issues of children and family.

Numerous researchers have found that women legislators feel a distinct interest in and responsibility for legislation concerning these "traditional women's" policy areas. For example, a study by the Center for the American Woman and Politics concludes that increased percentages of women in the state legislatures would mean higher priority for these issues (Thaemert, 1994:28). Sue Thomas's (1994a) comparative study of women state legislators of the early 1970s and those serving in the late 80s showed that both cohorts were more concerned with the issues than male legislators, but the early cohort, despite their concern, did not develop these issues as distinctive policy priorities. Many of the early female legislators commented on the need to be taken seriously in institutions. Deviation from the male-defined norms of the institution and perceptions that they were committed to "women's agendas" could cause them to be written off as "lightweights." The women who composed the later cohort, however, identified "women's" issues as their distinct policy priorities. Further, the study showed that women overall were *as* effective as men in securing passage of policies generally, and *more* effective than men in passing their policy priorities (Thomas, 1994a:78).

A few additional studies present a more complex picture. Research on the Arizona state legislature from 1969 to 1986 showed that greater numbers of women legislators resulted in increases in legislation dealing with both traditional women's concerns, such as child care, education, welfare, and public health, and feminist issues that explicitly dealt with improving the status of women (Saint-Germain, 1989). This study further suggested that proportional group size increases the impact of gender on public policy. Other studies showed that increases in the percentages of female legislators had minimal impact on education policies, medical issues, crime, the environment, energy, and public land use (Thomas, 1994a:63). Scholars found that women were somewhat less likely than men to give priority to bills supporting business and they tended to be less hawkish on defense issues (Welch and Thomas, 1991:14; Frankovic, 1977:315). Evidently there are policy areas where women have distinctly different views from men and areas where views are similar.

Researchers have also found statistically significant differences in the ideological orientation of men and women legislators. In a 1988 study that asked state legislators to identify themselves as "conservative," "liberal," or "middle of the road," higher proportions of women than men described themselves as "liberal" (32 percent of the women labeled themselves liberal vs. 15 percent men; 48 percent of the men labeled themselves conservative vs. 21 percent of the women) (Thomas, 1994a:63).

The current crop of conservative Republican women in Congress, however, illustrates how the tenor of the times affects the ideological mix of women as well as men in office. As Debra Dodson notes in this volume, six of the new Republican women elected to the House of Representatives are strongly opposed to abortion. All of these women were elected with strong support from the religious right. Two-thirds of them became politically active through working on religious right causes. For example, prior to running for Congress Linda Smith (R-Wash.) was the chair of a local chapter of the Eagle Forum. Helen Chenoweth (R-Idaho) was founder of a branch of Focus on the Family, a conservative Christian group that is more militant than the Christian Coalition (Melich, 1996:284). Since coming to Congress, Chenoweth has taken strong positions against the 1973 Endangered Species Act, supported metal mining in state recreation areas, and been outspoken in support of gun owners' rights (Koszczuk, 1995:3266).

In summary, women and men apparently come to office with certain distinctive policy and attitudinal differences, but the validating presence of other women legislators is an important precondition for women to act on parts of their agendas that differ from those of their male colleagues. Under these conditions women have been successful at passing into legislation policies they favored, particularly those dealing with women, children, and the family. It is, however, important not to overstate the ideological and policy differences between male and female elected officials. Positions on many policies do not reflect distinctly different male and female viewpoints—e.g., views on street sweeping appear to be gender neutral. Moreover, there are indications that as the two political parties become more ideologically polarized, party affiliation may become far more important than gender in predicting policy preferences.

Differences and Commonalities in Governing Style

As Lyn Kathlene highlights in Chapter 13 of this book, studies of differences in gender style indicate that as a group women differ from men along several dimensions. Women generally are more conscious of the web of relationships in which people are enmeshed, and they tend to be relatively more caring and nurturing, to emphasize expressive aspects of relationship, and to be more cooperative and nonhierarchical (see Chodorow, 1978; Gilligan, 1982; Tannen, 1990). Most feminists believe these differences are due to gender socialization. Men are raised to view the world as a hierarchy rather than a web of relationships, with the result that hierarchical public discourse emphasizes control and domination rather than cooperation and interdependence. Moreover, men and women tend to have very different views about the nature of power. Whereas men perceive power as capacity to control and dominate ("power over"), women tend to see it as a process through which voices can be heard and tasks accomplished ("power to") (Carroll, 1972:604). In Kathlene's study of the Colorado state house, male-sponsored education bills assumed that the target population needed to be influenced by negative sanctions, but those sponsored by women assumed that the population was already motivated and that including them in the process of reform was likely to unearth new ways to address problems in education (Kathlene, Clarke, and Fox, 1991:34).

As Carey, Niemi, and Powell illustrate in Chapter 6, differences in gender style often are reflected in differences in governing style. Researchers have found that women had a more hands-on style and emphasized collegiality and teamwork more than men (Melich, 1996:298). Women legislators report that they deal with legislative tasks differently than men, being "more thorough and detail-oriented in preparing, advocating, and opposing legislation and more attentive to various consequences of policy actions" (Thomas, 1994a:142). An example from the all-female Missoula County Board of Commissioners illustrates some of these differences. The board needed to find ways to overcome strong public opposition to efforts to reduce pollution from wood-burning stoves. After discovering that most of the opposition came from people who were unable to pay for alternative heating sources, the commissioners decided to provide assistance grants so low income people could shift to alternative sources.

Again, however, it is important that we not overstate the differences between the governing styles of men and women. Just because women as a group tend to have a more consensus-oriented governing style does not mean that any individual woman will behave in that manner. For example, Ellen Sauerbrey, the first woman elected to the position of minority leader in the Maryland state assembly, chose to pursue a more aggressive and confrontational style than had been followed by her male predecessors (Jewell and Whicker, 1994:81, 138). In a similar vein, one cannot predict the governing style of a male politician simply on the basis of biology. As noted in this volume, Jewell and Whicker (1994:177), in their comparative study of leadership styles in state legislatures, found that some male leaders were shifting away from the traditionally "male" form of command leadership toward a more "female" form of consensus and process leadership.

Moreover, there are important commonalities in the governing styles of men and women. Both men and women in leadership positions are expected to behave in an assertive manner. However, the degree of assertiveness that is considered appropriate for male and female leaders appears to be different. According to Duerst-Lahti and Kelly, assertiveness can be located at roughly the midpoint of a continuum ranging from fully aggressive behavior at one end to fully passive behavior at the other. Although both male and female leaders receive high marks for behaving in an assertive fashion, the appropriate range of women's behaviors is narrower than men's and is located nearer to the passive end of the continuum (Duerst-Lahti and Kelly, 1995:28).

The preceding summaries indicate that increasing the numbers of women in elective office produces two types of changes: innovations in policies and differences in governing style. Group and organizational theory also suggests that the presence of women affects the style of male legislators. Men feel freer to adopt nonhierarchical modes, consensual modes, and approaches which would not have been accepted under rigid male institutional norms. The question which remains is, How many women are necessary to effect these changes? Is 15 percent enough? Is 50 percent required? Research on groups and organizations provides us with some insights into the dynamics that emerge when a group moves from minority status to near parity.

Contributions from Group and Organizational Theory

Organizational theorists studying group dynamics within corporations have found that when only a few of any underrepresented group are included in a group, they take on "token" status and their behavior is constrained by that status. In order to be effective, tokens need to retain the credibility that "professionalism" can afford, and "professionalism" in organizations is measured by strict adherence to organizational norms. Should they deviate from those norms, tokens readily become a target for stereotyping, which undermines their credibility. Rosabeth Moss Kanter's seminal study of women in corporations showed that at numbers lower than 15 percent women are perceived as tokens and the dominant institutional norms prevail. When the proportion of women reaches between 15 and 30 percent, Kanter found that women "have potential allies among each other, can form coalitions, and can affect the culture of the group" (Kanter, 1977:209).

Numerous political scientists have attempted to determine whether political organizations exhibit a similar pattern of interaction between men and women. Initially, scholars simply found evidence indicating that the degree to which women are numerical minorities within government bodies influences the women's effectiveness and their willingness to pursue policies of importance to women. For example, Carroll noted that women are most likely to succeed under conditions of extreme minority status when they act like male politicians, and that when they express views on women's interests, they find no support among their male colleagues (Carroll, 1994). Extreme minority status also affects the political atmosphere and the tenor of debate. Thomas (1994a:88) found that "rather than blending into the mainstream, the female tokens continuously respond to their differential status—usually in an extreme fashion, such as accepting the isolation or defining themselves as exceptions to their social category and distancing themselves from other women."

Researchers discovered that changes occurred in the quality of interaction when the proportions of women in elected offices increased. One of the more interesting findings from studies of state legislatures is that somewhere near the 25 percent mark women become such a sizable minority that individual women legislators no longer feel as strong a personal responsibility to represent women as they do when women are a smaller minority (Carroll and Taylor, 1989:19–20). This finding supports the argument that the priority given to issues of women, children, and families among women legislators appears to be the need to deal with neglected business and not a reflection of narrowness of focus.

As we move into the twenty-first century we are on the brink of experiencing what it means to move from women as "tokens" in Congress to their having sufficient numbers to begin to affect the overall institutional culture and force other groups to seek them out as allies. This could qualitatively change both policy outcomes and the ways that Congress conducts the nation's business. The impact within state legislatures could be even more dramatic because the range is so great.

Future Prospects and Pitfalls

Predicting the future is fun, but it is also risky, for several reasons. First, the nature of electoral politics is undergoing a transition. As Carey, Niemi, and Powell point out in Chapter 6, some factors may provide additional opportunities for female candidates, but others work against the interests of women. Second, the devolution of political responsibility from the national to the state and local level has contradictory effects on the achievement of women's policy aims. Third, the interests and types of women elected to public office are undergoing dramatic shifts—some of which make predictions based on past behaviors suspect. Finally, more attention is being paid to the relationship between institutional roles and political influence. We consider each of these in turn and then make prescriptions about ways to improve the prospects for women.

Electoral Factors and Changes in Political Mobilization

Although the electoral system is always undergoing modification as new methods of campaigning evolve, women are particularly affected by four types of electoral changes or possible changes: the enactment of term limits on state elected officials, changes in campaign finance laws, modifications in discriminatory electoral arrangements, and shifts in voter mobilization.

Between 1990 and 1995, 23 states passed initiatives and referenda limiting the terms of some elected officials (Beyle, 1995b:24). Assessing the impact of these initiatives is difficult because the laws differ a great deal across the different states. When the limitations only apply to consecutive terms, the impact will be less than in states where there are lifetime limits. For example, the effect in Washington and Wyoming, where members of the assembly are limited to six years service out of twelve years, will be less severe than in the six states (California, Oklahoma, Arkansas, Michigan, Missouri, and Oregon) that have lifetime limits on legislative service. In California, an individual is limited to six years service in the assembly and eight years in the senate (Jewell and Whicker, 1994:193). Although most term limit restrictions apply to state legislatures, many apply to other statewide offices. For example, in 1994 Idaho and Massachusetts limited the terms that a person can serve as governor to eight years out of any fifteen and two consecutive terms in an eleven-year period, respectively (Beyle, 1995b:14).

At the current time it is virtually impossible to assess the long-term effects of the term limitation movement. Not only do the laws cover different offices and impose different restrictions, there is no reason to believe that the movement has run its course. However, as California state senator Marian Bergeson (R-Orange County) noted, "[term limits] give more women a chance to get elected to office" (Benjamin and Malbin, 1992:133). Because women are still a relatively small proportion of elected officials and generally have less seniority than their male counterparts, the initial impact will be to provide additional opportunities for women to gain political office and achieve institutional leadership positions. One study found that 93 percent of state legislators initially affected by term limits are men (Darcy, Welch, and Clark, 1994:146).

The second electoral factor that could affect women involves possible changes in campaign finance laws. As we noted earlier, both major political parties have, for the first time, a relatively large pool of qualified and well-funded women candidates. However, Republican and Democratic women receive political training and funding from very different sources. Because the Republican Party often has been characterized as antiwomen, the party has spent a great deal of money and time in grooming women candidates. Since the 1980s the Republican Party has run special workshops on political campaigning to train women with the potential to run for political office. Promising women are given scholarships and other inducements that allow them to attend these workshops (Darcy, Welch, and Clark, 1994:188). In contrast, the Democratic Party no longer singles out women for special funding or training. Democratic women interested in running for political office are more likely to rely on feminist PACs, such as EMILY's List, for fund-raising. This reliance on women's PACs means that Democratic women are vulnerable to charges of serving "special interests." More important, they are vulnerable to changes in the laws governing campaign contributions. Current Republican proposals for reforming election laws call for limits or prohibitions on PACs, such as EMILY's List, which solicit funds that are then "bundled" prior to being sent to candidates. If the Republican Party succeeds in enacting these reforms, Democratic women will be at a serious disadvantage.

Important changes are also taking place in the nature of political mobilization. Candidates do not win unless they succeed in mobilizing and turning out their supporters on election day. One of the main reasons for the Republican swing in 1994 was the failure to mobilize women voters. Sixteen million women who voted in 1992 failed to vote in the 1994 elections. Most of these nonvoters fall into the demographic category of "noncollege educated" women (*Notes from Emily*, 1995b:4). EMILY's List recently launched a major initiative, WOMEN VOTE, to convince women who sat out the 1994 elections that it is important for them to vote for female candidates. An early version of WOMEN VOTE was tested in the 1994 senatorial race between Dianne Feinstein and Michael Huffington. Proponents of the initiative argue that it boosted the number of women voters who had indicated that they would probably not vote by 415,000 (*Notes from Emily*, 1995a:5). Before the year 2000, EMILY's List plans to spend $10 million to mobilize nonvoting women in 15 states (*Notes from Emily*, 1995a:5). In 1995 the American Association of University Women (AAUW) started a similar get-out-the-vote campaign, which gained the support of 35 other organizations in its first year (Reed, 1996:11–12). The AAUW is using the Internet in its campaign to mobilize women voters. Although women currently comprise only 34 percent of all Internet users, women could achieve gender parity in Internet usage as early as 1997 (DeFazio, 1996:8). Potentially, WOMEN VOTE and the AAUW campaign could significantly increase the voting gender gap and mark a shift toward greater support for Democratic women candidates.[2]

The special election held in early 1996 to elect a replacement for Oregon senator Robert Packwood showed the potential impact of mobilizing women voters. Women's groups played a major role in turning out record numbers of women voters. Women comprised 57 percent of the electorate and they supported Democrat Ron Wyden over Republican Gordon Smith by an eight-point margin. In contrast, male voters preferred Smith by a margin of eight points. CNN's political analyst, William Schneider, called the women's vote the "key factor" in Wyden's victory (*Notes from Emily*, 1996). If the groups committed to mobilizing women voters continue to be successful in convincing women that they have a stake in turning out and voting as a bloc, it would mark one of the most significant transformations in our electoral system.

Although the country has spent many years struggling with how to devise electoral rules that provide fair representation to African-Americans and Latinos, little attention has been paid to ensuring that electoral arrangements are not biased against women. That is starting to change. For the first time, there is an awareness that some traditional electoral arrangements, which appear to be gender neutral on the surface, systematically discriminate against women running for political office. One of the most important structural differences between electoral systems is whether representation is chosen through single-member or multimember districts. Cross-national research, and analyses of different types of elections within the United States have shown that the use of multimember district systems favors the election of women.[3]

Because single-member districts are so much more prevalent than multimember districts, the research on the United States is still in its early stages. However, as Thomas notes in this volume's Introduction, researchers have identified four reasons why women may do better when running for offices that utilize multimember forms of representation. First, party leaders, who are under pressure to be responsive to different interest groups, may be more willing to include and support women candidates when they are part of a slate rather than the single party nominee. Second, voters may be more comfortable voting for women as part of a slate of representatives than as their single representative. Third, because it is more difficult to achieve name recognition as part of a large number of candidates running in a multimember district, a woman running against a group of men may have an advantage in generating media attention. Finally, women themselves appear to be more willing to become candidates for multimember seats than for single-member seats (Darcy, Welch, and Clark, 1994:158).

Although legal challenges to multimember district systems are a possibility, the political climate and concerns about undercutting the efforts of African-Americans and Latinos to achieve representation may work against this response. Even if legal remedies are not pursued, attention could be paid to changing some of the underlying reasons for the systematic underrepresentation of women in single-member districts. For example, party leaders need to begin thinking of women candidates as representing the majority of American citizens—not a special interest. At the same time, the reasons why women are less comfortable running in single-member districts need to be clearly identified and then addressed in training programs directed at recruiting women candidates. Although the strategy or strategies chosen are important, the essential first step in remedying the problem is the recognition that electoral arrangements are systematically biased against women. This is just beginning to occur.

The Devolution of Political Responsibility

The devolution of political responsibility from the national level of government to the state and local level has contradictory impacts on women's political efficacy. On the one hand, women comprise a far larger proportion of elected officials at the state and local level, than at the national level which means that women's concerns are more likely to be addressed. As we noted earlier, women currently comprise more than 20 percent of the members of state assemblies, and that figure is increasing by approximately 1 percent annually. Women's representation at the municipal and county level is slightly higher than within state legislatures and has increased dramatically over the past 20 years (Darcy, Welch, and Clark, 1994:31–32). The higher numbers of women officeholders would lead one to believe that women's issues would be treated more favorably at the state and local level than at the national level. On the other hand, returning primary responsibility for policy making to the state and local levels of government will likely translate into even greater interstate disparities in governmental services and regulations. We expect that the overall impact of de-federalizing the responsibilities for many policy areas will on the whole work against the interests of the most vulnerable elements in our society.

The 1996 law reforming the welfare system ended a more than six-decade long federal government guarantee to provide income support to all eligible low-income women with children. The reform measure replaces Aid to Families with Dependent Chidlren (AFDC) with block grants. Because the new law gives the states wide latitude in setting eligibility requirements, and benefits levels, the already dramatic differences between states are likely to become even greater. In 1993 the average monthly (AFDC) payment ranged from $120 in Mississippi to $748 in Alaska (Bureau of the Census, 1995). Equally stark interstate differences can be found for all types of social welfare spending, and they would almost certainly become more pronounced if federal minimums were abolished.

However, the most needy citizens are not the only group that would be adversely affected if policy responsibilities are returned to the state level. Women as a whole are likely to find their fundamental rights undermined. The actions of state governments following the recent Supreme Court decisions (*Webster v. Reproductive Health Services, Inc.* and *Planned Parenthood v. Casey*), which returned much of the power to regulate abortions to state governments, provide indications of the types of disparities that are likely to occur when policy making is de-federalized. Thirty-one states have enacted "informed" consent laws which require pregnant women to receive lectures and materials on fetal development and adoption prior to obtaining abortions. Half of these states require a woman to wait a specified period after receiving the lecture before she can obtain an abortion. Despite the Supreme Court's ruling in *Planned Parenthood v. Casey* (1992) that such provisions are unconstitutional, eleven states have statutes requiring husband notification or consent prior to a married woman obtaining an abortion. Thirty-five states have passed parental notification or consent laws that limit a minor's ability to obtain an abortion (NARAL Foundation, 1995).

The Diversification of Women Officeholders

Among the changes in the type of women elected to political office, the most dramatic have been the partisan affiliation and ideological orientation of women candidates and officeholders. Until recently significant majorities of women candidates and elected officials were Democrats. In recent years, however, the number of Republican women serving in all types of political offices has increased at a faster rate than that of Democratic women. By early 1996 Republicans comprised 44 percent of women serving in state legislatures (CAWP, 1996c). The effects of this party shift will not be apparent for some time, although Janet Clark's chapter in this volume gives preliminary evidence that Republican women in the House are still more liberal than their male counterparts. Having said this, however, the new Republican women are more conservative than those who have longer tenure in Congress.

Although Republican women do appear to be more ideologically conservative than in the past, it is important not to assume that they are all ideological clones. Conservative women (and men) are split into two broad camps: social conservatives and laissez-faire conservatives. Social conservatives adhere to the belief that gender roles are divinely ordained, with men exercising authority over women. In contrast, laissez-faire conservatives reflect a more libertarian view of politics where both men and women are considered to be rational, autonomous, and self-interested political actors. Unlike the social conservatives, many laissez-faire conservatives support feminist policies (Klatch, 1987:9).

In addition, splits are beginning to occur among social conservatives. For example, in 1995 the Oregon Citizens Alliance (OCA), the anti-gay rights group led by conservative Christians, attempted to seize control of the state Republican party apparatus. The OCA failed when some religious conservatives, whose votes they had counted on, chose to vote for Republicans not associated with the Christian right. One of the important defectors was state senator Marilyn Shannon (R-Clear Lake), an evangelical Christian and social conservative. Despite attempts by the OCA to engineer her defeat in the May 1995 Republican primary election, Shannon prevailed and was reelected (O'Keefe, 1996:A1, A16). Given their belief about the need for women to be subservient toward men, male leaders of the religious right will probably find it more difficult to mend fences with women who defect from their ranks than men. This, in turn, could lead socially conservative women to seek other political alliances and lead to the emergence of a more diverse Republican Party.

The Republican Party still includes politically moderate women. One of the leading moderates is Susan Molinari (R-N.Y.), who earned an AFL-CIO support score of 44 percent in 1994. Molinari is part of speaker Newt Gingrich's inner circle and is vice-chair of the Republican Conference. The party also has two organizations of pro-choice women, the National Republican Coalition for Choice and Republicans for Choice (Mclich, 1996:298). The New York state party platform includes a pro-choice plank, and many other state party platforms do not take positions on abortion.

The Limits of Position Power

Initially, many people believed that policies favorable to women would be enacted as soon as women got elected to some political offices. When that did not occur, there was a shift toward studying the relationship between institutional roles and political influence. As we noted earlier, women are just beginning to move into positions of leadership at the national and state levels of government. Scholars are beginning to discover that institutional leadership positions, although essential prerequisites for political influence, do not necessarily translate into the expected degree of political clout. Men and women in leadership positions, such as committee chairs, may not be equally influential. Because men are generally in a more powerful position than are women in our society, there is sometimes cognitive dissonance when women occupy leadership positions. The women have position power but not gender power. As a result women leaders may have greater power than rank-and-file men and women, but less than male leaders. Kathlene's study, discussed in Chapter 13 of this volume, showed that women committee chairs had a different leadership style than male committee chairs (see also Kathlene, 1995b:173). The women chairs spoke less frequently in meetings and were less likely to interrupt other speakers. More important, the other committee members and outsiders accorded the women chairs less respect and deference than was typically given to male chairs.

Does this mean that women cannot succeed in achieving equality in the political arena? In the relatively near future that may be true. As long as gender power in the broader society favors men, women achieving position power will be contravening social expectations and will be subject to having their authority challenged. However, this does not mean that women should give up their quest for political influence and wait for some mythical better future. Researchers have identified three strategies that can be used to enhance women's political power. First, when women committee members sit next to one another in meetings, they are accorded more respect. Second, if a woman sponsor is worried that her bill will not be taken seriously, she should attempt to get it referred to a committee chaired by another woman. Finally, seating arrangements in meetings are very important. If the table's shape does not allow every person sitting at it to see each other clearly, the women need to seat themselves strategically so they can make eye contact with as many other women as possible. Not only does this make it easier for the women to support each other, it makes the men more conscious of the women's power (Kathlene, 1995b:173–86).

Breaking the Political Glass Ceiling

We believe that the twenty-first century will provide both challenges and opportunities for women. As we have shown, the political glass ceiling has only begun to be scratched. If women wish to make significant inroads, it is essential that they take a proactive stance and aggressively pursue strategies to enhance their power. No one will hand women political power and influence on a silver platter. Instead, they must grasp hold of it. Opportunities to make gains, such as those presented by term limits legislation, will be squandered without preparation and planning. To that end, we make the following suggestions:

1. Women and men need to give money to strengthen organizations that support women candidates.

2. Activism on behalf of women needs to go beyond monetary contributions. There must be a redoubling of efforts to build a grass-roots movement to empower women.

3. Women need to encourage greater cooperation among a broad range of women's groups with similar goals.

4. Efforts must be made to reach out to non–college educated women, who sat out the 1994 election.

5. New means of mobilizing people, such as using the Internet, need to be aggressively pursued.

6. Women's organizations and the parties need to make greater efforts to not only fund viable women candidates, but also expand the pool of potentially viable candidates. This implies recruiting and training the next generation of women politicians.

7. Women need to consciously seek out opportunities for women office-holders to achieve leadership positions. Efforts must not stop there. Women's groups and political parties need to work with women in leadership to develop strategies that increase their effectiveness.

8. Women's groups need to strengthen existing links to traditional and non-traditional allies and build alliances with broader sectors of the populace.

9. Feminists need to open up networks of communication with politically conservative women so that they will be able to work together across ideological lines.

10. Above all, women must be willing to learn, grow, and change.[4]

Conclusion

We believe that the prospects for women to achieve political influence are greater than at any time in the past. Naomi Wolf (1994) pursues the implications of representation based on the true percentages of women and men in the population, which is not 50–50 but 51–49. She calls this difference the crucial 2 percent and reminds us that this crucial 2 percent means that women have tremendous potential to influence the political life of this nation. This difference, at minimum, means that women need not be supplicants at the political table and, at maximum, should they follow the road of identity politics, that they stand to be the majority partners in this political system. These prospects will be heartening to some, and perhaps worrisome to others. To the latter, be reminded that women legislators do not tend toward identity politics. Women officeholders cross-cut every economic group, every ethnic group, and every ideological stripe. They care about the welfare of their sons as well as their daughters. Women's beliefs and worldviews are forged in an environment that has consistently legitimated traditional male concerns. There is ample evidence that female politicians, just like their male counterparts, must be responsive to the prevailing societal values and the wishes and needs of those who put them in office. It is true, however, that increased female representation does mean that a broader range of political issues and positions will become part of the policy process. Yet, we would argue that the increased presence of women in office is less a prospect to be feared than it is a prescription for a nation disenchanted with its political leaders.

Notes

1. Due to redistricting, reapportionment, and voluntary retirements, there were an extraordinary number of open-seat congressional races in 1992. For the first time there was a relatively large pool of well-qualified and funded women available to take advantage of the political opportunity. Three-quarters of the new women elected to Congress in 1992 had previously held elected offices. See Mandel, Kleeman, and Baruch, 1995:8.
2. According to *Notes from Emily* (1995a:1), polling data and election returns form 1995 indicate that women voters already are strongly swinging back to the Democratic Party.
3. See Darcy, Welch, and Clark (1994:138–71) for a summary of the research on how women candidates are affected by different electoral arrangements. It is worth noting that racial and ethnic considerations also have an impact on how a candidate does in a particular electoral system. White women's representation is clearly enhanced by multimember electoral systems. African-American men do better in single-member districts than in multimember districts, but black women do better in multimember districts. Hispanics also appear to do somewhat better in single-member district races.
4. For further suggestions, see Urvashi Vaid's thoughtful discussion of ways that gays, lesbians, and transgendered people might enhance their political power (Vaid, 1995:395–401).

References

Academy of Life Insurance, and National Women's Political Caucus. 1993. *Women's Political Progress*. Fact sheet. Washington, D.C. June.

Acker, Joan. 1992. "Gendering Organization Theory." In *Gendering Organizational Analysis*, ed. Albert J. Mills and Peta Tancred. Newbury Park, Calif.: Sage.

Alexander, Deborah, and Kristi Andersen. 1993. "Gender as a Factor in the Attribution of Leadership Traits." *Political Research Quarterly* 46 (3): 527–46.

Alexander, Herbert E., ed. 1989. *Comparative Political Finance in the 1980s*. New York: Cambridge University Press.

Andersen, Kristi, and Stuart J. Thorson. 1984. "Congressional Turnover and the Election of Women." *Western Political Quarterly* 37:143–56.

Argyris, Chris. 1964. *Integrating the Individual and the Organization*. New York: Wiley.

Astin, Helen S., and Carole Leland. 1991. *Women of Influence, Women of Vision: A Cross-Generational Study of Leaders and Social Change*. San Francisco: Jossey-Bass.

Barone, Michael, and Grant Ujifusa. 1995. *The Almanac of American Politics 1996*. Washington, D.C.: National Journal.

Baruch, L., and K. McCormick. 1993. "Women's PACs Dramatically Increase Their Support in 1992: An Overview." *CAWP News and Notes* (Winter): 10.

Bass, Bernard M. 1990. *Bass and Stodgill's Handbook of Leadership*. New York: The Free Press.

Bass, Jack, and Walter DeVries. 1976. *The Transformation of Southern Politics: Social Change and Political Consequence Since 1945*. New York: New American Library.

Baxter, Janeen, and Emily W. Kane. 1995. "Dependence and Independence: A Cross-National Analysis of Gender Inequality and Gender Attitudes." *Gender and Society* 9 (2): 193–215.

Baxter, Sandra, and Marjorie Lansing. 1983. *Women in Politics: The Visible Majority*. Rev. ed. Ann Arbor, Mich.: University of Michigan Press.

Beck, Susan Abrams. 1991. "Rethinking Municipal Governance: Gender Distinctions on Local Councils." In *Gender and Policy Making: Studies of Women in Office*. Eagleton Institute of Politics, Rutgers University: Center for the American Woman and Politics.

Becker, Robin A. 1989. "Explaining Sex Roles of Women State Legislators in the Mid-Atlantic Region." Paper presented at the annual meeting of the Midwest Political Science Association, Chicago.

Bendyna, Mary, and Celinda Lake. 1994. "Gender and Voting in the 1994 Presidential Election." In *The Year of the Woman: Myths and Realities*, eds. E. Cook, S. Thomas, and C. Wilcox. Boulder, Colo.: Westview Press.

Benjamin, Gerald, and Michael J. Malbin. 1992. *Limiting Legislative Terms*. Washington, D.C.: Congressional Quarterly Press.

Benze, James G., and Eugene R. Declercq. 1985. "Content of Television Political Spot Ads for Female Candidates." *Journalism Quarterly* 62:278–83, 288.

Berkman, Michael B., and Robert E. O'Connor. 1993. "Do Women Legislators Matter? Female Legislators and State Abortion Policy." *American Politics Quarterly* 21:102–24.

Beyle, Thad L. 1995a. "Pete Wilson for President." In *State Government*, ed. Thad L. Beyle. Washington, D.C.: Congressional Quarterly Press.

———. 1995b. "Politics: Direct Democracy." In *State Government*, ed. Thad L. Beyle. Washington, D.C.: Congressional Quarterly Press.

Biersack, Robert, and Paul S. Herrnson. 1994. "Political Parties and the Year of the Woman." In *Year of the Woman: Myths and Realities*, ed. Elizabeth Adell Cook, Sue Thomas, and Clyde Wilcox. Boulder, Colo.: Westview Press.

Biocca, Frank. 1991. "Looking for Units of Meaning in Political Ads." In *Television and Political Advertising, Vol. II: Signs, Codes, and Images*, ed. Frank Biocca. Hillsdale, N.J.: Erlbaum.

Blair, Diane D., and Jeanie R. Stanley. 1991. "Personal Relationships and Legislative Power: Male and Female Perceptions." *Legislative Studies Quarterly* 16:495–507.

Blake, R., and J. S. Mouton. 1985. *Managerial Grid III*. Houston: Gulf.

Boneparth, Ellen. 1977. "Women in Campaigns: From Lickin' and Stickin' to Strategy." *American Politics Quarterly* 5:289–300.

Bositis, David. 1992. *Black State Legislators: A Survey and Analysis of Black Leadership in State Capitals*. Washington, D.C.: Joint Center for Political and Economic Studies.

Broder, David S. 1971. *The Party's Over: The Failure of Politics in America*. New York: Harper and Row.

———. 1993. "After 'Year of the Woman,' Feminists See '94 Elections as Daunting Test." *Washington Post*, July 12.

Bryce, Herrington J., and Alan E. Warrick. 1977. "Black Women in Electoral Politics." In *Portrait in Marginality: The Political Behavior of the American Woman*, ed. Marianne Githens and Jewel L. Prestage, 395–400. New York: David McKay Co.

Buck, Ross W., Virginia J. Savin, Robert E. Miller, and William F. Caul. 1972. "Communication of Affect through Facial Expressions in Humans." *Journal of Personality and Social Psychology* 23:362–71.

Bullock, Charles S. III, and Loch K. Johnson. 1985. "Sex and the Second Primary." *Social Science Quarterly* 66:933–44.

Bureau of the Census. 1995. *Statistical Abstract of the United States 1995*. Washington, D.C.: U.S. Government Printing Office.

Burns, James MacGregor. 1978. *Leadership*. New York: Harper & Row.

Burrell, Barbara C. 1988. "The Political Opportunity of Women Candidates for the U.S. House of Representatives in 1984." *Women and Politics* 8 (1): 51–69.

———. 1992. "The Presence and Performance of Women Candidates in Open-Seat Primaries for the U.S. House of Representatives: 1968–1990." *Legislative Studies Quarterly* 17 (November): 493–508.

———. 1993. "Party Decline, Party Transformation and Gender Politics: The USA." In *Gender and Party Politics*, eds. Joni Lovenduski and Pippa Norris, 291–308. Thousand Oaks, Calif.: Sage Publications.

Burrell, Barbara C. 1994. *A Woman's Place Is in the House: Campaigning for Congress in the Feminist Era*. Ann Arbor: University of Michigan Press.

Bystrom, Dianne. 1994. "Gender Differences and Similarities in the Presentation of Self: The Videostyles of Female vs. Male U.S. Senate Candidates in 1992." Paper presented at the annual meeting of the Speech Communication Association, New Orleans.

Bystydzienski, Jill M. 1985. "Public Politics in Norway." *Women Transforming Politics*. Bloomington: Indiana University Press.

Caldeira, Gregory A., and Samuel C. Patterson. 1987. "Political Friendship in the Legislature." *Journal of Politics* 49:953–75.

Cantor, Dorothy W., and Toni Bernay, with Jean Stoess. 1992. *Women in Power: The Secrets of Leadership*. Boston: Houghton Mifflin.

Carroll, Bernice. 1972. "Peace Research: The Cult of Power." *Journal of Conflict Resolution* 6 (4): 585–616.

Carroll, Susan J. 1994. *Women as Candidates in American Politics*. 2d ed. Bloomington: Indiana University Press.

Carroll, Susan J., and Ella Taylor. 1989. "Gender Differences in Policy Priorities of U.S. State Legislators: Preferences or Discrimination?" Paper presented at the Midwest Political Science Association Conference, April 13–16, Chicago.

Center for the American Woman and Politics (CAWP). 1978. *Women in Public Office: A Biographical Directory and Statistical Analysis*. 2d ed. Metuchen, N.J.: Scarecrow Press.

———. 1989. "Women in State Legislatures 1989." Fact sheet. New Brunswick, N.J.: Eagleton Institute of Politics, Rutgers University.

———. 1990. *Women State Legislators: Leadership Positions and Committee Chairs*. New Brunswick, N.J.: Eagleton Institute of Politics, Rutgers University.

———. 1991. "Women State Legislators: Leadership Positions and Committee Chairs 1991." Fact sheet. New Brunswick, N.J.: Eagleton Institute of Politics, Rutgers University.

———. 1993. "Women State Legislators: Leadership Positions and Committee Chairs 1993." Fact sheet. New Brunswick, N.J.: Eagleton Institute of Politics, Rutgers University.

———. 1995a. "Women in State Legislatures, 1995b." Fact sheet. New Brunswick, N.J.: Eagleton Institute of Politics, Rutgers University.

———. 1995b. "Women In the U.S. Congress 1995." Fact sheet. New Brunswick, N.J.: Eagleton Institute of Politics, Rutgers University.

———. 1996a. "Statewide Elective Executive Women 1996." New Brunswick, N.J.: Eagleton Institute of Politics, Rutgers University.

———. 1996b. "Women In Elective Office 1996." Fact sheet. New Brunswick, N.J.: Eagleton Institute of Politics, Rutgers University.

———. 1996c. "Women In State Legislatures 1996." Fact sheet. New Brunswick, N.J.: Eagleton Institute of Politics, Rutgers University.

———. 1996d. "Women of Color In Elective Office 1996." Fact sheet. New Brunswick, N.J.: Eagleton Institute of Politics, Rutgers University.

Chafe, William H. 1977. *Women and Equality*. New York: Oxford University Press.

Chodorow, Nancy. 1974. "Family Structure and Feminine Personality." In *Women, Culture and Society*, eds. Michelle Zimbalist Rosaldo and Louis Lamphere. Stanford, Calif.: Stanford University Press.

————. 1978. *The Reproduction of Mothering: Psychoanalysis and the Sociology of Gender.* Berkeley: University of California Press.

Clark, Cal, and Janet Clark. 1996. "Whither the Gender Gap? Converging and Conflicting Attitudes among Women." In *Women in Politics: Outsiders or Insiders?* 2d ed., ed. Lois L. Duke. Upper Saddle River, N.J.: Prentice Hall.

Clark, Janet, Robert Darcy, Susan Welch, and M. Ambrosius. 1985. "Women as Legislative Candidates in Six States." In *Political Women: Current Roles in State and Local Government*, ed. J.A. Flammang. Beverly Hills, Calif.: Sage Publications.

Clay, William L. 1993. *Just Permanent Interests: Black Americans in Congress, 1870–1992.* New York: Amistad Press.

Congressional Caucus for Women's Issues. 1993. "Women's Caucus Calls for Equitable Treatment of Women in Health Care Reform." Press release, September 14.

————. 1994a. "Funding of Women's Programs Continues to Rise in FY95." *Update* (September/October): 15.

————. 1994b. "Record Accomplishments for Women in Congress." Press release, October 13.

————. 1994c. "Summary of Health Care Reform Proposals." *Update* (June): 10.

Conover, Pamela. 1988. "Feminists and the Gender Gap." *Journal of Politics* 50:985–1010.

Cook, Elizabeth Adell. 1994. "Voter Responses to Women Candidates." In *The Year of the Woman: Myths and Realities*, eds. E. Cook, S. Thomas, and C. Wilcox. Boulder, Colo.: Westview Press.

Cook, Elizabeth Adell, and Clyde Wilcox. 1991. "Feminism and the Gender Gap—A Second Look." *Journal of Politics* 53:1111–22.

Cook, Elizabeth Adell, Sue Thomas, and Clyde Wilcox, eds. 1994. *The Year of the Woman: Myths and Realities.* Boulder, Colo.: Westview Press.

Costantini, Edmond. 1990. "Political Women and Political Ambition: Closing the Gender Gap." *Journal of Political Science* 34 (August): 741–70.

Council of State Governments. 1992. *Book of the States: 1992–93 Edition.* Lexington, Ky.: Council of State Governments.

————. 1993. *State Legislative Leadership, Committees and Staff: 1993–94.* Lexington, Ky.: Council of State Governments.

Cox, Elizabeth M. 1994. "The Three Who Came First." *State Legislatures* 20 (November): 12–19.

D'Amico, Francine. 1995. "Women National Leaders." In *Women in World Politics*, eds. Francine D'Amico and Peter R. Beckman. Westport, Conn: Bergin and Garvey.

Darcy, Robert, Margaret Brewer, and Judy Clay. 1984. "Women in the Oklahoma Political System: State Legislative Elections." *Social Science Journal* 21:67–78.

Darcy, Robert, and Sarah Slavin Schramm. 1977. "When Women Run Against Men." *Public Opinion Quarterly* 41:1–12.

Darcy, Robert, Susan Welch, and Janet Clark. 1994. *Women, Elections and Representation.* 2d ed. Lincoln: University of Nebraska Press.

Darling, Marsha J. 1992. "Lifting As We Rise: Black Women in America." In *Introduction to Africana Studies*, ed. Mario Azevedo. Durham, N.C.: Carolina Academic Press.

Davidson, Chandler, and Bernard Grofman, eds. 1994. *Quiet Revolution in the South:*

The Impact of the Voting Rights Act, 1965–1990. Princeton, N.J.: Princeton University Press.

Davidson, JoAnn. 1994. "Women in Legislative Leadership." Panel presentation at the annual meeting of the National Conference of State Legislatures. July 25, New Orleans.

Davis, Marianna W., ed. 1982. *Contributions of Black Women to America.* VII. Columbia, S.C.: Kenday Press.

DeFazio, Jackie. 1996. "Voters on Line." *Outlook* 90 (Spring): 6–9.

Deutchman, Iva Ellen. 1991. "The Politics of Empowerment." *Women & Politics* 11:1–18.

Diamond, Irene. 1977. *Sex Roles in the State House.* New Haven, Conn.: Yale University Press.

Dodson, Debra L. 1994. "Women Officeholders: Continuity and Change across Two Decades." Paper delivered at the annual meeting of the Southern Political Science Association, Atlanta, Ga.

———. 1995a. "The Impact of Congresswomen on Reproductive Rights Policies in the 103rd Congress." Paper presented at the Annual Meeting of the Midwest Political Science Association, April 6–8.

———. 1995b. "The Impact of Women on Health Care Reform: The Case of the 103rd Congress." Paper presented at the Annual Meeting of the American Political Science Association.

Dodson, Debra L., and Susan J. Carroll. 1991. *Reshaping the Agenda: Women in State Legislatures.* New Brunswick, N.J.: Center for the American Woman and Politics, Rutgers University.

Dodson, Debra L., Susan J. Carroll, Ruth B. Mandell, Katherine E. Kleeman, Ronnee Schreiber, and Debra Liebowitz. 1995. *Voices, Views, Votes: The Impact of Women in the 103rd Congress.* New Brunswick, N.J.: Center for the American Woman and Politics, Rutgers University.

Dolan, Kathleen, and Lynne E. Ford. "Change and Continuity Among Women State Legislators: Evidence from Three Decades." *Political Research Quarterly,* forthcoming.

DuBerry, Lois. 1994. "Women in Legislative Leadership." Panel presentation at the annual meeting of the National Conference of State Legislatures. New Orleans, July 25.

Duerst-Lahti, Georgia. 1993. "Year of the Woman, Decade of Women: Wisconsin Legislative Elections." Paper presented at the annual meeting of the Midwest Political Science Association, April 15–18, Chicago.

———. 1994. "Candidate Debriefing." Workshop presented at National Steering Committee meeting, September, Denver.

Duerst-Lahti, Georgia, and Rita Mae Kelly, eds. 1995. *Gender Power, Leadership and Governance.* Ann Arbor: University of Michigan Press.

Duerst-Lahti, Georgia, and Dayna Verstegen. 1995. "Making Something of Absence." In *Gender Power, Leadership and Governance,* eds. Georgia Duerst-Lahti and Rita Mae Kelly. Ann Arbor: University of Michigan Press.

Duke, Lois Lovelace, ed. 1996. *Women In Politics: Outsiders or Insiders?* 2d ed. Upper Saddle River, N.J.: Prentice Hall.

Eagly, Alice H., and Blair T. Johnson. 1990. "Gender and Leadership Style: A Meta-Analysis." *Psychological Bulletin* 108:233–56.

Eakins, Barbara Westbrook, and R. Gene Eakins. 1978. *Sex Differences in Human Communication.* Boston: Houghton Mifflin.

Edelsky, C. 1981. "Who's Got the Floor?" *Language in Society* 10:383–421.

Ekstrand, Laurie, and William Eckert. 1981. "The Impact of Candidate's Sex on Voter Choice." *Western Political Quarterly* 34:78–87.

Elazar, Daniel. 1984. *American Federalism: A View from the States.* 3d ed. New York: Harper and Row.

Fenno, Richard R., Jr. 1978. *Home Style: House Members in Their Districts.* Boston: Little, Brown.

Ferguson, Kathy. 1984. *The Feminist Case against Bureaucracy.* Philadelphia: Temple University Press.

Fiedler, Fred E. 1967. *A Theory of Leadership Effectiveness.* New York: McGraw-Hill.

Fiedler, Fred E., and Joseph E. Garcia. 1987. *New Approaches to Effective Leadership: Cognitive Resources and Organizational Performance.* New York: John Wiley & Sons.

Flammang, Janet A. 1985. "Female Officials in the Feminist Capital: The Case of Santa Clara County." *Western Political Quarterly* 38:94–118.

Foerstel, Karen. 1994. "Voters Favor Term Limits, Reject Tax Restrictions." *Congressional Quarterly*, November 12, 3251.

Foerstel, Karen, and Herbert N. Foerstel. 1996. *Climbing the Hill: Gender Conflict in Congress.* Westport, Conn.: Praeger.

Frankovic, Kathleen. 1977. "Sex and Voting In the U.S. House of Representatives: 1961–1975." *American Politics Quarterly* 5(3): 315–31.

Freeman, Jo. 1995. *Women: A Feminist Perspective,* 5th ed. Mountain View, Calif.: Mayfield.

Gehlen, Frieda L. 1977. "Women Members of Congress: A Distinctive Role." In *A Portrait of Marginality: the Political Behavior of American Woman,* eds. Marianne Githens and Jewel L. Prestage. New York: David McKay.

Gelb, Joyce, and Marian Palley. 1987. *Women and Public Policies.* Princeton, N.J.: Princeton University Press.

Gertzog, Irwin N. 1995. *Congressional Women.* 2d ed. Westport, Conn.: Praeger.

Gilligan, Carol. 1982. *In a Different Voice: Psychological Theory and Women's Development.* Cambridge, Mass.: Harvard University Press.

Gilligan, Carol, Nona Lyons, and Trudy J. Hanmer, eds. 1990. *Making Connections.* Cambridge, Mass.: Harvard University Press.

Gilligan, Carol, Janie V. Ward, Jill McLean Taylor, and Betty Bardige, eds. 1988. *Mapping the Moral Domain.* Cambridge, Mass.: Harvard University Press.

Githens, Marianne, and Jewel L. Prestage. 1977. *Portrait in Marginality: The Political Behavior of the American Woman.* New York: David McKay.

Glazer, Sarah. 1994. "Women's Health Issues." *CQ Researcher,* May 13, 414.

Hakim, Catherine. 1987. *Research Design: Strategies and Choices in the Design of Social Research.* London: Unwin Hyman.

Hansen, Susan B. 1995. "Was Susan B. Anthony Wrong? State Public Policy and the Representation of Women's Interests." Paper presented at the annual meeting of the American Political Science Association, Chicago.

Haussman, Melissa H. 1985. "The Personal is Constitutional: Feminist Struggles for Equality Rights in the United States and Canada." In *Women Transforming Politics.* Bloomington: Indiana University Press.

Hedlund, Ronald D., Patricia K. Freeman, Keith E. Hamm, and Robert M. Stein.

"The Electability of Women Candidates: The Effects of Sex Role Stereotypes." *Journal of Politics* 41(1–2): 513–24.

Helgesen, Sally. 1990. *The Female Advantage: Women's Ways of Leadership.* New York: Doubleday.

Herrick, Rebekah. 1995. "A Reappraisal of the Quality of Women Candidates." *Women & Politics* 15:25–38.

Herrick, Rebekah, and Susan Welch. 1991. "The Impact of At-Large Elections on the Representation of Black and White Women." In *Ethnic Politics and Civil Liberties,* ed. Lucius J. Barker. New Brunswick, N.J.: Transaction.

Hersey, Paul, and Kenneth H. Blanchard. 1977. *Management of Organization Behavior: Utilizing Human Resources.* Englewood Cliffs, N.J.: Prentice- Hall.

Hershey, Marjorie R. 1977. "The Politics of Androgyny: Sex Roles and Attitudes Toward Women in Politics." *American Politics Quarterly* 5:261–87.

Higginbotham, Evelyn Brooks. 1993. *Righteous Discontent: The Women's Movement in the Black Baptist Church, 1880–1920.* Cambridge, Mass.: Harvard University Press.

Hill, David B. 1981. "Political Culture and Female Political Representation." *Journal of Politics* 43:159–68.

Hockmeyer, Anne. 1988. "Object Relations Theory and Feminism: Strange Bedfellows." *Frontiers* 10:20–28.

Hook, Janet. 1993. "Women Remain on Periphery Despite Electoral Gains." *Congressional Quarterly,* Oct. 9, 2707–13.

Huddy, Leonie, and Nayda Terkildsen. 1993a. "The Consequences of Gender Stereotypes for Women Candidates at Different Levels and Types of Office." *Political Research Quarterly* 46(3): 503–26.

———. 1993b. "Gender Stereotypes and the Perception of Male and Female Candidates." *American Journal of Political Science* 37:119–47.

Jacobson, Gary C. 1992. *The Politics of Congressional Elections.* 3d ed. New York: HarperCollins.

Jamieson, Kathleen Hall. 1995. *Beyond the Double Bind.* New York: Oxford University Press.

Jaquette, Jane S., ed. 1974. *Women in Politics.* New York: John Wiley & Sons.

Jaynes, Gerald David, and Robin M. Williams, Jr., eds. 1989. *A Common Destiny: Blacks and American Society.* Washington, D.C.: National Academy Press.

Jewell, Malcolm E., and Marcia Lynn Whicker. 1993. "The Feminization of Leadership in State Legislatures." *PS: Political Science and Politics* 26(4): 705–8.

———. 1994. *Legislative Leadership in the American States.* Ann Arbor: University of Michigan Press.

Johnston, Anne, and Anne Barton White. 1994. "Communication Styles and Female Candidates: A Study of the Political Advertising during the 1986 Senate Elections." *Journalism Quarterly* 71:321–29.

Joint Center for Political and Economic Studies. 1994. *Black Elected Officials: A National Roster, 1993.* 21st ed. Washington, D.C.: Joint Center for Political and Economic Studies.

———. 1973. "Black Women in Electoral Politics." *Focus* 1(10): A–D.

Joslyn, Richard A. 1986. "Political Advertising and the Meaning of Elections." In *New Perspectives in Political Advertising,* eds. Lynda Lee Kaid, Dan Nimmo, and Keith R. Sanders. Carbondale: Southern Illinois University Press.

———. 1990. "Election Campaigns as Occasions for Civic Education." In *New*

Directions in Political Communication: A Resource Book, eds. David L. Swanson and Dan Nimmo. Newbury Park, Calif.: Sage.

Kahn, Kim Fridkin. 1992. "Does Being Male Help? An Investigation of Gender and Media Effects in U.S. Senate Races." *Journal of Politics* 54:497–517.

———. 1993. "Gender Differences in Campaign Messages: The Political Advertisements of Men and Women Candidates for U.S. Senate." *Political Research Quarterly* 46:481–502.

———. 1994a. "The Distorted Mirror: Press Coverage of Women Candidates for Statewide Office." *Journal of Politics* 56:154–73.

———. 1994b. "Does Gender Make a Difference? An Experimental Examination of Sex Stereotypes and Press Patterns in Statewide Campaigns." *American Journal of Political Science* 38:162–95.

Kahn, Kim Fridkin, and Edie N. Goldenberg. 1991. "Women Candidates in the News: An Examination of Gender Differences in U.S. Senate Campaigns." *Public Opinion Quarterly* 55:180–99.

Kanter, Rosabeth Moss. 1977. *Men and Women of the Corporation*. New York: Basic Books.

Kathlene, Lyn. 1989. "Uncovering the Political Impacts of Gender: An Exploratory Study." *Western Political Quarterly* 42:397–421.

———. 1992. "Studying the New Voice of Women in Politics." *The Chronicle of Higher Education*, November 18, B1–2.

———. 1994. "Power and Influence in State Legislative Policy Making: The Interaction of Gender and Position in Committee Hearing Debates." *American Political Science Review* 88:560–75.

———. 1995a. "Alternative Views of Crime: Legislative Policy Making in Gendered Terms." *The Journal of Politics* 57:696–723.

———. 1995b. "Position Power versus Gender Power: Who Holds the Floor?" In *Gender Power, Leadership, and Governance*, eds. Georgia Duerst-Lahti and Rita Mae Kelly. Ann Arbor: University of Michigan Press.

Kathlene, Lyn, Susan E. Clarke, and Barbara A. Fox. 1991. "Ways Women Politicians are Making a Difference." In *Gender and Policy Making: Studies of Women in Office*. New Brunswick, N.J.: Center for American Women and Politics, Rutgers University.

Katz, J. L. 1995. "House Passes Welfare Bill; Senate Likely to Alter It." *Congressional Quarterly*, March 25, 872.

Katz, J. L., and A. J. Rubin. 1995. "House Panel Poised to Approve GOP Welfare Overhaul Bill." *Congressional Quarterly*, March 4, 689–92.

Kelly, Rita Mae, Michelle Saint-Germain, and Jody Horn. 1991. "Female Public Officials: A Different Voice?" *Annals*, American Academy of Political and Social Science, 515 (May): 77–87.

Kern, Montague. 1989. *30-Second Politics: Political Advertising in the Eighties*. New York: Praeger.

Kern, Montague, and Paige P. Edley. 1994. "Women Candidates Going Public: The 30-Second Format." *Argumentation and Advocacy* 31:80–95.

Key, V. O., Jr. 1949. *Southern Politics in State and Nation*. New York: Vintage Books.

Kirkpatrick, Jeane. 1974. *Political Woman*. New York: Basic Books.

Klatch, Rebecca E. 1987. *Women of the New Right*. Philadelphia: Temple University Press.

Koszczuk, Jackie. 1995. "Freshmen: New, Powerful Voice." *Congressional Quarterly Weekly Report*, October 28, 3251–54.

Lake, Celinda. 1995. Interview. August 5, Nashville.

Lang-Takac, Ester, and Zahava Osterweil. 1992. "Separateness and Connectedness: Differences between the Genders." *Sex Roles* 27:277–89.

Lawson, Steven F. 1976. *Black Ballots: Voting Rights in the South, 1944–1969.* New York: Columbia University Press.

———. 1991. *Running for Freedom: Civil Rights and Black Politics in America Since 1941.* New York: McGraw-Hill.

Leader, Shelah G. 1977. "The Policy Impact of Elected Women Officials." In *The Impact of the Electoral Process*, eds. Louis Maisel and Joseph Cooper. Beverly Hills. Calif.: Sage Publications.

Lee, Marcia Manning. 1976. "Why Few Women Hold Public Office: Democracy and Sex Roles." *Political Science Quarterly* 91(1–2): 297–314.

Leeper, Mark Stephen. 1991. "The Impact of Prejudice on Female Candidates: An Experimental Look at Voter Inference." *American Politics Quarterly* 19:248–61.

Likert, Rensis. 1961. *New Patterns of Management.* New York: McGraw-Hill.

Lilley, William III, Laurence J. DeFranco, and William M. Diefenderfer III. 1994. *State Data Atlas: Almanac of State Legislatures.* Washington, D.C.: CQ Press.

Lips, Hilary M. 1981. *Women, Men, and the Psychology of Power.* Englewood Cliffs, N.J.: Prentice-Hall.

———. 1995. "Gender-Role Socialization: Lessons in Femininity." In *Women: A Feminist Perspective*, 5th ed., ed. Jo Freeman. Mountain View, Calif.: Mayfield.

Luntz, Frank I. 1988. *Candidates, Consultants, and Campaigns: The Style and Substance of American Electioneering.* Oxford: Basil Blackwell.

Lusane, Clarence. 1994. *African-Americans at the Crossroads: The Restructuring of Black Leadership and the 1992 Elections.* Boston: South End Press.

Maccoby, Michael B. 1976. *The Gamesman: Winning and Losing the Career Game.* New York: Bantam Books.

Mandel, Ruth B. 1981. *In the Running: The New Woman Candidate.* New Haven, Conn.: Ticknor and Fields.

Mandel, Ruth B., and Debra Dodson. 1992. "Do Women Officeholders Make a Difference?" In *The American Woman*, ed. Sara E. Rix. New York: Norton.

Mandel, Ruth B., Kathy Kleeman, and Lucy Baruch. 1995. "No Year of the Woman, Then or Now." *Extensions* (Spring): 7–10.

Manning, Richard D. 1988. "How Three Women Took Over Missoula County and the 'Gender Factor' Became an Edge." *Governing* (May): 44–50.

Margolies-Mezvinsky, Marjorie. 1994. *A Woman's Place . . . The Freshmen Women Who Changed the Face of Congress.* New York: Crown.

Mathis, Nancy. 1993. "Will 1994 Be Another 'Year of the Woman'?" *Houston Chronicle*, July 12.

Matland, Richard E., and Deborah Dwight Brown. 1992. "District Magnitude's Effect on Female Representation in U.S. State Legislatures." *Legislative Studies Quarterly* 17: 469–92.

Matthews, D. A., and J. W. Prothro. 1966. *Negroes and the New Southern Politics.* New York: Harcourt Brace Jovanovich.

Matthews, Glenna. 1992. *The Rise of Public Woman: Woman's Power and Woman's Place in the United States, 1630–1970.* New York: Oxford University Press.

Mayhew, David. 1974. *Congress: The Electoral Connection*. New Haven: Yale University Press.

McGlen, Nancy E., and Karen O'Connor. 1995. *Women, Politics and American Society*. Englewood Cliffs, N.J.: Prentice-Hall.

McGregor, David. 1960. *The Human Side of Enterprise*. New York: McGraw-Hill.

Melich, Tanya. 1996. *The Republican War Against Women*. New York: Bantam Books.

Mezey, Susan Gluck. 1978a. "Does Sex Make a Difference? A Case Study of Women in Politics." *Western Political Quarterly* 31:492–501.

———. 1978b. "Support for Women's Rights Policy: An Analysis of Local Politicians." *American Politics Quarterly* 6:496.

———. 1980. "The Effects of Sex on Recruitment: Local Connecticut Offices." In *Women in Local Politics*, ed. Debra W. Stewart. Metchen, N.J.: Scarecrow Press.

Morrison, Ann M., Randall P. White, and Ellen Van Velson. 1987. *Breaking the Glass Ceiling*. Reading, Mass.: Addison-Wesley.

Nails, D., M. A. O'Loughlin, and J. G. Walker, eds. 1983. "Women and Morality." *Social Research* 50:487–695.

Nakashima, Ellen. 1996. "Women are Being Seen, Heard in Va. Assembly." *Washington Post*, March 4.

NARAL Foundation. 1995. *A State-by-State Review of Abortion and Reproductive Rights: Who Decides?* 5th ed. Washington, D.C.: NARAL.

National Black Caucus of State Legislators. 1995. *1995–96 Directory of African-American State Legislators*. Washington, D.C.: National Black Caucas of State Legislators.

National Council of State Legislatures (NCSL). 1994. *State Legislatures*, January, 28–32.

National Women's Political Caucus (NWPC). 1994. *Why Don't More Women Run?* a Study prepared by Mellman, Lazurus and Lake. December 15. Washington, D.C.: National Women's Political Caucus.

———. 1995a. *Moving More Women into Public Office: A Three-Step Candidate Recruitment Guide for State and Local Caucus Leaders*. a Study prepared by Jean Dugan. Washington, D.C.: National Women's Political Caucus.

———. 1995b. *Women's Political Progress*. Fact sheet, March 23.

———. 1995c. *Women's Political Times*, Fall.

———. 1995d. *Women's Political Times*, Spring.

Natividad, Irene. 1992. "Women of Color and the Campaign Trail." In *The American Woman, 1992–93: A Status Report*, ed. Paula Ries and Anne J. Stone, 127–48. New York: W. W. Norton.

Nechemias, Carol. 1985. "Geographic Mobility and Women's Access to State Legislatures." *Western Political Quarterly* 38:119–31.

———. 1987. "Changes in the Election of Women to U.S. State Legislative Seats." *Legislative Studies Quarterly* 12:125–42.

Nelson, Albert J. 1991. *Emerging Influentials in State Legislatures: Women, Blacks, and Hispanics*. New York: Praeger.

Nelson, Candice. 1994. "Women's PACs in the Year of the Woman." In *Year of the Woman: Myths and Realities*, ed. Elizabeth Adell Cook, Sue Thomas, and Clyde Wilcox. Boulder, Colo.: Westview Press.

Nesbit, Dorothy Davidson. 1988. *Videostyle in Senate Campaigns*. Knoxville: University of Tennessee Press.

Newman, Jody. 1994. *Perception and Reality: A Study Comparing the Success of Men and Women Candidates.* Washington, D.C.: National Women's Political Caucus.

———. 1995. Interview. September 18, Washington, D.C.

Niemi, Richard G., Simon Jackman, and Laura Winsky. 1991. "Candidacies and Competitiveness in Multimember Districts. *Legislative Studies Quarterly* 16:91–109.

Norton, Noelle. 1995. "Women, It's Not Enough to be Elected: Committee Position Makes a Difference." In *Gender Power, Leadership and Governance*, ed. Georgia Duerst-Lahti and Rita Mae Kelly. Ann Arbor: University of Michigan Press.

Notes from Emily. 1995a. September. EMILY's List.

———. 1995b. December. EMILY's List.

———. 1996. March. EMILY's List.

O'Keefe, Mark. 1996. "Mabon's Despotic Style Erodes OCA Faithful." *Sunday Oregonian*, March 10, A1, A16.

Ouchi, William G. 1981. *Theory Z: How American Business Can Meet the Japanese Challenge.* New York: Avon Books.

Paizis, Suzanne. 1977. *Getting Her Elected: A Political Woman's Handbook.* Sacramento, Calif.: Creative Editions.

Patterson, Thomas E. 1994. *Out of Order.* New York: Vintage.

Pfau, Michael, and Henry C. Kenski. 1990. *Attack Politics: Strategy and Defense.* New York: Praeger.

Pierce, John C., William P. Avery, and Addison Carey Jr. 1977. "Sex Differences in Black Political Beliefs and Behavior." In *Portrait in Marginality: The Political Behavior of the American Woman*, ed. Marianne Githens and Jewel L. Prestage, 66–74. New York: David McKay.

Pitkin, Hanna F. 1967. *The Concept of Representation.* Berkeley: University of California Press.

Plutzer, Eric, and John F. Zipp. 1996. "Identity Politics, Partisanship, and Voting for Women Candidates." *Public Opinion Quarterly* 60:30–57.

Poole, Keith T., and L. Harmon Zeigler. 1985. *Women, Public Opinion, and Politics: The Changing Political Attitudes of American Women.* New York: Longman.

Powell, Lynda. 1991. "Changes in the Liberalism-Conservatism of House Members: 1978–1988." Paper presented at the annual meeting of the American Political Science Association, Washington, D.C.

Prestage, Jewel L. 1977. "Black Women State Legislators: A Profile." In *Portrait in Marginality: The Political Behavior of the American Woman*, ed. Marianne Githens and Jewel L. Prestage, 401–18. New York: David McKay.

———. 1980. "Political Behavior of American Black Women: An Overview." In *The Black Woman*, ed. La Frances Rodgers-Rose, 233–45. Beverly Hills, Calif.: Sage.

Procter, David E., Roger C. Aden, and Phyllis Japp. 1988. "Gender/Issue Interaction in Political Identity Making: Nebraska's Woman vs. Woman Gubernatorial Campaign." *Central States Speech Journal* 39:190–203.

Procter, David E., William J. Schenck-Hamlin, and Karen A. Haase. 1994. "Exploring the Role of Gender in the Development of Negative Political Advertisements." *Women and Politics* 14:1–22.

Ragins, Belle Rose, and Eric Sundstrom. 1989. "Gender and Power in Organizations: A Longitudinal Perspective." *Psychological Bulletin* 105:51–88.

Rahn, Wendy. 1993. "The Role Of Partisan Stereotypes in Information Processing about Political Candidates." *American Journal of Political Science* 37:472–96.

Randall, Vicky. 1987. *Women and Politics.* Chicago: University of Chicago Press.

Reed, Deborah. 1996. "Getting Out the Facts." *Outlook* 90 (Spring): 10–12.

Rieselbach, Leroy N. 1992. " 'Fools Rush In . . .': Thinking about Power and Leadership in Congressional Committees." Paper presented at the annual meeting of the American Political Science Association, Chicago.

Rinehart, Sue Tolleson. 1991. "Do Women Leaders Make a Difference? Substance, Style and Perceptions." *Gender and Policy Making: Studies of Women in Office.* New Brunswick, N.J.: Center for the American Woman and Politics, Rutgers University.

Romney, Ronna, and Beppie Harrison. 1988. *Momentum: Women in American Politics Now.* New York: Crown.

Rosenthal, Cindy Simon. 1995a. "Once They Get There: The Role of Gender in Legislative Careers." *Extensions: A Journal of the Carl Albert Congressional Research and Studies Center* (Spring): 15–17.

———. 1995b. "Women's Ways of Political Leadership: A Cross-Jurisdictional Study of State Legislative Committee Chairs." Ph.D dissertation, University of Oklahoma, 1995.

Rossi, Alice S. 1983. "Beyond the Gender Gap: Women's Bid for Political Power." *Social Science Quarterly* 64: 718–33.

Rule, Wilma. 1981. "Why Women Don't Run: The Critical Contextual Factors in Women's Legislative Recruitment." *Western Political Quarterly* 34:60–77.

———. 1987. "Electoral Systems, Contextual Factors and Women's Opportunities for Election to Parliament in Twenty-Three Democracies." *Western Political Quarterly* 40:477–98.

———. 1993. "Why Are More Women State Legislators?" In *Women in Politics: Outsiders or Insiders?*, ed. Lois Lovelace Duke. Englewood Cliffs, N.J.: Prentice Hall.

———. 1994. "Women's Underrepresentation and Electoral Systems." *PS: Political Science & Politics* (December): 689–92.

Rule, Wilma, and Joseph Zimmerman, eds. 1995. *The United States Electoral Systems: Their Impact on Women and Minorities.* New York: Greenwood Press.

Ryan, Barbara. 1992. *Feminism and the Women's Movement.* New York: Routledge.

Saint-Germain, Michelle A. 1989. "Does Their Difference Make a Difference? The Impact of Women on Public Policy in the Arizona Legislature." *Social Science Quarterly* 70 (4): 956–68.

Salant, Jonathan D. 1996. "Republicans Must be Squeezed in Defending the 'Contract.' " *Congressional Quarterly Weekly Report* 54 (February 24): 448–50.

Sapiro, Virginia. 1981. "Research Frontier Essay: When Are Interests Interesting? The Problem of Political Representation for Women." *American Political Science Review* 75:496.

———. 1981–2. "If U.S. Senator Baker Were a Woman: An Experimental Study of Candidate Images." *Political Psychology* 3 (1–2): 61–83.

Schreiber, R. 1995. " 'To Vote Against Breast Cancer Research is to Vote Against Women': The Rise of Women's Health on the National Agenda." Paper presented at the annual meeting of the Midwest Political Science Association, April 6–8.

Sharkansky, Ira. 1969. "The Utility of Elazar's Political Culture." *Polity* 2: 66–83.

Seligman, Lee, et al. 1974. *Patterns of Recruitment: A State Chooses Its Lawmakers.* Chicago: Rand McNally.

Sigel, Roberta S. 1996. *Ambition and Accommodation: How Women View Gender Relations.* Chicago: University of Chicago Press.

Sigelman, Lee, and Carol K. Sigelman. 1982. "Sexism, Racism, and Ageism in Voting Behavior: An Experimental Analysis." *Social Psychology Quarterly* 45:263–69.

Sigelman, Lee, Carol K. Sigelman, and Christopher Fowler. 1987. "A Bird of a Different Feather? An Experimental Investigation of Physical Attractiveness and the Electability of Female Candidates." *Social Psychology Quarterly* 50:32–43.

Southern, Terry. 1994. "Political Piety." *The Nation*, March 14.

Spain, Daphne. 1992. *Gendered Spaces.* Chapel Hill, N.C.: University of North Carolina Press.

Squire, Peverill. 1990. "Legislative Professionalization and Membership Diversity in State Legislatures." *Legislative Studies Quarterly* 17: 69–82.

Swann, Joan. 1988. "Talk Control: An Illustration from the Classroom of Problems in Analyzing Male Dominance of Conversation." In *Women in Their Speech Communities*, eds. Jennifer Coates and Deborah Cameron. London: Longman.

Tamerius, Karen L. 1995. "Sex, Gender, and Leadership in the Representation of Women." In *Gender Power, Leadership, and Governance*, eds. Georgia Duerst-Lahti and Rita Mae Kelly, 93–112. Ann Arbor: University of Michigan Press.

Tannen, Deborah. 1990. *You Just Don't Understand: Women and Men in Conversation.* New York: Ballantine Books.

Thaemert, Rita. 1994. "Twenty percent and Climbing." *State Legislatures* 20 (January): 20: 28–32.

Thomas, Sue. 1990. "Voting Patterns in the California Assembly: The Role of Gender." *Women & Politics* 9:43–56.

———. 1991a. "Evaluating the Impact of Women Legislators on Political Policies and Processes: The Content of Success." Paper presented at the Midwest Political Science Association, April, Chicago.

———. 1991b. "The Impact of Women on State Legislative Policies." *Journal of Politics* 53 (November): 958–76.

———. 1994a. *How Women Legislate.* New York: Oxford University Press.

———. 1994b. "Women in State Legislatures: One Step at a Time." In *The Year of the Woman: Myths and Realities*, ed. Elizabeth Adell Cook, Sue Thomas, and Clyde Wilcox. Boulder, Colo.: Westview.

Thomas, Sue, and Susan Welch. 1991. "The Impact of Gender on Activities and Priorities of State Legislators." *Western Political Quarterly* 44:445–56.

Trent, Judith S., and Robert V. Friedenberg. 1995. *Political Campaign Communication: Principles and Practices.* 3rd ed. New York: Praeger.

Trent, Judith S., and Teresa Sabourin. 1993a. "Sex Still Counts: Women's Use of Televised Advertising During the Decade of the 80's." *Journal of Applied Communication Research* 21:21–40.

———. 1993b. "When the Candidate Is a Woman: The Content and Form of Televised Negative Advertising." In *Communication and Sex-Role Socialization*, eds. Cynthia Berryman- Fink, Deborah Ballard-Reisch, and Lisa H. Newman. New York: Garland.

Turner, Lynn H. 1992. "An Analysis of Words Coined by Women and Men: Reflections on the Muted Group Theory and Gilligan's Model." *Women and Language* 15:21–26.

United Nations. 1995. *The World's Women 1995: Trends and Statistics.* New York: The United Nations.

United States House Historian's Office. 1995. Interview. December 3.

U.S. News & World Report. 1995. Database. February 13.

Vaid, Urvashi. 1995. *Virtual Equality: The Mainstreaming of Gay and Lesbian Liberation.* New York: Anchor Books.

Van Dunk, Emily, and Thomas M. Holbrook. 1994. "The 1994 State Legislative Elections." *Extensions of Remarks.* December 11.

Vega, Arturo, and Juanita M. Firestone. 1995. "The Effects of Gender on Congressional Behavior and the Substantive Representation of Women." *Legislative Studies Quarterly* 20:213–22.

Volgy, Thomas J., John E. Schwarz, and Hildy Gottlieb. 1986. "Female Representation and the Quest for Resources: Feminist Activism and Electoral Success." *Social Science Quarterly* 67:156–68.

Voter News Service. 1995. "Voter News Service General Election Exit Polls, 1994." Computer file. Ann Arbor, Mich.: Inter University Consortium for Political and Social Research (distributor).

Voter Research and Surveys. 1991. "Voter Research and Surveys General Election Exit Polls, 1990." Computer file. Ann Arbor, MI: Inter University Consortium for Political and Social Research (distributor).

————. 1993. "Voter Research and Surveys General Election Exit Polls, 1992." Computer file. Ann Arbor, Mich.: Inter University Consortium for Political and Social Research (distributor).

Wattenberg, Martin P. 1991. *The Rise of Candidate-Centered Politics.* Cambridge, Mass.: Harvard University Press.

Weisman, Leslie Kanes. 1992. *Discrimination by Design: A Feminist Critique of the Man-Made Environment.* Chicago: University of Illinois Press.

Welch, Susan. 1978. "Recruitment of Women to Public Office: A Discriminant Analysis." *Western Political Quarterly* 31:372–80.

————. 1985. "Are Women More Liberal than Men in the U.S. Congress?" *Legislative Studies Quarterly* 10 (1): 125–34.

Welch, Susan, and Donley Studlar. 1990. "Multimember Districts and the Representation of Women: Evidence from Britain and the United States." *Journal of Politics* 52:391–412.

Welch, Susan, and Sue Thomas. 1991. "Do Women in Public Office Make A Difference?" In *Gender and Policy Making: Studies of Women in Office,* ed. Debra Dodson. New Brunswick, N.J.: Center for the American Woman and Politics, Rutgers University.

Werner, Emmy. 1968. "Women in State Legislatures." *Western Political Quarterly* 21:40–50.

West, Darrell M. 1994. "Political Advertising and News Coverage in the 1992 California U.S. Senate Campaigns." *Journal of Politics* 56:1053–75.

Wheeler, Marjorie Spruill. 1993. *New Women of the New South: The Leaders of the Women's Suffrage Movement in the Southern States.* New York: Oxford University Press.

Whicker, Marcia Lynn, and Jennie J. Kronenfeld. 1986. *Sex Roles: Technology, Politics, and Policy.* New York: Praeger.

Whicker, Marcia Lynn, Malcolm Jewell, and Lois Duke. 1993. "Women in Congress." In *Women in Politics: Outsiders, Have They Become Insiders?,* 136–51. Englewood Cliffs, N.J.: Prentice-Hall.

Whillock, Rita Kirk. 1991. *Political Empiricism: Communication Strategies in State and Regional Elections*. New York: Praeger.

Wilcox, Clyde. 1994. "Why Was 1992 the 'Year of the Woman'? Explaining Women's Gains in 1992." In *The Year of the Woman: Myths and Realities*, ed. Elizabeth Adell Cook, Sue Thomas, and Clyde Wilcox. Boulder, Colo.: Westview Press.

———. n.d. "From the Ballot Box to the White House: Gender, Public Opinion, and the Presidency." In *The Other Elites: Women, Politics, and Power in the Executive Branch*, eds. MaryAnne Borrelli and Janet M. Martin. Boulder, Colo.: Lynne Reinner, forthcoming.

Wiley, Mary Glenn, and Arlene Eskilson. 1985. "Speech Style, Gender Stereotypes, and Corporate Success: What If Women Talk More Like Men?" *Sex Roles* 12:993–1007.

Williams, Leonard. 1994. "Political Advertising in the Year of the Woman: Did X Mark the Spot?" In *The Year of the Woman: Myths and Realities*, eds. Elizabeth Adell Cook, Sue Thomas, and Clyde Wilcox. Boulder, Colo.: Westview.

Witt, Linda, Karen M. Paget, and Glenna Matthews. 1994. *Running As a Woman: Gender and Power in American Politics*. New York: Free Press.

Wolf, Naomi. 1994. *Fire with Fire*. New York: Fawcett.

Wollstonecraft, Mary. [1792] 1975. *A Vindication of the Rights of Woman*. Harmondsworth, U.K.: Penguin Press.

Woloch, Nancy. 1984. *Women and the American Experience*. New York: Alfred A. Knopf.

Women's Policy, Inc. 1995. "Special Report: Actions of the 104th Congress." *The Source on Women's Issues in Congress* 8: September 8.

———. 1996a. "President Clinton Promotes Conciliation in State of the Union Address." *The Source on Women's Issues in Congress* 3: January 26.

———. 1996b. *Special Report: First Session of the 104th Congress*, February 2.

Yoder, Janice D. 1991. "Rethinking Tokenism: Looking Beyond Numbers." *Gender and Society* 5:178–92.

Zipp, John F., and Eric Plutzer. 1985. "Gender Differences in Voting for Female Candidates: Evidence from the 1982 Election." *Public Opinion Quarterly* 49:179–97.

Index